14th SIGMORPHON Workshop on Computational Research in Phonetics, Phonology, and Morphology 2016

Held at ACL 2016

Berlin, Germany
11 August 2016

ISBN: 978-1-5108-2774-5

ACL 2016

**The 54th Annual Meeting of the
Association for Computational Linguistics**

**Proceedings of the 14th SIGMORPHON Workshop on
Computational Research in Phonetics, Phonology, and
Morphology**

August 11, 2016
Berlin, Germany

Introduction

Welcome to the 14th SIGMORPHON Workshop on Computational Research in Phonetics, Phonology, and Morphology. The workshop aims to bring together researchers interested in applying computational techniques to problems in morphology, phonology, and phonetics. Our program this year highlights the ongoing and important interaction between work in computational linguistics and work in theoretical linguistics. We received 23 submissions and accepted 11.

The volume of submissions made it necessary to recruit several additional reviewers. We'd like to thank all of these people for agreeing to review papers on what seemed like impossibly short notice.

This year also marks the first SIGMORPHON shared task, on morphological reinflection. The shared task received 9 submissions, all of which were accepted, and greatly advanced the state of the art in this area.

We thank all the authors, reviewers and organizers for their efforts on behalf of the community.

Organizers:

Micha Elsner, The Ohio State University
Sandra Kübler, Indiana University

Program Committee:

Adam Albright, MIT
Kelly Berkson, Indiana University
Damir Cavar, Indiana University
Grzegorz Chrupała, Tilburg University
Çağrı Çöltekin, University of Tübingen
Ewan Dunbar, Laboratoire de Sciences Cognitives et Psycholinguistique, Paris
Jason Eisner, Johns Hopkins University
Valerie Freeman, University of Washington
Sharon Goldwater, University of Edinburgh
Nizar Habash, NYU Abu Dhabi
David Hall, Semantic Machines
Mike Hammond, University of Arizona
Jeffrey Heinz, University of Delaware
Colin de la Higuera, University of Nantes
Ken de Jong, Indiana University
Gaja Jarosz, Amherst
Greg Kobele, University of Chicago
Greg Kondrak, University of Alberta
Kimmo Koskenniemi, University of Helsinki
Karen Livescu, TTI Chicago
Kemal Oflazer, CMU Qatar
Jeff Parker, Brigham Young
Jelena Prokic, Philipps-Universität Marburg
Andrea Sims, OSU
Kairit Sirts, Macquarie University
Richard Sproat, Google
Reut Tsarfaty, Weizmann Institute
Sami Virpioja, Aalto University
Shuly Wintner, University of Haifa

Invited Speaker:

Colin Wilson, Johns Hopkins University

Table of Contents

Conference Program

Thursday, August 11, 2016

9:00–9:30   **Phonetics**

09:00–09:30   *Mining linguistic tone patterns with symbolic representation*
SHUO ZHANG

09:30–10:30   *Invited Talk*
Colin Wilson

10:30–11:00   *Coffee Break*

11:00–11:30   *The SIGMORPHON 2016 Shared Task—Morphological Reinflection*
Ryan Cotterell, Christo Kirov, John Sylak-Glassman, David Yarowsky, Jason Eisner and Mans Hulden

11:30–12:30   **Shared task poster session**

Morphological reinflection with convolutional neural networks
Robert Östling

EHU at the SIGMORPHON 2016 Shared Task. A Simple Proposal: Grapheme-to-Phoneme for Inflection
Iñaki Alegria and Izaskun Etxeberria

Morphological Reinflection via Discriminative String Transduction
Garrett Nicolai, Bradley Hauer, Adam St Arnaud and Grzegorz Kondrak

Morphological reinflection with conditional random fields and unsupervised features
Ling Liu and Lingshuang Jack Mao

Improving Sequence to Sequence Learning for Morphological Inflection Generation: The BIU-MIT Systems for the SIGMORPHON 2016 Shared Task for Morphological Reinflection
Roee Aharoni, Yoav Goldberg and Yonatan Belinkov

Evaluating Sequence Alignment for Learning Inflectional Morphology
David King

Using longest common subsequence and character models to predict word forms
Alexey Sorokin

MED: The LMU System for the SIGMORPHON 2016 Shared Task on Morphological Reinflection
Katharina Kann and Hinrich Schütze

The Columbia University - New York University Abu Dhabi SIGMORPHON 2016 Morphological Reinflection Shared Task Submission
Dima Taji, Ramy Eskander, Nizar Habash and Owen Rambow

12:00–14:00 *Lunch Break*

14:00–15:00 **Workshop poster session**

Letter Sequence Labeling for Compound Splitting
Jianqiang Ma, Verena Henrich and Erhard Hinrichs

Automatic Detection of Intra-Word Code-Switching
Dong Nguyen and Leonie Cornips

Read my points: Effect of animation type when speech-reading from EMA data
Kristy James and Martijn Wieling

Predicting the Direction of Derivation in English Conversion
Max Kisselew, Laura Rimell, Alexis Palmer and Sebastian Padó

Morphological Segmentation Can Improve Syllabification
Garrett Nicolai, Lei Yao and Grzegorz Kondrak

Towards a Formal Representation of Components of German Compounds
Thierry Declerck and Piroska Lendvai

Thursday, August 11, 2016 (continued)

Mining linguistic tone patterns with symbolic representation

Shuo Zhang

Department of Linguistics, Georgetown University
`ssz6@georgetown.edu`

Abstract

This paper conceptualizes speech prosody data mining and its potential application in data-driven phonology/phonetics research. We first conceptualize Speech Prosody Mining (SPM) in a time-series data mining framework. Specifically, we propose using efficient symbolic representations for speech prosody time-series similarity computation. We experiment with both symbolic and numeric representations and distance measures in a series of time-series classification and clustering experiments on a dataset of Mandarin tones. Evaluation results show that symbolic representation performs comparably with other representations at a reduced cost, which enables us to efficiently mine large speech prosody corpora while opening up to possibilities of using a wide range of algorithms that require discrete valued data. We discuss the potential of SPM using time-series mining techniques in future works.

1 Introduction

Current investigations on the phonology of intonation and tones (or pitch accent) typically employ data-driven approaches by building research on top of manual annotations of a large amount of speech prosody data (for example, (Morén and Zsiga, 2006; Zsiga and Zec, 2013), and many others). Meanwhile, researchers are also limited by the amount of resources invested in such expensive endeavor of manual annotations. Given this paradox, we believe that this type of data driven approach in phonology-phonetics interface can benefit from tools that can efficiently index, query, classify, cluster, summarize, and discover meaningful prosodic patterns from a large speech prosody corpus.

The data mining of f_0[1] (pitch) contour patterns from audio data has recently gained success in the domain of Music Information Retrieval (aka MIR, see (Gulati and Serra, 2014; Gulati et al., 2015; Ganguli, 2015) for examples). In contrast, the data mining of speech prosody f_0 data (here on referred to as Speech Prosody Mining (SPM)[2]) is a less explored research topic (Raskinis and Kazlauskiene, 2013). Fundamentally, SPM in a large prosody corpus aims at discovering meaningful patterns in the f_0 data using efficient time-series data mining techniques adapted to the speech prosody domain. Such knowledge has many potential applications in prosody-related tasks, including speech prosody modeling and speech recognition. Moreover, a Speech Prosody Query and Retrieval (SPQR) tool can be also of great utility to researchers in speech science and theoretical phonology/phonetics (tone and intonation).

Due to the nature of speech prosody data, SPM in a large prosody corpus faces classic time-series data mining challenges such as high dimensionality, high feature correlation, and high time complexity in operations such as pair-wise distance computation. Many of these challenges have been addressed in the time-series data mining literature by proposing heuristics that make use of cheaper and more efficient approximate representations of time-series (e.g., symbolic representations). However, a central question to be addressed in SPM is how to adapt these generic techniques to develop the most efficient methods for computing similar-

---

[1]In this paper we use the terms *fundamental frequency*, f_0, and *pitch* somewhat interchangably.

[2]As the previous research in this specific area is sparse, we have coined this term for the current paper as we conceptualize the time-series data mining based framework for the pattern discovery, similarity computation and content retrieval from speech prosody databases.

Proceedings of the 14th Annual SIGMORPHON Workshop on Computational Research in Phonetics, Phonology, and Morphology, pages 1–9,
Berlin, Germany, August 11, 2016. ©2016 Association for Computational Linguistics

ity for the speech prosody time-series data (that also preserves the most meaningful information within this domain).

In this paper, we first conceptualize SPM in a time-series mining framework. We outline the various components of SPM surrounding the central question of efficiently computing similarity for speech prosody time-series data. In particular, we propose using Symbolic Aggregate approXimation (SAX) representation for time-series in various SPM tasks. We then evaluate the use of SAX against several alternative representations for f_0 time-series in a series of classic data mining tasks using a data set of Mandarin tones(Gauthier et al., 2007). Finally we discuss potential challenges and SPM applications to be addressed in future works.

2 SPM framework: Computing similarity for speech prosody time-series

2.1 Overview

Formally, a time series T = $t_1,...,t_p$ is an ordered set of p real-valued variables, where i is the time index. Speech prosody consists of time-ordered fundamental frequency f_0 data points computed at a specified hop size, which can be naturally viewed as a time-series.

Due to the typical large size of data mining tasks and the high dimensionality of time-series, it is often impossible to fit the data into main memory for computation. A generic time-series mining framework is proposed as follows (Faloutsos et al., 1994): (1)Create an *approximation* of the data, which will fit in main memory, yet retains the essential features of interest; (2) Approximately solve the task at hand in main memory; (3)Make few accesses to the original data on disk to confirm/modify the solution obtained in Step 2. In practice, however, the success of this generic framework depends on the efficient time-series representation and distance measure in the approximated space that allows the lower bounding of true distances in the original space, along with the appropriate and tractable distance computation(Lin et al., 2007).

2.2 Subsequence generation

There are two ways to generate time-series subsequences (such as sequences of syllabic tones). In the first mode ("long sequence"), we store time-series as a long sequence (e.g., one audio recording file lasting an hour), and we extract subsequences (such as tones or tone n-grams) on the fly while performing data mining tasks by sliding a moving window across the entire time-series. In this mode, the two parameters to be specified are: (1) the length of the desired subsequence; (2) hop size, i.e., the distance between two consecutive windowing (such as n samples, where $n \geq 1$). Most time-series mining applications work in this way (e.g., financial, weather, DNA, EKG, etc). The second mode is to store pre-extracted time-series as individual subsequences and perform experiments on these subsequences directly. The first mode usually generates much more numerous (partially overlapping) subsequences due to the small hop size used in practice.

In speech prosody, however, it is meaningful to store tone or intonation time-series as subsequences. For example, it is generally acknowledged that tones are associated with each syllable (or some sub-syllabic structure like the mora(Morén and Zsiga, 2006)). Intuitively, we are only interested in tone time-series that have beginning and ending points at syllable boundaries. This is true for tone syllable n-grams as well. On the other hand, in a motif discovery[3] context, it is conceivable that f_0 patterns that begin or end in the middle of the syllable could still be of interest (due to misalignment of tone and syllable, such as peak delay (Xu, 2001)). In that case, using the long sequence mode, we might discover novel, previously unknown patterns and knowledges about interesting phenomena in a large prosody corpus.

2.3 F_0 time-series representations and Symbolic Aggregate approXimation

A great deal of effort has been devoted to developing efficient approximate representations for time-series data(Debarr et al., 2012). The limitations of real-valued approaches [4] have led researchers to consider using a symbolic representation of time series. A symbolic approach that allows lower bounding of the true distance would not only satisfy the requirement of the generic framework outlined in Section 2.1, but also enables us to use a

---

[3]As will be discussed later, motif discovery is a classic time-series mining task that searches for all previously unspecified recurring time-series subsequence patterns in the data set in an exhaustive manner.

[4]Since in many contexts the probability of observing any real number is zero, this may limit the types of algorithms that can work with these representations.

variety of algorithms and data structures that are only defined for discrete data, including hashing, Markov models, and suffix trees (Lin et al., 2007).

Symbolic Aggregation approXmation (or SAX (Lin et al., 2003)) is the first symbolic representation for time series that allows for dimensionality reduction and indexing with a lower-bounding distance measure at the same time. The SAX algorithm first transforms the original time-series into a representation with a lower time resolution, using Piecewise Aggregate Approximation technique (PAA, (Keogh et al., 2001)) as an intermediate step. Then it quantizes the pitch space using an alphabet, therefore transforms the entire time-series into a string. It has two parameters: a *word size*(w=desired length of the symbolic feature vector) and an *alphabet size* (a), the latter being used to divide the pitch space of the contour into a equiprobable parts assuming a Gaussian distribution of F0 values (the breakpoints are obtained from a lookup statistical table). After we obtain the breakpoints, each segment of the time-series can be assigned a letter based on the alphabet bin it is in. Figure 1 shows an example of SAX transformation of a time-series of length 128 into the string 'baabccbc'.

In the current paper, we consider several other representations of f_0 time-series data for evaluation against the SAX representation:

(1) *Non-parametric f_0 representation.* f_0 contour units can be directly represented by down-sampled or transformed f_0 data points (originally in Hertz, or transformed to Cent or Bark scale[5]). (Gauthier et al., 2007) showed that unsupervised classification using Self-Organizing Map yielded a 80% correct result with 30-point f_0 vectors. In the same study, the First Derivative Vector (D1) is shown to be a more effective feature than f_0.

(2) *Prosody modeling phonetic model representation.* In speech prosody modeling, the most straightforward phonetic model representation of pitch contours is to use polynomial functions(Hirst et al., 2000) to fit the f_0 contour of each utterance unit (such as a tone). A f_0 contour can thus be represented by the coefficient vector $[c_1, c_2, ..., c_{n+1}]$ of a n-th order polynomial. An alternative and linguistically more meaningful model is the quantitative Target Approximation(qTA)(Prom-on et al., 2009). qTA models tone/intonation production as

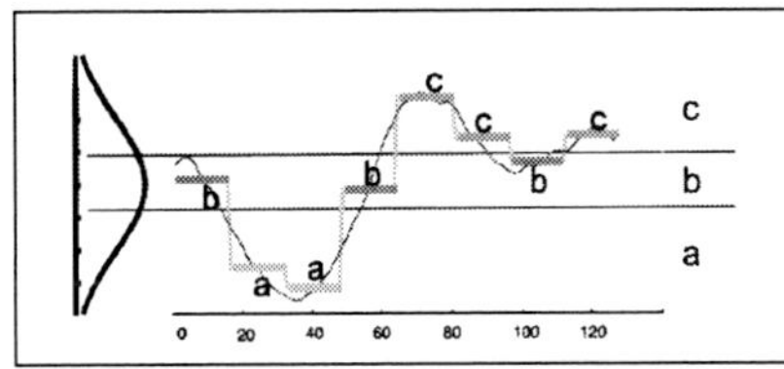

Figure 1: Symbolic Aggregate Approximation, with original length n = 128, number of segments w = 8 and alphabet size a = 3, with output word **baabccbc** (adpated from Lin et al 2007)

Euclidean	DTW(LB_Keogh)	MINDIST
(30)norm-f_0 (30)norm-f_0-bk (30)norm-f_0-ct (30)D1 (4)polynomial (3)qTA	(30)norm-f_0 (30)norm-f_0-bk (30)norm-f_0-ct (30)D1	(10,20)SAX

Table 1: Experiments on distance measures and time-series (TS) representations. Each column shows various TS representations with a distance measure in the top row, with the dimensionality or dimensionality range of the TS-representation in the preceding parenthesis (norm=normalized, bk=Bark, ct=Cent, D1=first derivative)

a process of syllable-wise pitch target approximation, where the target is defined by a linear equation with slope m and intercept b. The actual realization of the f_0 contour is constrained by articulatory factors, characterized by a third-order critically damped system with parameter λ.

2.4 Distance computation

The first two of the following three distance measures work on numeric representation of time-series data, while the third works on symbolic data.

(1) *Euclidean Distance* is an effective and economic distance measure in many contexts despite its simplicity. (Mueen et al., 2009) shows that the difference between Euclidean and DTW distance (discussed next) becomes smaller as the data gets bigger.

(2) *Dynamic time warping* (DTW, see (Rakthanmanon et al., 2012)) is an algorithm for measuring similarity between two temporal sequences which may vary in time or speed in a non-linear fashion. The optimal (shortest) DTW distance, or the best alignment between two time series is obtained with dynamic programming (similar to edit distance for string alignment). It is described

---

[5]Cent and Bark scales are transformations of Hertz values in order to more closely reflect the human perception of pitch differences.

in the literature as being extremely effective for computing distances for time-series data (Xi et al., 2006) and has become indispensable for many domains. In practice, due to its high cost, various lower-bounding techniques are proposed to speed up DTW distance computation in a large database. The LB_Keogh lower bounding technique (Keogh, 2002), for example, speeds up the computation by first taking an approximated distance between the time-series that is both fast to compute and lower bounds the true distance. Only when this approximated distance is better than the best-so-far do we need to actually compute the DTW distance between the pair. This makes DTW essentially an $O(n)$ algorithm. However, in general DTW distance matrix computation in a big data set remains a more expensive operation in practice. By using symbolic representation, our goal is to find a more efficient representation and distance measure that perform comparably to DTW.

(3) *MINDIST distance function* returns the minimum distance between two SAX strings. It lower bounds the true distances of original data (Lin et al., 2003). It can be computed efficiently by summing up the letter-wise distances in the SAX string (letter-wise distance can be obtained from a lookup table using the Gaussian-equiprobable breakpoints mentioned before). For a given value of the alphabet size a, the table needs only be calculated once, then stored for fast lookup.

Table 1 gives an overview of all the time-series representations and distance measures evaluated in this paper.

2.5 Pitch normalization

Many literature reviews(Lin, 2005) in time-series mining assert that time series must be normalized using the z-score transformation normalization strategy so that each contour has a standard deviation of 1 and mean of 0. However, we observe that z-score transformation distorts the shapes of tone or intonation contours with a relatively flat shape. Since z-score transformation expresses each data point in a time series by its relative value to the mean in terms of standard deviation, it would magnify the differences in the values of the flat or near flat contours, and turn such contours into a significantly un-flat contour. To solve this problem, we propose the Subtract-Mean normalization strategy:

$$z_0 = (x_i - \mu) \tag{1}$$

SAX has a requirement to first normalize the time-series using the standard-deviation normalized z-score transformation. In our implementation, when the standard deviation of a subsequence time-series is less than a pre-set threshold (a very small number), all of its segments will be assigned the same symbol.

3 Related work

There has been limited amount of previous works on f_0 pattern data mining, including MIR f_0 melodic pattern mining, and corpus based speech intonation research.

(Gulati and Serra, 2014) mined a database of melodic contour patterns in Indian Art Music. Due to its astronomical size (over 14 trillion pairs of distance computation), various techniques are used to speed up the computation, including lower bounding in DTW distance computation (Keogh, 2002) and early abandoning techniques for distance computation (Rakthanmanon et al., 2012). The goal is to discover highly similar melodic time-series patterns that frequently occur in the collection (motifs) in an unsupervised manner, and the result is evaluated using the query-by-content paradigm (in which a seed query pattern is provided and top-K similar patterns are returned). The meaningfulness of the discovered pattern is then assessed by experts of Indian music.

(Gulati et al., 2015) experimented with 560 different combinations of procedures and parameter values (including sampling rate of the melody representation, pitch quantization levels, normalization techniques and distance measures) in a large-scale evaluation for the similarity computation in MIR domain. The results showed that melodic fragment similarity is particularly sensitive to distance measures and normalization techniques, while sampling rate plays a less important role.

(Valero-Mas et al., 2015) experimented with SAX representation for the computation of F0 contour similarity from music audio signals in a Query-By-Humming (QBH) task[6] in MIR. Results suggest that SAX does not perform well for music

---

[6]In a query by humming task, a user hums a subsection of the melody of a desired song to search for the song from a database of music recordings.

TSR-DIST	SAX-MINDIST				BK-EU	HERTZ-EU	HERTZ-DTW	D1	qTA	polynomial
K	1	3	5	7	1	1	1	1	1	1
dimension	20	20	20	20	30	30	30	30	3	4
accuracy	0.81	0.87	0.87	0.89	0.92	0.92	0.93	0.93	0.73	0.70
CR	0.66	0.66	0.66	0.66	1	1	1	1	0.1	0.13

Table 2: K-Nearest Neighbor tone classification results, with 10-fold cross validation (CR=compression rate, TSR=time-series representation, DIST=distance measure, EU=Euclidean Distance, SAX parameters (w,a)=(20,17), test_size=1600, training_size=320)

time-series data in the context of QBH. The authors attribute this to the fact that the SAX representation loses information important in music melodic retrieval through its dimensionality reduction process.

To the best of our knowledge, the only work that attempted at data mining of speech prosody is (Raskinis and Kazlauskiene, 2013)'s work on clustering intonation patterns in Lithuanian (although it did not explicitly employ any time-series data mining techniques). While this work examined the use of a number of distance measures (mainly Euclidean vs. DTW), it is a early-stage research and no clear conclusion was reached regarding either the effectiveness of the discussed methods or the significance of the patterns discovered.

4 Case study: mining Mandarin tones with symbolic representation

In this section we report our initial experimentation using SAX and other types of time-series representations and distance measures discussed above. We evaluate on a data set of pre-extracted subsequences of Mandarin tone time-series. The current experiment aims at a focused evaluation of these techniques on a controlled and relatively small data set in order to study their behaviors when dealing with speech prosody time-series data. Therefore, we have deliberately chosen a smaller and relatively clean dataset from which we can clearly see the consequences when we vary the parameters. The ultimate goal is of course to use this framework to mine large databases of tone and intonation corpora.

4.1 Experimental setup

Our evaluation data set of Mandarin tones is drawn from the (Gauthier et al., 2007) data used for unsupervised learning of Mandarin tones with the Self-Organizing Map. This data set contains lab speech (480*4=1920 tones, three speakers each produced 160 instances of each of the four tone

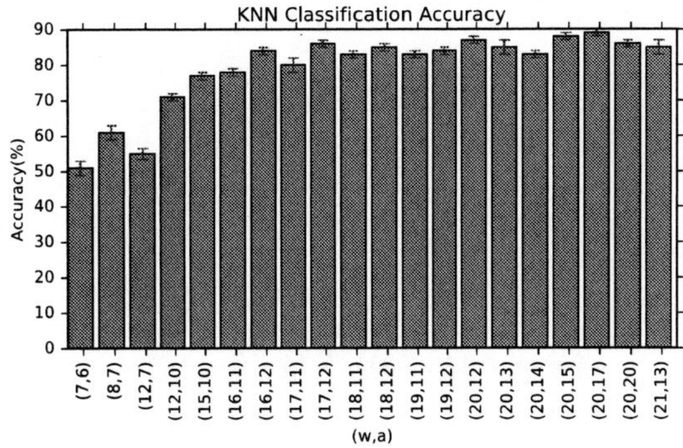

Figure 2: Classification accuracy(%) by SAX parameters w and a

categories), where all possible tone combinations are permuted with the original intention to study the variability of tone shapes in running speech. The tonal environments introduce noisy deviation of tone shapes from tone templates, making tone recognition a mildly challenging task. The target tones are spoken in a carrier sentence and later extracted as syllable-length subsequences.

Table 1 shows the time-series representations and distance measures to be evaluated in this paper. Following conventions in time-series data mining literature, we evaluate these combinations using time-series classification and clustering. For classification, we use k-nearest neighbor (KNN) and Decision Tree, both of which are widely used in time-series classification[7]. We report only accuracy on the classification experiments considering the balanced nature of the data set. All classification experiments are done with 10-fold cross validation with randomized split of data.

Following the convention of using a smaller training size in time-series data mining literature (and considering the optimal time complexity for splitting data size in KNN), the classification ex-

---

[7]In practice, KNN is an expensive algorithm that scale more poorly than decision trees.

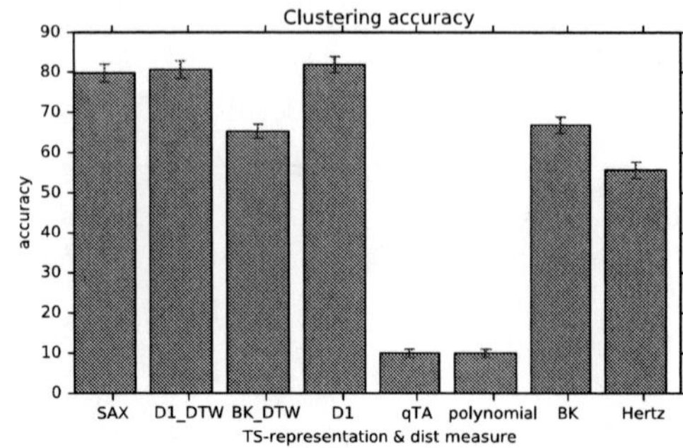

Figure 3: Average clustering accuracy for 1920 Mandarin tones (%) from 5 iterations. For numeric representations, Euclidean distance is used by default unless otherwise noted

periments are carried out using 1600 samples for testing and 320 samples for training (with total size of the data set being 1920 samples of tone contour time-series). To optimize SAX parameters (with MINDIST distance measure), for w, we search from 6 up to $2n/3$ (n is the length of the time series); for a, we search each value between 6 and 20. It is observed that low value for a results in poor classification results (since the MINDIST is a sum of pairwise letter distance between two strings). Figure 2 shows how classification accuracy varies depending on w and a.

For clustering experiments we use the k-means clustering algorithm, where accuracy is computed against true tone labels for each instance. [8]

4.2 Results

First we report time-series classification results on the Mandarin dataset using K-Nearest Neighbor (KNN) and Decision Trees (J48 as implemented in Weka). These classification results are presented in Table 2 and Table 3, respectively. First, we observe that the original f_0 (Hertz) representation performs comparably with normalized-Bark and First Derivative (D1) vectors, using Euclidean dis-

---

[8]The clustering accuracy measure is defined by comparing the assigned cluster labels to the true tone labels of each time series, obtaining a confusion matrix showing the true labels against the predicted labels of the cluster assignments, where predicted labels is the most predominant label (i.e., the tone category with the most number of instances among all tones assigned that label) within that cluster. If the the predominant label is not unique across clusters, then a low value of 0.1 is arbitrarily assigned to the accuracy to represent the accuracy is undecidable.

TSR	SAX	BK	Hertz	D1	qTA	poly
accuracy	0.88	0.93	0.92	0.93	0.83	0.79
CR	0.66	1	1	1	0.1	0.13

Table 3: Decision tree classification results (with 10-fold cross validation), CR=compression rate

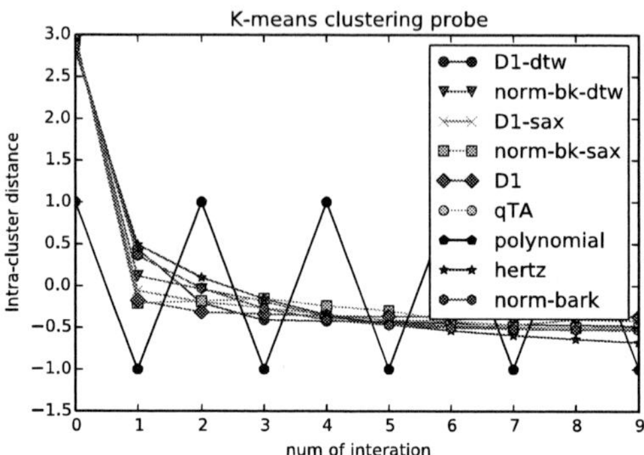

Figure 4: Kmeans clustering objective function by number of iteration. Intra-cluster distance (y axis) is normalized, distance measure noted except for Euclidean. Only polynomial and qTA (overlapped) showed periodic oscillation without a trend to converge.

tance and DTW distance[9]. All of these achieved above 90% accuracy and F1 score using $K = 1$. The DTW distance showed slight advantage over Euclidean distance. All of the numeric representations performed comparably when K varies, so only results for $K = 1$ are shown. Second, we note that the SAX representation achieved reasonable but lower score (with lower dimensionality, compression rate being 0.66). In particular, it performs worse on $K = 1$, and the performance improves significantly when we increase K to 3, 5, and 7. Third, the qTA and polynomial representations achieved significantly lower classification accuracy, at the advantage of having very low dimensionality (compression rate around 0.1). These trends also showed up in the Decision Tree classification, which has comparable classification accuracy with KNN (with lower cost). Overall, we note that SAX shows slight disadvantage in the time-series classification accuracy, while being able to achieve a 0.66 compression rate for time and space complexity.

The true utility of the SPM framework lies

---

[9]The difference between Bark and Cent features is small, so we only report results for Bark.

in detecting patterns in an unsupervised setting. Comparing to classification, SAX shows more distinct advantage in the clustering experiments. In the following discussion, we note that we are able to use a bigger compression rate for SAX in the clustering experiments (i.e., smaller word size), at $w = 13$, which gives a compression rate of approximately 0.43.

The clustering accuracy is summarized in Figure 3. We establish baseline accuracy of 56% with normalized f_0 representation, indicating the difficulty of this task (although this is still well above chance level of 25% for four tones). Clustering results suggest that (1) The D1 feature significantly outperforms the f_0-based features with Euclidean distance; (2) The DTW distance computed with LB_Keogh heuristic shows its clear advantage with f_0 features, although its utility is quite limited in this dataset, comparing to others; (3) it is noteworthy that SAX is in a much lower dimension yet performs comparably with D1; (4) polynomial and qTA model coefficient based features perform below chance in this task, indicating distances in the original space are not preserved in the ultra low dimensional parameter space. To probe into these behaviors, we plot the k-means objective function against the number of iteration in Figure 4. In particular, the polynomial and qTA parameters show periodic oscillation of intra-cluster distances, lacking a trend to converge. SAX shows quick convergence, ranking among the most effective.

Overall, in this unsupervised setting, it is noteworthy that DTW is not showing its advantage in computing time-series similarity for the current tone dataset as seen in literature in other domains (see previous discussion). We are yet to evaluate DTW on a harder and bigger dataset for its utility in speech prosody tasks (as comparing to SAX).

Finally, we plot distance matrixes in Figure 5, which may give a hint as to why SAX is a more effective representation than the f_0-Hertz vectors in clustering: In Figure 5 we can clearly see that the lower dimension SAX-MINDIST distance reflects the intrinsic structure of the clusters with lower distances along the diagonal, whereas the distances are all somewhat equalized in the f_0 distance matrix. Overall, SAX and its low dimensionality property may act as a noise-reduction mechanism for revealing the internal structure of the data, making it more suitable for speech tasks

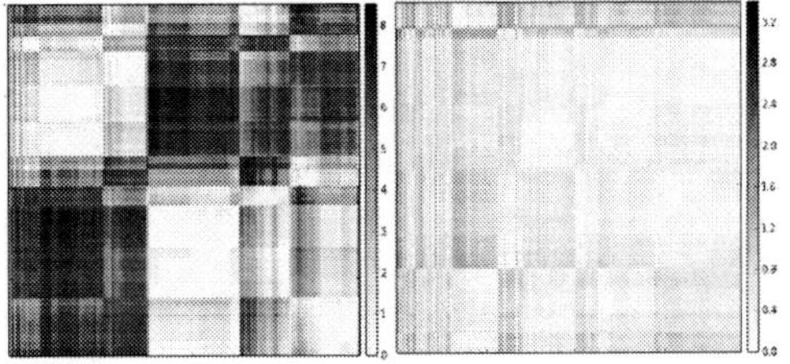

Figure 5: SAX-MINDIST(left) and f_0-Euclidean (right) Distance matrix of 1920 Mandarin tones sorted by tone category. Tones are ordered by tone categories along the x- and y-axis. Origin at top left corner (i.e., on both axis data points are ordered by 480 instances of tone 1, tone 2, tone 3, and tone 4 when moving away from origin).

comparing to MIR tasks.

5 Discussion

In the above experiments we showed the potential of how SPM could benefit from time-series mining techniques, such as low-dimension symbolic representation of time-series that can exploit computational gains from the data compression as well as the availability of efficient string matching algorithms(Ganguli, 2015) (whose utility in SPM is our future research task).

We observed one paradox in our evaluation of SAX, between KNN classification and k-means clustering: the latter is able to achieve better performance (comparing to other time-series representations within the same experiments) with a greater compression rate (0.4) of SAX, whereas the former performs relatively worse with a higher compression rate (0.7) while requiring a larger value of k ($k=7$ is with SAX performs comparably with $k=1$ for other representations). We attribute this difference to the nature of the two algorithms, KNN classification and k-means clustering. It is possible that in SAX-MINDIST space, data points have lower distances to cluster centers, but higher distances to its nearest k neighbors within the same tone category (that is, comparing to Euclidean distance).

Meanwhile, a property of SAX is that each segment used to represent the original time-series must be of the same length. This might not be an ideal situation in many applications (exemplified in (Ganguli, 2015)) where variable lengths segments are desired. The complexity of converting to such an variable-length representation may be greater than the original SAX, as one must design some criteria to decide whether the next frame of audio samples belong to the current segment or it should be the start of a new segment. One intuitive strategy is inactivity detection (i.e., flat period can be represented with a single symbol). Moreover, the utility and implications of symbolic representations (equal- or variable-length) for tones and intonation is also of great theoretical interest to phonology [10].

6 Future works

There are many research questions and applications to be addressed in future works of SPM. Our next step following the current experiments is to evaluate the various time-series representations and distance measures on a larger dataset of spontaneous speech (e.g., newscast speech) in order to find the most efficient methods of computing similarity for speech prosody time-series. Such methods will be useful for all SPM tasks in a large database.

Another useful SPM task is to perform time-series motif discovery in speech prosody data. Motif discovery aims at discovering previously unspecified patterns that frequently occur in the time-series database. Typically we perform motif discovery by generating time-series subsequences on-the-fly (original time-series stored as one long sequence), and then iteratively updating the most frequently occurring patterns. In this way we consider potential motifs in an almost exhaustive manner, with substantial overlaps between consecutive patterns extracted.

Motif discovery has great potential utility for discovering patterns in intonation and tone research. For example, to better understand the nature of contextual variability of Mandarin tone contour shapes in spontaneous speech[11], we might be interested in performing motif discovery with window length being equal to one syllable or syllable n-grams, which considers syllables along with its neighboring tones. Alternatively, we may use variable window length and discover motifs of any length. Of course, a challenge that follows is how

to assess the meaningfulness of the motifs discovered.

A direct application of SPM is a Speech Prosody Query and Retrieval (SPQR) tool that can assist phonologists, phoneticians, and speech prosody researchers in their daily research tasks (that might be done manually otherwise). The basic functionality of this tool is for the user to query a speech prosody corpus using a seed pattern (to be defined using a meaningful prosodic unit, such as a syllabic tone, tone n-gram, an intonation phrase), and retrieve the top k similar patterns in the corpus. The seed pattern can be selected using example top K-motifs extracted from the corpus, or using a user-supplied pattern (numeric, symbolic data points, or audio files). The researcher can further assess the meaningfulness of the patterns discovered by means of intrinsic (i.e., within the phonology/phonetics domain) or extrinsic evaluation (i.e., combined with annotations in other domains such as syntax, semantics, and information structure in discourse). Extended functionalities of the SPQR tool will showcase the motif discovery and other applications of SPM. The application can be implemented with a GUI web interface and use pre-computed time-series similarity indexes for faster retrieval[12].

References

David Debarr, Jessica Lin, Sheri Williamson, and Kirk Borne. 2012. Pattern recognition in time series. *Advances in Machine Learning and Data Mining for Astronomy*.

C Faloutsos, M Ranganathan, and Y Manolopulos. 1994. Fast subsequence matching in time-series database. *SIGMOD Record*, 23:419–429.

Rastog A Pandit V Kantan P Rao P. Ganguli, K. 2015. Efficient melodic query based audio search for hindustani vocal compositions. *Proceedings of ISMIR 2015*.

Bruno Gauthier, Rushen Shi, and Yi Xu. 2007. Learning phonetic categories by tracking movements. *Cognition*, 103(1):80–106, apr.

Sankalp Gulati and Joan Serra. 2014. Mining Melodic Patterns in Large Audio Collections of Indian Art Music. *Proceedings of International Conference on Signal Image Technology & Internet Based Systems*

---

[10]Personally communication with scholars in phonology.

[11]The variability problem refers to the fact that while there exists a canonical contour shape for each tone category, in spontaneous speech the shapes of tones are distorted greatly due to many contextual factors. This is a fundamental challenge in tone recognition.

---

[12]A similar application for querying melodic patterns in Indian music (developed by Sankalp Gulati at Music Technology Group, Universitat Pompeu Fabra) is available here: http://dunya.compmusic.upf.edu/motifdiscovery/.

(SITIS) - *Multimedia Information Retrieval and Applications, Marrakech, Morocco 2014*.

Sankalp Gulati, Joan Serr, and Xavier Serra. 2015. An Evaluation Of Methodologies For Melodic Similarity In Audio Recordings Of Indian Art Music. *Proceedings of IEEE Int. Conf. on Acoustics, Speech, and Signal Processing (ICASSP), Brisbane, Australia 2015*, pages 678–682.

Daniel Hirst, Albert Di Cristo, and Robert Espesser, 2000. *Prosody: Theory and Experiment: Studies Presented to Gösta Bruce*, chapter Levels of Representation and Levels of Analysis for the Description of Intonation Systems, pages 51–87. Springer Netherlands, Dordrecht.

E. Keogh, K. Chakrabarti, M. Pazzani, and S. Mehrotra. 2001. Dimensionality reduction for fast similarity search in large time series databases. *Knowledge and information Systems*, 3(3):263–286.

E Keogh. 2002. Exact indexing of dynamic time warping. *28th International Conference on Very Large Data Bases*, pages 406–417.

Jessica Lin, Eamonn Keogh, Stefano Lonardi, and Bill Chiu. 2003. A symbolic representation of time series, with implications for streaming algorithms. *Proceedings of the 8th ACM SIGMOD workshop on Research issues in data mining and knowledge discovery - DMKD '03*, page 2.

Jessica Lin, Eamonn Keogh, Li Wei, and Stefano Lonardi. 2007. Experiencing SAX: a novel symbolic representation of time series. *Data Min Knowl Disc*, 15:107–144.

Jessica Lin. 2005. Mining time-series data. *Data Mining and Knowledge Discovery Handbook*.

Bruce Morén and Elizabeth Zsiga. 2006. The lexical and post-lexical phonology of thai tones. *Natural Language & Linguistic Theory*, 24(1):113–178.

Abdullah Mueen, Eamonn Keogh, Qiang Zhu, Sydney Cash, and Brandon Westover. 2009. Exact Discovery of Time Series Motifs. *Proceedings of the 2009 SIAM International Conference on Data Mining*, pages 473–484.

Santitham Prom-on, Yi Xu, and Bundit Thipakorn. 2009. Modeling tone and intonation in Mandarin and English as a process of target approximation. *The Journal of the Acoustical Society of America*, 125(1):405–24, jan.

Thanawin Rakthanmanon, Bilson Campana, Abdullah Mueen, Gustavo Batista, Brandon Westover, Qiang Zhu, Jesin Zakaria, and Eamonn Keogh. 2012. Searching and mining trillions of time series subsequences under dynamic time warping. *Proceedings of the 18th ACM SIGKDD International Conference on Knowledge Discovery and Data Mining*, pages 262–270.

G Raskinis and A Kazlauskiene. 2013. From speech corpus to intonation corpus: clustering phrase pitch contours of lithuanian. *Proceedings of the 19th Nordic Conference of Computational Linguistics*.

Jose J Valero-Mas, Justin Salamon, and Emilia Gómez. 2015. Analyzing the influence of pitch quantization and note segmentation on singing voice alignment in the context of audio-based Query-by-Humming. *Sound and Music Computing Conference*.

Xiaopeng Xi, Eamonn Keogh, Christian Shelton, Li Wei, and Chotirat Ann Ratanamahatana. 2006. Fast time series classification using numerosity reduction. In *Proceedings of the Twenty-Third International Conference on Machine Learning*, pages 1033–1040.

Y Xu. 2001. Fundamental frequency peak delay in Mandarin. *Phonetica*, 58(1-2):26–52.

Elizabeth Zsiga and Draga Zec. 2013. Contextual evidence for the representation of pitch accents in standard serbian. *Language & Speech,*, 56(1):69–104.

The SIGMORPHON 2016 Shared Task—Morphological Reinflection

Ryan Cotterell
Dept. of Computer Science
Johns Hopkins University
ryan.cotterell@jhu.edu

Christo Kirov
Dept. of Computer Science
Johns Hopkins University
ckirov@gmail.com

John Sylak-Glassman
Dept. of Computer Science
Johns Hopkins University
jcsg@jhu.edu

David Yarowsky
Dept. of Computer Science
Johns Hopkins University
yarowsky@jhu.edu

Jason Eisner
Dept. of Computer Science
Johns Hopkins University
jason@jhu.edu

Mans Hulden
Dept. of Linguistics
University of Colorado
mans.hulden@colorado.edu

Abstract

The 2016 SIGMORPHON Shared Task was devoted to the problem of morphological reinflection. It introduced morphological datasets for 10 languages with diverse typological characteristics. The shared task drew submissions from 9 teams representing 11 institutions reflecting a variety of approaches to addressing supervised learning of reinflection. For the simplest task, inflection generation from lemmas, the best system averaged 95.56% exact-match accuracy across all languages, ranging from Maltese (88.99%) to Hungarian (99.30%). With the relatively large training datasets provided, recurrent neural network architectures consistently performed best—in fact, there was a significant margin between neural and non-neural approaches. The best neural approach, averaged over all tasks and languages, outperformed the best non-neural one by 13.76% absolute; on individual tasks and languages the gap in accuracy sometimes exceeded 60%. Overall, the results show a strong state of the art, and serve as encouragement for future shared tasks that explore morphological analysis and generation with varying degrees of supervision.

1 Introduction

Many languages use systems of rich overt morphological marking in the form of affixes (i.e. suffixes, prefixes, and infixes) to convey syntactic and semantic distinctions. For example, each English count noun has both singular and plural forms (e.g. *robot/robots*, *process/processes*), and these are known as the inflected forms of the noun. While English has relatively little inflectional morphology, Russian nouns, for example, can have a total of 10 distinct word forms for any given

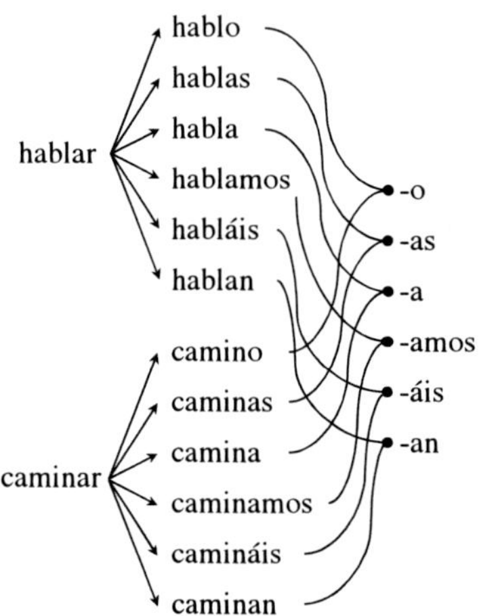

Figure 1: The relatedness of inflected forms, such as the present indicative paradigm of the Spanish verbs *hablar* 'speak' and *caminar* 'walk,' allows generalizations about the shape and affixal content of the paradigm to be extracted.

lemma and 30 for an imperfective verb.[1] In the extreme, Kibrik (1998) demonstrates that even by a conservative count, a verb conjugation in Archi (Nakh-Daghestanian) consists of 1,725 forms, and if all sources of complexity are considered, a single verb lemma may give rise to up to 1,502,839 distinct forms. The fact that inflected forms are systematically related to each other, as shown in Figure 1, is what allows humans to generate and analyze words despite this level of morphological complexity.

A core problem that arises in languages with rich morphology is data sparsity. When a single lexical item can appear in many different word

---

[1]This latter figure rises to 52 if the entire imperfective-perfective pair (e.g. *govorit'/skazat'* 'speak, tell') is considered to be a single lemma.

Proceedings of the 14th Annual SIGMORPHON Workshop on Computational Research in Phonetics, Phonology, and Morphology, pages 10–22,
Berlin, Germany, August 11, 2016. ©2016 Association for Computational Linguistics

forms, the probability of encountering any single word form decreases, reducing the effectiveness of frequency-based techniques in performing tasks like word alignment and language modeling (Koehn, 2010; Duh and Kirchhoff, 2004). Techniques like lemmatization and stemming can ameliorate data sparsity (Goldwater and McClosky, 2005), but these rely on morphological knowledge, particularly the mapping from inflected forms to lemmas and the list of morphs together with their ordering. Developing systems that can accurately learn and capture these mappings, overt affixes, and the principles that govern how those affixes combine is crucial to maximizing the cross-linguistic capabilities of most human language technology.

The goal of the 2016 SIGMORPHON Shared Task[2] was to spur the development of systems that could accurately generate morphologically inflected words for a set of 10 languages based on a range of training parameters. These 10 languages included low resource languages with diverse morphological characteristics, and the training parameters reflected a significant expansion upon the traditional task of predicting a full paradigm from a lemma. Of the systems submitted, the neural network-based systems performed best, clearly demonstrating the effectiveness of recurrent neural networks (RNNs) for morphological generation and analysis.

We are releasing the shared task data and evaluation scripts for use in future research.

2 Tasks, Tracks, and Evaluation

Up to the present, the task of morphological inflection has been narrowly defined as the generation of a complete inflectional paradigm from a lemma, based on training from a corpus of complete paradigms.[3] This task implicitly assumes the availability of a traditional dictionary or gazetteer, does not require explicit morphological analysis, and, though it mimics a common task in second language (L2) pedagogy, it is not a realistic learning setting for first language (L1) acquisition.

Systems developed for the 2016 Shared Task had to carry out *reinflection* of an already inflected form. This involved *analysis* of an already in-

---

[2]Official website: http://ryancotterell.github.io/sigmorphon2016/

[3]A paradigm is defined here as the set of inflected word forms associated with a single lemma (or lexeme), for example, a noun declension or verb conjugation.

	Task 1	Task 2	Task 3
Lemma	run	—	—
Source tag	—	PAST	—
Source form	—	ran	ran
Target tag	PRESPART	PRESPART	PRESPART
Target form	running	running	running
Lemma	decir	—	—
Source tag	—	PRESENT1S	—
Source form	—	digo	digo
Target tag	FUTURE2S	FUTURE2S	FUTURE2S
Target form	dirás	dirás	dirás

Table 1: Systems were required to generate the target form, given the information above the line. Two examples are shown for each task—one in English and one in Spanish. Task 1 is inflection; tasks 2–3 are reinflection.

	Restricted	Standard	Bonus
Task 1	1	1	1, M
Task 2	2	1, 2	1, 2, M
Task 3	3	1, 2, 3	1, 2, 3, M

Table 2: Datasets that were permitted for each task under each condition. Numbers indicate a dataset from that respective task, e.g. '1' is the dataset from Task 1, and 'M' indicates bonus monolingual text from Wikipedia dumps.

flected word form, together with *synthesis* of a different inflection of that form. The systems had to learn from limited data: they were not given complete paradigms to train on, nor a dictionary of lemmas.

Specifically, systems competed on the three tasks illustrated in Table 1, of increasing difficulty. Notice that each task can be regarded as mapping a source string to a target string, with other input arguments (such as the target tag) that specify which version of the mapping is desired.

For each language and each task, participants were provided with supervised training data: a collection of input tuples, each paired with the correct output string (target form).

Each system could compete on a task under any of three tracks (Table 2). Under the restricted track, only data for that task could be used, while for the standard track, data from that task and any from a lower task could be used. The bonus track was the same as the standard track, but allowed the use of monolingual data in the form of Wikipedia dumps from 2 November 2015.[4]

Each system was required to produce, for every input given at test time, either a single string or a ranked list of up to 20 predicted strings for each task. Systems were compared on the follow-

---

[4]https://dumps.wikimedia.org/backup-index.html

ing metrics, averaged over all inputs:

- Accuracy: 1 if the top predicted string was correct, else 0

- Levenshtein distance: Unweighted edit distance between the top predicted string and the correct form

- Reciprocal rank: $1/(1 + \text{rank}_i)$, where rank_i is the rank of the correct string, or 0 if the correct string is not on the list

The third metric allows a system to get partial credit for including a correct answer on its list, preferably at or near the top.

3 Data

3.1 Languages and Typological Characteristics

Datasets from 10 languages were used. Of these, 2 were held as surprise languages whose identity and data were only released at evaluation time.

- *Standard Release*: Arabic, Finnish, Georgian, German, Navajo, Russian, Spanish, and Turkish

- *Surprise*: Hungarian and Maltese

Finnish, German, and Spanish have been the subject of much recent work, due to data made available by Durrett and DeNero (2013), while the other datasets used in the shared task are released here for the first time. For all languages, the word forms in the data are orthographic (not phonological) strings in the native script, except in the case of Arabic, where we used the romanized forms available from Wiktionary. An accented letter is treated as a single character. Descriptive statistics of the data are provided in Table 3.

The typological character of these languages varies widely. German and Spanish inflection generation has been studied extensively, and the morphological character of the languages is similar: Both are suffixing and involve internal stem changes (e.g., a $\mapsto$ ä, e $\mapsto$ ie, respectively). Russian can be added to this group, but with consonantal rather than vocalic stem alternations. Finnish, Hungarian, and Turkish are all agglutinating, almost exclusively suffixing, and have vowel harmony systems. Georgian exhibits complex patterns of verbal agreement for which it utilizes circumfixal morphology, i.e. simultaneous prefixation and suffixation (Aronson, 1990).

	Split	Pairs	Lem	Full	T2T	I-Tag	O-Tag	Sync
Ar	train	12616	2130	225	1.57	72.23	56.57	1.10
	dev	1596	1081	220	1.08	9.13	7.26	1.08
	test	15643	2150	230	1.71	87.06	69.22	1.12
Fi	train	12764	9855	95	5.70	142.15	134.36	1.01
	dev	1599	1546	91	1.51	19.28	18.60	1.01
	test	23878	15128	95	9.87	261.00	251.34	1.01
Ge	train	12390	4246	90	14.02	152.38	137.67	1.06
	dev	1591	1274	77	5.31	24.25	23.40	1.03
	test	21813	4622	90	15.32	279.43	242.36	1.08
Ge	train	12689	6703	99	7.76	246.19	129.48	1.44
	dev	1599	1470	98	1.80	30.82	16.32	1.37
	test	15777	7277	100	9.48	300.49	159.37	1.50
Hu	train	18206	1508	87	9.05	231.13	211.70	1.04
	dev	2381	1196	83	2.14	30.27	29.04	1.02
	test	2360	1186	84	2.09	29.52	28.78	1.02
Ma	train	19125	1453	3607	1.00	6.00	6.01	1.00
	dev	2398	1033	1900	1.00	1.62	1.61	1.00
	test	2399	1055	1928	1.00	1.61	1.59	1.00
Na	train	10478	355	54	17.48	310.55	194.03	1.47
	dev	1550	326	47	2.80	44.93	33.69	1.17
	test	686	233	42	2.89	25.56	16.33	1.12
Ru	train	12663	7941	83	10.32	182.25	152.56	1.07
	dev	1597	1492	78	2.36	23.69	20.74	1.06
	test	23445	10560	86	17.87	320.28	282.47	1.09
Sp	train	12725	5872	84	3.24	186.38	151.48	1.06
	dev	1599	1406	83	1.41	23.08	19.26	1.07
	test	23743	7850	84	5.42	342.72	286.06	1.06
Tu	train	12645	2353	190	1.81	79.82	67.62	1.08
	dev	1599	1125	170	1.09	11.15	9.57	1.06
	test	1598	1128	170	1.08	10.99	9.57	1.05

Table 3: Descriptive statistics on data released to shared task participants. Figures represent averages across tasks. Abbreviations in the headers: 'Lem' = lemmas, 'Full' = number of full tags, T2T = average occurrences of tag-to-tag pairs, I-Tag & O-Tag = average occurrences of each input or output tag, resp., and 'Sync' = average forms per tag (syncretism).

Navajo, like other Athabaskan languages, has primarily prefixing verbal morphology with consonant harmony among its sibilants (Rice, 2000; Hansson, 2010). Arabic and Maltese, both Semitic languages, utilize templatic, non-concatenative morphology. Maltese, due partly to its contact with Italian, also uses concatenative morphology (Camilleri, 2013).

3.2 Quantifying Morphological Processes

It is helpful to understand how often each language makes use of different morphological processes and where they apply. In lieu of a more careful analysis, here we use a simple heuristic to estimate how often inflection involves prefix changes, stem-internal changes (apophony), or suffix changes (Table 4). We assume that each word form in the training data can be divided into three parts—prefix, stem and suffix—with the prefix and suffix possibly being empty.

To align a source form with a target form, we pad both of them with – symbols at their start and/or end (but never in the middle) so that they have equal length. As there are multiple ways

Language	Prefix	Stem	Suffix
Arabic	68.52	37.04	88.24
Finnish	0.02	12.33	96.16
Georgian	4.46	0.41	92.47
German	0.84	3.32	89.19
Hungarian	0.00	0.08	99.79
Maltese	48.81	11.05	98.74
Navajo	77.64	18.38	26.40
Russian	0.66	7.70	85.00
Spanish	0.09	3.25	90.74
Turkish	0.21	1.12	98.74

Table 4: Percentage of inflected word forms that have modified each part of the lemma, as estimated from the "lemma $\mapsto$ inflected" pairs in task 1 training data. A sum $< 100\%$ for a language implies that sometimes source and target forms are identical; a sum $> 100\%$ implies that sometimes multiple parts are modified.

to pad, we choose the alignment that results in minimum Hamming distance between these equal-length padded strings, i.e., characters at corresponding positions should disagree as rarely as possible. For example, we align the German verb forms brennen 'burn' and gebrannt 'burnt' as follows:

```
--brennen
gebrannt-
```

From this aligned string pair, we heuristically split off a prefix pair before the first matching character ($\emptyset \mapsto$ ge), and a suffix pair after the last matching character (en $\mapsto$ t). What is left is presumed to be the stem pair (brenn $\mapsto$ brann):

Pref.	Stem	Suff.
	brenn	en
ge	brann	t

We conclude that when correctly mapping this source form to this target form, the prefix, stem, and suffix parts all change. In what fraction of training examples does each change, according to this heuristic? Statistics for each language (based on task 1) are shown in Table 4.

The figures roughly coincide with our expectations. Finnish, Hungarian, Russian, Spanish, and Turkish are largely or exclusively suffixing. The tiny positive number for Finnish prefixation is due to a single erroneous pair in the dataset. The large rate of stem-changing in Finnish is due to the phenomenon of consonant gradation, where stems undergo specific consonant changes in cer-

tain inflected forms. Navajo is primarily prefixing,[5] and Arabic exhibits a large number of "stem-internal" changes due to its templatic morphology. Maltese, while also templatic, shows fewer stem-changing operations than Arabic overall, likely a result of influence from non-Semitic languages. Georgian circumfixal processes are reflected in an above-average number of prefixes. German has some prefixing, where essentially the only formation that counts as such is the circumfix ge____t for forming the past participle.

3.3 Data Sources and Annotation Scheme

Most data used in the shared task came from the English edition of Wiktionary.[6] Wiktionary is a crowdsourced, broadly multilingual dictionary with content from many languages (e.g. Spanish, Navajo, Georgian) presented within editions tailored to different reader populations (e.g. English-speaking, Spanish-speaking). Kirov et al. (2016) describe the process of extracting lemmas and inflected wordforms from Wiktionary, associating them with morphological labels from Wiktionary, and mapping those labels to a universalized annotation scheme for inflectional morphology called the UniMorph Schema (Sylak-Glassman et al., 2015b).

The goal of the UniMorph Schema is to encode the meaning captured by inflectional morphology across the world's languages, both high- and low-resource. The schema decomposes the morphological labels into universal attribute-value pairs. As an example, consider again Table 1. The FUT2S label for a Spanish future tense second-person singular verb form, such as dirás, is decomposed into [POS=VERB, mood=INDICATIVE, tense=FUTURE, person=2, number=SINGULAR].

The accuracy of data extraction and label association for data from Wiktionary was verified according to the process described in Kirov et al. (2016). However, verifying the full linguistic accuracy of the data was beyond the scope of preparation for the task, and errors that resulted from the original input of data by crowdsourced authors remained in some cases. These are noted in several of the system description papers. The full dataset from the English edition of Wiktionary, which in-

---

[5] The Navajo verb stem is always a single syllable appearing in final position, causing our heuristic to misclassify many stem changes as suffixal. In reality, verb suffixes are very rare in Navajo (Young and Morgan, 1987).

[6] https://en.wiktionary.org

cludes data from 350 languages, ≈977,000 lemmas, and ≈14.7 million inflected word forms, is available at `unimorph.org`, along with detailed documentation on the UniMorph Schema and links to the references cited above.

The Maltese data came from the Ġabra open lexicon[7] (Camilleri, 2013), and the descriptive features for inflected word forms were mapped to features in the UniMorph Schema similarly to data from Wiktionary. This data did not go through the verification process noted for the Wiktionary data.

Descriptive statistics for the data released to shared task participants are given in Table 3.

4　Previous Work

Much previous work on computational approaches to inflectional morphology has focused on a special case of reinflection, where the input form is always the lemma (i.e. the citation form). Thus, the task is to generate all inflections in a paradigm from the lemma and often goes by the name of *paradigm completion* in the literature. There has been a flurry of recent work in this vein: Durrett and DeNero (2013) heuristically extracted transformational rules and learned a statistical model to apply the rules, Nicolai et al. (2015) tackled the problem using standard tools from discriminative string transduction, Ahlberg et al. (2015) used a finite-state construction to extract complete candidate inflections at the paradigm level and then train a classifier, Faruqui et al. (2016) applied a neural sequence-to-sequence architecture (Sutskever et al., 2014) to the problem.

In contrast to paradigm completion, the task of reinflection is harder as it may require both morphologically analyzing the source form and transducing it to the target form. In addition, the training set may include only partial paradigms. However, many of the approaches taken by the shared task participants drew inspiration from work on paradigm completion.

Some work, however, has considered full reinflection. For example, Dreyer and Eisner (2009) and Cotterell et al. (2015) apply graphical models with string-valued variables to model the paradigm jointly. In such models it is possible to predict values for cells in the paradigm conditioned on sets of other cells, which are not required to include the lemma.

[7] `http://mlrs.research.um.edu.mt/resources/gabra/`

5　Baseline System

To support participants in the shared task, we provided a baseline system that solves all tasks in the standard track (see Tables 1–2).

Given the input string (source form), the system predicts a left-to-right sequence of edits that convert it to an output string—hopefully the correct target form. For example, one sequence of edits that could be legally applied to the Finnish input `katossa` is *copy*, *copy*, *copy*, *insert*(t), *copy*, *delete*(3). This results in the output `katto`, via the following alignment:

```
1   2   3   4   5    6
k   a   t   -   o   ssa
k   a   t   t   o    -
```

In general, each edit has the form *copy*, *insert*(string), *delete*(number), or *subst*(string), where *subst*(w) has the same effect as *delete*($|w|$) followed by *insert*(w).

The system treats edit sequence prediction as a sequential decision-making problem, greedily choosing each edit action given the previously chosen actions. This choice is made by a deterministic classifier that is trained to choose the correct edit on the assumption that that all previous edits on this input string were correctly chosen.

To prepare training data for the classifier, each supervised word pair in training data was aligned to produce a desired sequence of edits, such as the 6-edit sequence above, which corresponds to 6 supervised training examples. This was done by first producing a character-to-character alignment of the source and target forms (`katossa`, `katto`), using an iterative Markov Chain Monte Carlo method, and then combining consecutive deletions, insertions, or substitutions into a single compound edit. For example, *delete*(3) above was obtained by combining the consecutive deletions of `s`, `s`, and `a`.

The system uses a linear multi-class classifier that is trained using the averaged perceptron method (Freund and Schapire, 1999). The classifier considers the following binary features at each position:

- The previous 1, 2, and 3 input characters, e.g. `t`, `at`, `kat` for the 4th edit in the example.

- The previous 1, 2, and 3 output characters, e.g. `t`, `tt`, `att` for the 5th edit.

- The following 1, 2, and 3 input characters, e.g. `o`, `os`, `oss` for the 3rd edit.

- The previous edit. (The possible forms were given above.)

- The UniMorph morphosyntactic features of the source tag S or the target tag T (according to what type of mapping we are building—see below). For example, when lemmatizing `katossa` into `katto` as in the example above, $S = \big[$POS=NOUN, case=IN+ESS, number=SINGULAR$\big]$, yielding 3 morphosyntactic features.

- Each conjunction of two features from the above list where the first feature in the combination is a morphosyntactic feature and the second is not.

For task 1, we must edit from LEMMA $\rightarrow T$. We train a separate edit classifier for each part-of-speech, including the morphosyntactic description of T as features of the classifier. For task 2, we must map from $S \rightarrow T$. We do so by lemmatizing $S \rightarrow$ LEMMA (lemmatization) and then reinflecting LEMMA $\rightarrow T$ via the task 1 system.[8] For the lemmatization step, we again train a separate edit classifier for each part-of-speech, which now draws on source tag S features. For task 3, we build an additional classifier to analyze the source form to its morphosyntactic description S (using training data from all tasks, as allowed in the standard track). This classifier uses substrings of the word form as its features, and is also implemented by an averaged perceptron. The classifier treats each unique sequence of feature-value pairs as a separate class. Task 3 is then solved by first recovering the source tag and then applying the task 2 system.

The baseline system performs no tuning of parameters or feature selection. The averaged perceptron is not trained with early stopping or other regularization and simply runs for 10 iterations or until the data are separated. The results of the baseline system are given in Table 5. Most participants in the shared task were able to outperform the baseline, often by a significant margin.

Language	Task 1	Task 2	Task 3
Arabic	66.96	55.00	45.15
Finnish	64.45	59.59	56.95
Georgian	89.12	86.66	85.12
German	89.44	87.62	80.13
Hungarian	73.42	72.78	71.70
Maltese	38.49	27.54	26.00
Navajo	53.06	47.59	44.96
Russian	88.65	84.68	79.55
Spanish	95.72	94.54	87.51
Turkish	59.60	57.63	55.25

Table 5: Accuracy results for the baseline system on the standard track test set.

6 System Descriptions

The shared task received a diverse set of submissions with a total of 11 systems from 9 teams representing 11 different institutions. For the sake of clarity, we have grouped the submissions into three camps.

The first camp adopted a pipelined approach similar to that of the baseline system provided. They first employed an unsupervised alignment algorithm on the source-target pairs in the training data to extract a set of edit operations. After extraction, they applied a discriminative model to apply the changes. The transduction models limited themselves to monotonic transduction and, thus, could be encoded through weighted finite-state machine (Mohri et al., 2002).

The second camp focused on neural approaches, building on the recent success of neural sequence-to-sequence models (Sutskever et al., 2014; Bahdanau et al., 2014). Recently, Faruqui et al. (2016) found moderate success applying such networks to the inflection task (our task 1). The neural systems were the top performers.

Finally, the third camp relied on linguistically-inspired heuristic means to reduce the structured task of reinflection to a more reasonable multi-way classification task that could be handled with standard machine learning tools.

6.1 Camp 1: Align and Transduce

Most of the systems in this camp drew inspiration from the work of Durrett and DeNero (2013), who extracted a set of edit operations and applied the transformations with a semi-Markov

CRF (Sarawagi and Cohen, 2004).

EHU EHU (Alegria and Etxeberria, 2016) took an approach based on standard grapheme-to-phoneme machinery. They extend the Phonetisaurus (Novak et al., 2012) toolkit, based on the OpenFST WFST library (Allauzen et al., 2007), to the task of morphological reinflection. Their system is organized as a pipeline. Given pairs of input and output strings, the first step involves an unsupervised algorithm to extract an alignment (many-to-one or one-to-many). Then, they train the weights of the WFSTs using the imputed alignments, introducing morphological tags as symbols on the input side of the transduction.

Alberta The Alberta system (Nicolai et al., 2016) is derived from the earlier work by Nicolai et al. (2015) and is methodologically quite similar to that of EHU—an unsupervised alignment model is first applied to the training pairs to impute an alignment. In this case, they employ the M2M-aligner (Jiampojamarn et al., 2007). In contrast to EHU, Nicolai et al. (2016) do allow many-to-many alignments. After computing the alignments, they discriminatively learn a string-to-string mapping using the DirectTL+ model (Jiampojamarn et al., 2008). This model is state-of-the-art for the grapheme-to-phoneme task and is very similar to the EHU system in that it assumes a monotonic alignment and could therefore be encoded as a WFST. Despite the similarity to the EHU system, the model performs much better overall. This increase in performance may be attributable to the extensive use of language-specific heuristics, detailed in the paper, or the application of a discriminative reranker.

Colorado The Colorado system (Liu and Mao, 2016) took the same general tack as the previous two systems—they used a pipelined approach that first discovered an alignment between the string pairs and then discriminatively trained a transduction. The alignment algorithm employed is the same as that of the baseline system, which relies on a rich-get-richer scheme based on the Chinese restaurant process (Sudoh et al., 2013), as discussed in §5. After obtaining the alignments, they extracted edit operations based on the alignments and used a semi-Markov CRF to apply the edits in a manner very similar to the work of Durrett and DeNero (2013).

OSU The OSU system (King, 2016) also used a pipelined approach. They first extracted sequences of edit operations using Hirschberg's algorithm (Hirschberg, 1975). This reduces the string-to-string mapping problem to a sequence tagging problem. Like the Colorado system, they followed Durrett and DeNero (2013) and used a semi-Markov CRF to apply the edit operations. In contrast to Durrett and DeNero (2013), who employed a 0th-order model, the OSU system used a 1st-order model. A major drawback of the system was the cost of inference. The unpruned set of edit operations had over 500 elements. As the cost of inference in the model is quadratic in the size of the state space (the number of edit operations), this created a significant slowdown with over 15 days required to train in some cases.

6.2 Camp 2: Revenge of the RNN

A surprising result of the shared task is the large performance gap between the top performing neural models and the rest of the pack. Indeed, the results of Faruqui et al. (2016) on the task of morphological inflection only yielded modest gains in some languages. However, the best neural approach outperformed the best non-neural approach by an average (over languages) of 13.76% absolute accuracy, and at most by 60.04%!

LMU The LMU system (Kann and Schütze, 2016) was the all-around best performing system in the shared task. The system builds off of the encoder-decoder model for machine translation (Sutskever et al., 2014) with a soft attention mechanism (Bahdanau et al., 2014). The architecture is identical to the RNN encoder-decoder architecture of Bahdanau et al. (2014)—a stacked GRU (Cho et al., 2014). The key innovation is in the formatting of the data. The input word along with both the source and target tags were fed into the network as a *single string* and trained to predict the target string. In effect, this means that if there are n elements in the paradigm, there is a single model for all n^2 possible reinflectional mappings. Thus, the architecture shares parameters among all reinflections, using a single encoder and a single decoder.

BIU-MIT The BIU-MIT (Aharoni et al., 2016) team submitted two systems. Their first model, like LMU, built upon the sequence-to-sequence architecture (Sutskever et al., 2014; Bahdanau et al., 2014; Faruqui et al., 2016), but with several im-

System	Standard			Restricted			Bonus		
	Task 1	Task 2	Task 3	Task 1	Task 2	Task 3	Task 1	Task 2	Task 3
LMU-1	1.0 (95.56)	1.0 (96.35)	1.0 (95.83)	1.0 (95.56)	1.0 (95.34)	1.0 (90.95)	1.0 (96.71)	1.0 (96.35)	1.0 (95.83)
LMU-2	2.0 (95.56)	2.0 (96.23)	2.0 (95.83)	2.0 (95.56)	2.0 (95.27)	2.0 (90.95)	—	—	—
BIU/MIT-1	—	—	—	4.2 (92.65)	5.2 (77.70)	3.8 (76.39)	—	—	—
BIU/MIT-2	—	—	—	4.2 (93.00)	4.2 (81.29)	—	—	—	—
HEL	—	—	—	3.9 (92.89)	3.5 (86.30)	3.2 (86.48)	—	—	—
MSU	3.8 (84.06)	3.6 (86.06)	3.8 (84.87)	6.2 (84.06)	6.0 (79.68)	6.2 (62.16)	—	—	—
CU	4.6 (81.02)	5.0 (72.98)	5.0 (71.75)	7.3 (81.02)	6.9 (69.89)	5.5 (67.91)	—	—	—
EHU	5.5 (79.24)	—	—	8.0 (79.67)	—	—	—	—	—
COL/NYU	6.5 (67.86)	4.7 (75.59)	4.8 (67.61)	9.2 (67.86)	7.2 (77.34)	6.3 (53.56)	2.7 (72.30)	2.5 (71.74)	2.6 (67.61)
OSU	—	—	—	9.0 (72.71)	—	—	—	—	—
UA	4.6 (81.83)	4.7 (74.06)	4.4 (71.23)	—	—	—	2.3 (79.95)	2.5 (71.56)	2.4 (70.04)
ORACLE.E	97.49	98.15	97.97	98.32	97.84	95.80	98.14	97.80	97.57

Table 6: Summary of results, showing average rank (with respect to other competitors) and average accuracy (equally weighted average over the 10 languages and marked in parentheses) by system. Oracle ensemble (ORACLE.E) accuracy represents the probability that at least one of the submitted systems predicted the correct form.

provements. Most importantly, they augment the encoder with a bidirectional LSTM to get a more informative representation of the context and they represent individual morphosyntactic attributes as well. In addition, they include template-inspired components to better cope with the templatic morphology of Arabic and Maltese. The second architecture, while also neural, more radically departs from previously proposed sequence-to-sequence models. The aligner from the baseline system is used to create a series of edit actions, similar to the systems in Camp 1. Rather than use a CRF, the BIU-MIT team predicted the sequence of edit actions using a neural model, much in the same way as a transition-based LSTM parser does (Dyer et al., 2015; Kiperwasser and Goldberg, 2016). The architectural consequence of this is that it replaces the soft alignment mechanism of (Bahdanau et al., 2014) with a hard attention mechanism, similar to Rastogi et al. (2016).

Helsinki The Helsinki system (Östling, 2016), like LMU and BIU-MIT, built off of the sequence-to-sequence architecture, augmenting the system with several innovations. First, a single decoder was used, rather than a unique one for all possible morphological tags, which allows for additional parameter sharing, similar to LMU. More LSTM layers were also added to the decoder, creating a deeper network. Finally, a convolutional layer over the character inputs was used, which was found to significantly increase performance over models without the convolutional layers.

6.3 Camp 3: Time for Some Linguistics

The third camp relied on linguistics-inspired heuristics to reduce the problem to multi-way classification. This camp is less unified than the other two, as both teams used very different heuristics.

Columbia – New York University Abu Dhabi The system developed jointly by Columbia and NYUAD (Taji et al., 2016) is based on the work of Eskander et al. (2013). It is unique among the submitted systems in that the first step in the pipeline is segmentation of the input words into prefixes, stems, and suffixes. Prefixes and suffixes are directly associated with morphological features. Stems within paradigms are further processed, using either linguistic intuitions or an empirical approach based on string alignments, to extract the stem letters that undergo changes across inflections. The extracted patterns are intended to capture stem-internal changes, such as vowel changes in Arabic. Reinflection is performed by selecting a set of changes to apply to a stem, and attaching appropriate affixes to the result.

Moscow State The Moscow State system (Sorokin, 2016) is derived from the work of Ahlberg et al. (2014) and Ahlberg et al. (2015). The general idea is to use finite-state techniques to compactly model all paradigms in an abstract form called an 'abstract paradigm'. Roughly speaking, an abstract paradigm is a set of rule transformations that derive all slots from the shared string subsequences present in each slot. Their method relies on the computation of longest common subsequence (Gusfield, 1997) to derive the abstract paradigms, which is similar to its use in the related task of lemmatization (Chrupała et al., 2008;

Müller et al., 2015). Once a complete set of abstract paradigms has been extracted from the data, the problem is reduced to multi-way classification, where the goal is to select which abstract paradigm should be applied to perform reinflection. The Moscow State system employs a multiclass SVM (Bishop, 2006) to solve the selection problem. Overall, this was the best-performing non-neural system. The reason for this may be that the abstract paradigm approach enforces hard constraints between reinflected forms in a way that many of the other non-neural systems do not.

6.4 Performance of Submitted Systems

Relative system performance is described in Table 6, which shows the average rank and per-language accuracy of each system by track and task. The table reflects the fact that some teams submitted more than one system (e.g. LMU-1 & LMU-2 in the table). Full results can be found in the appendix. Table 7 shows that in most cases, competing systems were significantly different (average $p < 0.05$ across 6 unpaired permutation tests for each pair with 5000 permutations per test). The only case in which this did not hold true was in comparing the systems submitted by LMU to one another.

Three teams exploited the bonus resources in some form: LMU, Alberta and Columbia/NYUAD. In general, gains from the bonus resources were modest. Even in Arabic, where the largest benefits were observed, going from track 2 to track 3 on task 1 resulted in an absolute increase in accuracy of only $\approx 3\%$ for LMU's best system.

The neural systems were the clear winner in the shared task. In fact, the gains over classical systems were quite outstanding. The neural systems had two advantages over the competing approaches. First, all these models learned to align and transduce *jointly*. This idea, however, is not intrinsic to neural architectures; it is possible—in fact common—to train finite-state transducers that sum over all possible alignments between the input and output strings (Dreyer et al., 2008; Cotterell et al., 2014).

Second, they all involved massive parameter sharing between the different reinflections. Since the reinflection task entails generalizing from only a few data pairs, this is likely to be a boon. Interestingly, the second BIU-MIT system, which

trained a neural model to predict edit operations, consistently ranked behind their first system. This indicates that pre-extracting edit operations, as all systems in the first camp did, is not likely to achieve top-level performance.

Even though the top-ranked neural systems do very well on their own, the other submitted systems may still contain a small amount of complementary information, so that an ensemble over the different approaches has a chance to improve accuracy. We present an upper bound on the possible accuracy of such an ensemble. Table 6 also includes an 'Oracle' that gives the correct answer if *any* of the submitted systems is correct. The average potential ensemble accuracy gain across tasks over the top-ranked system alone is 2.3%. This is the proportion of examples that the top system got wrong, but which some other system got right.

7 Future Directions

Given the success of the submitted reinflection systems in the face of limited data from typologically diverse languages, the future of morphological reinflection must extend in new directions. Further pursuing the line that led us to pose task 3, the problem of morphological reinflection could be expanded by requiring systems to learn with less supervision. Supervised datasets could be smaller or more weakly supervised, forcing systems to rely more on inductive bias or unlabeled data.

One innovation along these lines could be to provide multiple unlabeled source forms and ask for the rest of the paradigm to be produced. In another task, instead of using source and target morphological tags, systems could be asked to induce these from context. Such an extension would necessitate interaction with parsers, and would more closely integrate syntactic and morphological analysis.

Reflecting the traditional linguistic approaches to morphology, another task could allow the use of phonological forms in addition to orthographic forms. While this would necessitate learning a grapheme-to-phoneme mapping, it has the potential to actually simplify the learning task by removing orthographic idiosyncrasies (such as the Spanish 'c/qu' alternation, which is dependent on the backness of the following vowel, but preserves the phoneme /k/).

Traditional morphological analyzers, usually

	EHU	BI/M-1	BI/M-2	CU	COL/NYU	HEL	MSU	LMU-1	LMU-2	OSU
UA	90% (10)	—	—	67% (30)	93% (58)	—	79% (28)	100% (60)	100% (30)	—
EHU	—	100% (10)	100% (10)	85% (20)	100% (18)	100% (10)	85% (20)	100% (20)	100% (20)	100% (9)
BI/M-1	—	—	70% (20)	86% (28)	100% (22)	67% (30)	93% (28)	100% (30)	100% (30)	100% (9)
BI/M-2	—	—	—	95% (19)	100% (12)	80% (20)	79% (19)	95% (20)	95% (20)	100% (9)
CU	—	—	—	—	86% (49)	96% (28)	84% (56)	100% (58)	100% (58)	100% (9)
COL/NYU	—	—	—	—	—	95% (22)	96% (47)	100% (80)	100% (50)	100% (8)
HEL	—	—	—	—	—	—	89% (28)	97% (30)	97% (30)	100% (9)
MSU	—	—	—	—	—	—	—	96% (56)	96% (56)	100% (9)
LMU-1	—	—	—	—	—	—	—	—	3% (60)	100% (9)
LMU-2	—	—	—	—	—	—	—	—	—	100% (9)

Table 7: How often each pair of systems had significantly different accuracy under a paired permutation test ($p < 0.05$), as a fraction of the number of times that they competed (on the same language, track and task). The number of such competitions is in parentheses.

implemented as finite state transducers (Beesley and Karttunen, 2003), often return all morphologically plausible analyses if there is ambiguity. Learning to mimic the behavior of a hand-written analyzer in this respect could offer a more challenging task, and one that is useful within unsupervised learning (Dreyer and Eisner, 2011) as well as parsing. Existing wide-coverage morphological analyzers could be leveraged in the design of a more interactive shared task, where hand-coded models or approximate surface rules could serve as informants for grammatical inference algorithms.

The current task design did not explore all potential inflectional complexities in the languages included. For example, cliticization processes were generally not present in the language data. Adding such inflectional elements to the task can potentially make it more realistic in terms of real-world data sparsity in L1 learning scenarios. For example, Finnish noun and adjective inflection is generally modeled as a paradigm of 15 cases in singular and plural, i.e. with 30 slots in total—the shared task data included precisely such paradigms. However, adding all combinations of clitics raises the number of entries in an inflection table to 2,253 (Karlsson, 2008).

Although the languages introduced in this year's shared task were typologically diverse with a range of morphological types (agglutinative, fusional; prefixing, infixing, suffixing, or a mix), we did not cover reduplicative morphology, which is common in Austronesian languages (and elsewhere) but is avoided by traditional computational morphology since it cannot be represented using finite-state transduction. Furthermore, the focus was solely on inflectional data. Another version of the task could call for learning derivational morphology and predicting which derivational forms led to grammatical output (i.e. existing words or neologisms that are not subject to morphological blocking; Poser (1992)). This could be extended to learning the morphology of polysynthetic languages. These languages productively use not only inflection and derivation, which call for the addition of bound morphemes, but also incorporation, which involves combining lexical stems that are often used to form independent words (Mithun, 1984). Such languages combine the need to decompound, generate derivational alternatives, and accurately inflect any resulting words.

8 Conclusion

The SIGMORPHON 2016 Shared Task on Morphological Reinflection significantly expanded the problem of morphological reinflection from a problem of generating complete paradigms from a designated lemma form to generating requested forms based on arbitrary inflected forms, in some cases without a morphological tag identifying the paradigm cell occupied by that form. Furthermore, complete paradigms were not provided in the training data. The submitted systems employed a wide variety of approaches, both neural network-based approaches and extensions of non-neural approaches pursued in previous works such as Durrett and DeNero (2013), Ahlberg et al. (2015), and Nicolai et al. (2015). The superior performance of the neural approaches was likely due to the increased parameter sharing available in those architectures, as well as their ability to discover subtle linguistic features from these relatively large training sets, such as weak or long-distance contextual features that are less likely to appear in hand-engineered feature sets.

References

Roee Aharoni, Yoav Goldberg, and Yonatan Belinkov. 2016. Improving sequence to sequence learning for morphological inflection generation: The BIU-MIT systems for the SIGMORPHON 2016 shared task for morphological reinflection. In *Proceedings of the 2016 Meeting of SIGMORPHON*, Berlin, Germany. Association for Computational Linguistics.

Malin Ahlberg, Markus Forsberg, and Mans Hulden. 2014. Semi-supervised learning of morphological paradigms and lexicons. In *Proceedings of the 14th EACL*, pages 569–578, Gothenburg, Sweden. Association for Computational Linguistics.

Malin Ahlberg, Markus Forsberg, and Mans Hulden. 2015. Paradigm classification in supervised learning of morphology. In *Human Language Technologies: The 2015 Annual Conference of the North American Chapter of the ACL*, pages 1024–1029, Denver, CO. Association for Computational Linguistics.

Iñaki Alegria and Izaskun Etxeberria. 2016. EHU at the SIGMORPHON 2016 shared task. A simple proposal: Grapheme-to-phoneme for inflection. In *Proceedings of the 2016 Meeting of SIGMORPHON*, Berlin, Germany, August. Association for Computational Linguistics.

Cyril Allauzen, Michael Riley, Johan Schalkwyk, Wojciech Skut, and Mehryar Mohri. 2007. OpenFST: A general and efficient weighted finite-state transducer library. In *Implementation and Application of Automata, 12th International Conference, CIAA 2007, Prague, Czech Republic, July 16-18, 2007, Revised Selected Papers*, pages 11–23.

Howard I. Aronson. 1990. *Georgian: A Reading Grammar*. Slavica, Columbus, OH.

Dzmitry Bahdanau, Kyunghyun Cho, and Yoshua Bengio. 2014. Neural machine translation by jointly learning to align and translate. *arXiv preprint arXiv:1409.0473*.

Kenneth R. Beesley and Lauri Karttunen. 2003. *Finite State Morphology*. CSLI Publications, Stanford, CA.

Christopher M. Bishop. 2006. *Pattern Recognition and Machine Learning*. Springer.

John J. Camilleri. 2013. A computational grammar and lexicon for Maltese. Master's thesis, Chalmers University of Technology. Gothenburg, Sweden.

Kyunghyun Cho, Bart Van Merriënboer, Dzmitry Bahdanau, and Yoshua Bengio. 2014. On the properties of neural machine translation: Encoder-decoder approaches. *arXiv preprint arXiv:1409.1259*.

Grzegorz Chrupała, Georgiana Dinu, and Josef van Genabith. 2008. Learning morphology with Morfette. In *LREC*.

Ryan Cotterell, Nanyun Peng, and Jason Eisner. 2014. Stochastic contextual edit distance and probabilistic fsts. In *Proceedings of the 52nd Annual Meeting of the Association for Computational Linguistics (Volume 2: Short Papers)*, pages 625–630, Baltimore, Maryland. Association for Computational Linguistics.

Ryan Cotterell, Nanyun Peng, and Jason Eisner. 2015. Modeling word forms using latent underlying morphs and phonology. *Transactions of the Association for Computational Linguistics*, 3:433–447.

Markus Dreyer and Jason Eisner. 2009. Graphical models over multiple strings. In *Proceedings of the 2009 Conference on Empirical Methods in Natural Language Processing: Volume 1*, pages 101–110. Association for Computational Linguistics.

Markus Dreyer and Jason Eisner. 2011. Discovering morphological paradigms from plain text using a Dirichlet process mixture model. In *Proceedings of EMNLP 2011*, pages 616–627, Edinburgh. Association for Computational Linguistics.

Markus Dreyer, Jason R. Smith, and Jason Eisner. 2008. Latent-variable modeling of string transductions with finite-state methods. In *EMNLP*, pages 1080–1089.

Kevin Duh and Katrin Kirchhoff. 2004. Automatic learning of language model structure. In *Proceedings of the 20th International Conference on Computational Linguistics (COLING)*, pages 148–154, Stroudsburg, PA. Association for Computational Linguistics.

Greg Durrett and John DeNero. 2013. Supervised learning of complete morphological paradigms. In *Proceedings of the 2013 Conference of the North American Chapter of the Association for Computational Linguistics: Human Language Technologies*, pages 1185–1195, Atlanta. Association for Computational Linguistics.

Chris Dyer, Miguel Ballesteros, Wang Ling, Austin Matthews, and Noah A. Smith. 2015. Transition-based dependency parsing with stack long short-term memory. In *ACL*.

Ramy Eskander, Nizar Habash, and Owen Rambow. 2013. Automatic extraction of morphological lexicons from morphologically annotated corpora. In *Proceedings of the 2013 Conference on Empirical Methods in Natural Language Processing, EMNLP 2013*, pages 1032–1043.

Manaal Faruqui, Yulia Tsvetkov, Graham Neubig, and Chris Dyer. 2016. Morphological inflection generation using character sequence to sequence learning. In *Proceedings of the 2016 Conference of the North American Chapter of the Association for Computational Linguistics: Human Language Technologies*, San Diego, California. Association for Computational Linguistics.

Yoav Freund and Robert E. Schapire. 1999. Large margin classification using the perceptron algorithm. *Machine Learning*, 37(3):277–296.

Sharon Goldwater and David McClosky. 2005. Improving statistical MT through morphological analysis. In *Proceedings of the Conference on Human Language Technology and Empirical Methods in Natural Language Processing (HLT-EMNLP)*, pages 676–683, Stroudsburg, PA. Association for Computational Linguistics.

Dan Gusfield. 1997. *Algorithms on strings, trees and sequences: Computer science and computational biology*. Cambridge University Press.

Gunnar Ólafur Hansson. 2010. *Consonant Harmony: Long-Distance Interaction in Phonology*. University of California Publications in Linguistics. University of California Press, Berkeley, CA.

Daniel S. Hirschberg. 1975. A linear space algorithm for computing maximal common subsequences. *Communications of the ACM*, 18(6):341–343.

Sittichai Jiampojamarn, Grzegorz Kondrak, and Tarek Sherif. 2007. Applying many-to-many alignments and hidden Markov models to letter-to-phoneme conversion. In *Proceedings of the Human Language Technology Conference of the North American Chapter of the Association of Computational Linguistics*, pages 372–379.

Sittichai Jiampojamarn, Colin Cherry, and Grzegorz Kondrak. 2008. Joint processing and discriminative training for letter-to-phoneme conversion. In *ACL 2008, Proceedings of the 46th Annual Meeting of the Association for Computational Linguistics*, pages 905–913.

Katharina Kann and Hinrich Schütze. 2016. MED: The LMU system for the SIGMORPHON 2016 shared task on morphological reinflection. In *Proceedings of the 2016 Meeting of SIGMORPHON*, Berlin, Germany. Association for Computational Linguistics.

Fred Karlsson. 2008. *Finnish: An essential grammar*. Routledge.

Aleksandr E. Kibrik. 1998. Archi. In Andrew Spencer and Arnold M. Zwicky, editors, *The Handbook of Morphology*, pages 455–476. Blackwell, Oxford.

David King. 2016. Evaluating sequence alignment for learning inflectional morphology. In *Proceedings of the 2016 Meeting of SIGMORPHON*, Berlin, Germany, August. Association for Computational Linguistics.

Eliyahu Kiperwasser and Yoav Goldberg. 2016. Simple and accurate dependency parsing using bidirectional LSTM feature representations. *arXiv preprint arXiv:1603.04351*.

Christo Kirov, John Sylak-Glassman, Roger Que, and David Yarowsky. 2016. Very-large scale parsing and normalization of Wiktionary morphological paradigms. In *Proceedings of the Tenth International Conference on Language Resources and Evaluation (LREC 2016)*, pages 3121–3126, Paris, France. European Language Resources Association (ELRA).

Philipp Koehn. 2010. *Statistical Machine Translation*. Cambridge University Press, Cambridge.

Ling Liu and Lingshuang Jack Mao. 2016. Morphological reinflection with conditional random fields and unsupervised features. In *Proceedings of the 2016 Meeting of SIGMORPHON*, Berlin, Germany. Association for Computational Linguistics.

Marianne Mithun. 1984. The evolution of noun incorporation. *Language*, 60(4):847–894, December.

Mehryar Mohri, Fernando Pereira, and Michael Riley. 2002. Weighted finite-state transducers in speech recognition. *Computer Speech & Language*, 16(1):69–88.

Thomas Müller, Ryan Cotterell, Alexander Fraser, and Hinrich Schütze. 2015. Joint lemmatization and morphological tagging with LEMMING. In *Empirical Methods in Natural Language Processing*.

Garrett Nicolai, Colin Cherry, and Grzegorz Kondrak. 2015. Inflection generation as discriminative string transduction. In *NAACL HLT 2015, The 2015 Conference of the North American Chapter of the Association for Computational Linguistics: Human Language Technologies*, pages 922–931.

Garrett Nicolai, Bradley Hauer, Adam St. Arnaud, and Grzegorz Kondrak. 2016. Morphological reinflection via discriminative string transduction. In *Proceedings of the 2016 Meeting of SIGMORPHON*, Berlin, Germany. Association for Computational Linguistics.

Josef R. Novak, Nobuaki Minematsu, and Keikichi Hirose. 2012. WFST-based grapheme-to-phoneme conversion: Open source tools for alignment, model-building and decoding. In *10th International Workshop on Finite State Methods and Natural Language Processing (FSMNLP)*, pages 45–49.

Robert Östling. 2016. Morphological reinflection with convolutional neural networks. In *Proceedings of the 2016 Meeting of SIGMORPHON*, Berlin, Germany. Association for Computational Linguistics.

William J. Poser. 1992. Blocking of phrasal constructions by lexical items. In Ivan Sag and Anna Szabolcsi, editors, *Lexical Matters*, pages 111–130, Palo Alto, CA. CSLI.

Pushpendre Rastogi, Ryan Cotterell, and Jason Eisner. 2016. Weighting finite-state transductions with neural context. In *NAACL*.

Keren Rice. 2000. *Morpheme Order and Semantic Scope: Word Formation in the Athapaskan Verb*. Cambridge University Press, Cambridge, UK.

Sunita Sarawagi and William W. Cohen. 2004. Semi-Markov conditional random fields for information extraction. In *Advances in Neural Information Processing Systems 17 [Neural Information Processing Systems, NIPS 2004]*, pages 1185–1192.

Alexey Sorokin. 2016. Using longest common subsequence and character models to predict word forms. In *Proceedings of the 2016 Meeting of SIGMOR-PHON*, Berlin, Germany. Association for Computational Linguistics.

Katsuhito Sudoh, Shinsuke Mori, and Masaaki Nagata. 2013. Noise-aware character alignment for bootstrapping statistical machine transliteration from bilingual corpora. In *Proceedings of the 2013 Conference on Empirical Methods in Natural Language Processing, EMNLP 2013*, pages 204–209.

Ilya Sutskever, Oriol Vinyals, and Quoc V. Le. 2014. Sequence to sequence learning with neural networks. In *Advances in Neural Information Processing Systems*, pages 3104–3112.

John Sylak-Glassman, Christo Kirov, Matt Post, Roger Que, and David Yarowsky. 2015a. A universal feature schema for rich morphological annotation and fine-grained cross-lingual part-of-speech tagging. In Cerstin Mahlow and Michael Piotrowski, editors, *Proceedings of the 4th Workshop on Systems and Frameworks for Computational Morphology (SFCM)*, pages 72–93. Springer, Berlin.

John Sylak-Glassman, Christo Kirov, David Yarowsky, and Roger Que. 2015b. A language-independent feature schema for inflectional morphology. In *Proceedings of the 53rd Annual Meeting of the Association for Computational Linguistics and the 7th International Joint Conference on Natural Language Processing (ACL-IJCNLP)*, pages 674–680, Beijing. Association for Computational Linguistics.

Dima Taji, Ramy Eskander, Nizar Habash, and Owen Rambow. 2016. The Columbia University - New York University Abu Dhabi SIGMORPHON 2016 morphological reinflection shared task submission. In *Proceedings of the 2016 Meeting of SIGMOR-PHON*, Berlin, Germany. Association for Computational Linguistics.

Robert W. Young and William Morgan. 1987. *The Navajo Language: A Grammar and Colloquial Dictionary*. University of New Mexico Press, Albuquerque.

Morphological reinflection with convolutional neural networks

Robert Östling

Department of Modern Languages, University of Helsinki
PL 24 (Unionsgatan 40, A316)
00014 Helsingfors universitet, Finland
`robert.ostling@helsinki.fi`

Abstract

We present a system for morphological reinflection based on an encoder-decoder neural network model with extra convolutional layers. In spite of its simplicity, the method performs reasonably well on all the languages of the SIGMORPHON 2016 shared task, particularly for the most challenging problem of limited-resources reinflection (track 2, task 3). We also find that using *only* convolution achieves surprisingly good results in this task, surpassing the accuracy of our encoder-decoder model for several languages.

1 Introduction

Morphological reinflection is the task of predicting one form from a morphological paradigm given another form, e.g. predicting the English present participle *ringing* given the past tense *rang*. The SIGMORPHON shared task considers three variants of this problem, with decreasing amounts of information available beyond the source form and the morphological features of the target form:

1. The source form is always the citation form.
2. The source form's morphological features are not fixed, but given.
3. Only the source form itself is given.

The first and simplest case is the most well-researched, and is essentially equivalent to the task of predicting morphological paradigms.

This paper presents our system for morphological reinflection, which was submitted for the SIGMORPHON 2016 shared task. To complement the description given here, the source code of our implementation is available as free software.[1]

---

[1] `https://github.com/robertostling/`
`sigmorphon2016-system`

2 Background

In general, morphological reinflection can be solved by applying any technique for morphological analysis followed by morphological generation. These tasks have traditionally been performed using manually specified rules, a slow and expensive process. Recently, there has been an increased interest in methods for learning morphological transformations automatically from data, which is also the setting of the SIGMORPHON 2016 shared task.

This work is based on that of Faruqui et al. (2016), who use a sequence-to-sequence model similar to that commonly used in machine translation (Sutskever et al., 2014). Their method is very simple: for each language and morphological feature set, they train a separate model with a character-level bidirectional LSTM encoder (where only the final hidden states are used), and an LSTM decoder whose inputs are the encoded input as well as the input character sequence.

3 Model

We propose modifying the model of Faruqui et al. (2016) by:

1. using a single decoder, rather than one for each combination of morphological features (which could lead to data sparsity for languages with complex morphology and large paradigms),
2. using both the raw letter sequence of the source string and its convolution as inputs,
3. using deeper LSTM units for the decoder.

Although this model was originally designed for inflection generation given a lemma, it can trivially be used for reinflection by using inflected forms rather than lemmas as input. Thus, we use exactly the same model for the first and third task,

Proceedings of the 14th Annual SIGMORPHON Workshop on Computational Research in Phonetics, Phonology, and Morphology, pages 23–26,
Berlin, Germany, August 11, 2016. ©2016 Association for Computational Linguistics

Figure 1: Structure of our convolutional encoder-decoder model (note that convolutional layers are not present in all configurations).

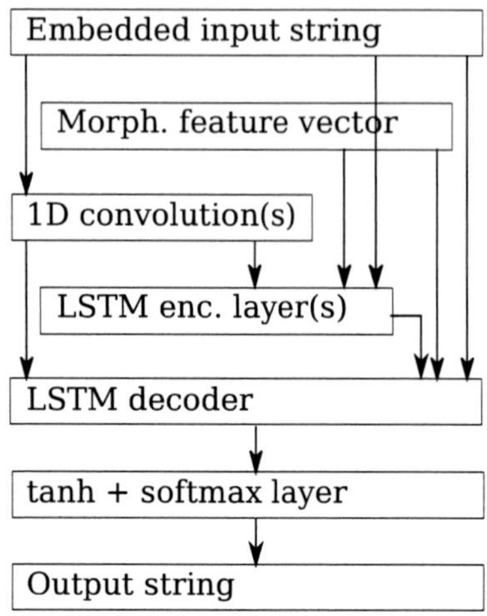

Figure 2: Structure of our purely convolutional model (note that GRU layers are not present in all configurations).

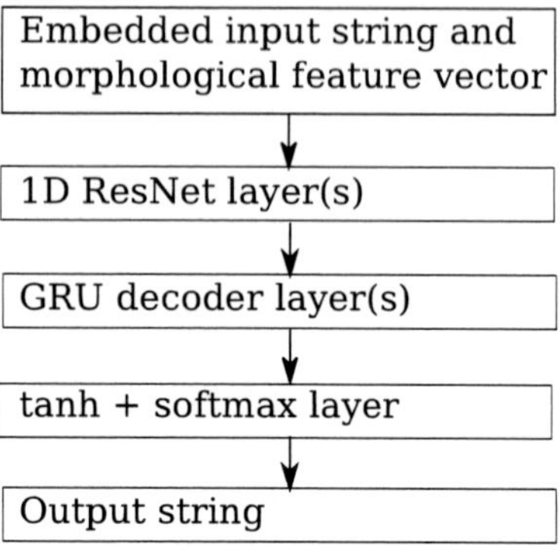

and for the second task where morphological features are given for the source form, we include those features along with the target form features (which are given in all three tasks).

In our experiments, we use 4 convolutional layers and 2 stacked LSTMs (Hochreiter and Schmidhuber, 1997). We use 256 LSTM units (for both the encoder and decoder), 64-dimensional character embeddings and 64 convolutional filters of width 3 for each layer. The LSTM outputs were projected through a fully connected hidden layer with 64 units, and finally through a fully connected layer with softmax activations over the alphabet of the language in question. Morphological features are encoded as binary vectors, which are concatenated with the character embeddings (and, when used, convolved character embeddings) to form the input of the decoder. We then used the Adam algorithm (Kingma and Ba, 2014) for optimization, where the training objective is the cross-entropy of the target strings. For decoding, we use beam search with a beam size of 4. The model architecture is summarized in figure 1.

To further explore the effect of using convolutional layers in isolation, we also performed follow-up experiments after the shared task submission. In these experiments we used an even simpler architecture without any encoder, instead we used a 1-dimensional residual network architecture (He et al., 2016, figure 1b) with constant size across layers, followed by either one or zero Gated Recurrent Unit layers (Cho et al., 2014). The output vector of each residual layer (which contains two convolutional layers with Batch Normalization (Ioffe and Szegedy, 2015) and rectified linear units after each) is combined with the vector of the previous layer by addition, which means that the output is the sum of the input and the output of each layer. This direct additive coupling between layers at different depth allows very deep networks to be trained efficiently. In this work we use up to 12 residual layers, corresponding to a total of 24 convolutional layers.

In these experiments (unlike the encoder-decoder model), dropout (Srivastava et al., 2014) was used for regularization, with a dropout factor of 50%. The morphological features of the target form are concatenated to the 128-dimensional character embeddings at the top convolutional layer, so the total number of filters for each layer is $128 + n$ in order to keep the architecture simple and uniform, where n is the number of different morphological features in the given language. Decoding is done by choosing the single most probable symbol at each letter position, according to the final softmax layer. This model is summarized in figure 2.

4 Evaluation

All results reported in this section refer to accuracy, computed using the official SIGMORPHON 2016 development data and scoring script. Table 1 on the following page shows the result on the official test set, and a full comparison to other systems

Table 1: Results of our convolutional encoder-decoder system on the official SIGMORPHON shared task test set.

Language	Accuracy (percent)		
	Task 1	Task 2	Task 3
Arabic	89.52	69.53	70.43
Finnish	95.14	88.42	87.55
Georgian	97.02	92.84	91.85
German	94.40	91.73	89.14
Hungarian	98.38	96.25	96.46
Maltese	86.16	73.17	75.54
Navajo	82.10	77.37	83.21
Russian	89.94	86.60	84.59
Spanish	98.35	95.35	94.85
Turkish	97.93	91.69	91.25

is available on the shared task website[2] (our system is labeled 'HEL').

We participate only in track 2, which only allows training data from the same task that is evaluated. Training data from other (lower-numbered) tasks, as track 1 allows, could trivially be appended to the training data of our model, but this was not done since we focused on exploring the core problem of learning reinflection. The same constraints are followed in all experiments described here.

Note that due to time constraints, we were not able to explore the full set of parameters before submitting the test set results. Of the models that had finished training by the deadline, we chose the one which had the highest accuracy on the development set. The results reported here are from later experiments which were carried out to systematically test the effects of our proposed changes. Table 2 shows that using convolutional layers improves accuracy in almost all cases, whereas adding an extra LSTM layer does not bring any systematic improvement.

Results when using only convolutional layers or convolutional layers followed by a GRU recurrent layer can be found in table 3 on the following page. To our surprise, we found that convolution alone is sufficient to achieve results comparable to or better than several of the other systems in the shared task, and for some languages it beats our own submitted results. There is no clear benefit across languages of adding a final GRU decoder

Table 2: Results of our convolutional encoder-decoder system on the official SIGMORPHON shared task development set for task 3 (reinflection). The first column contains results of models with both convolutions (4 layers) and deep LSTMs (2 layers), the second uses a single LSTM layer, and the third one uses no convolutional layers.

Language	Accuracy (percent)		
	both	-deep	-conv
Arabic	66.9	70.8	**75.8**
Finnish	85.5	**88.4**	80.9
Georgian	**92.3**	91.9	87.1
German	**89.6**	87.2	88.7
Hungarian	**97.1**	94.0	95.6
Maltese	**76.1**	74.0	74.9
Navajo	**89.6**	87.2	85.1
Russian	83.2	**84.1**	82.2
Spanish	93.6	**94.3**	91.1
Turkish	**89.7**	88.8	80.4

layer, but increasing the depth of the network and in particular the width of the convolution seem to benefit accuracy.

5 Conclusions

We find that the model of Faruqui et al. (2016) can be extended to the task of reinflection and delivers very good levels of accuracy across languages, and that adding convolutional layers consistently improves accuracy.

Further experiments show, to our surprise, that a simple and purely convolutional architecture designed for image classification in many cases achieves an even higher accuracy. Although convolutional architectures have become standard (along with recurrent neural networks) in many text *encoding* tasks, this is one of rather few examples of where they have been successfully used for text *generation*.

Acknowledgments

This work was carried out using the computing resources of CSC.[3]

[2] http://ryancotterell.github.io/sigmorphon2016/

[3] https://www.csc.fi/

Table 3: Results of our purely convolution system (not submitted) on the official SIGMORPHON shared task development set for task 3 (reinflection). System configurations are given on the form "convolutional layers–filter size".

Language	Accuracy (percent)									
	With GRU decoder					Without GRU decoder				
	24–7	16–7	8–7	24–5	24–3	24–7	16–7	8–7	24–5	24–3
Arabic	**74.2**	69.6	63.7	71.8	47.7	71.9	68.1	67.4	65.0	55.5
Finnish	89.6	90.9	84.9	85.5	90.4	**91.3**	89.2	91.0	88.8	86.9
Georgian	91.2	91.4	91.3	**91.5**	90.1	89.9	89.7	90.3	91.0	89.6
German	89.0	89.8	89.1	89.6	88.8	88.9	**89.9**	89.6	89.8	88.9
Hungarian	93.5	**96.0**	89.8	93.8	92.0	92.2	90.0	88.0	90.9	90.0
Maltese	63.0	63.2	60.4	50.1	63.2	**66.0**	61.1	54.1	61.2	64.6
Navajo	78.8	81.9	72.4	78.8	50.0	**84.3**	80.5	49.6	68.5	31.4
Russian	84.8	85.0	**86.1**	85.4	83.2	85.4	86.0	85.0	86.1	82.2
Spanish	**95.5**	92.6	94.5	95.3	92.7	94.7	94.8	94.9	94.1	95.2
Turkish	91.4	91.4	92.1	90.8	89.7	**92.8**	91.1	90.7	90.7	90.4

References

Kyunghyun Cho, Bart van Merrienboer, Caglar Gulcehre, Dzmitry Bahdanau, Fethi Bougares, Holger Schwenk, and Yoshua Bengio. 2014. Learning phrase representations using RNN encoder–decoder for statistical machine translation. In *Proceedings of the 2014 Conference on Empirical Methods in Natural Language Processing (EMNLP)*, pages 1724–1734, Doha, Qatar, October. Association for Computational Linguistics.

Manaal Faruqui, Yulia Tsvetkov, Graham Neubig, and Chris Dyer. 2016. Morphological inflection generation using character sequence to sequence learning. In *Proc. of NAACL*.

Kaiming He, Xiangyu Zhang, Shaoqing Ren, and Jian Sun. 2016. Identity mappings in deep residual networks. *CoRR*, abs/1603.05027.

Sepp Hochreiter and Jürgen Schmidhuber. 1997. Long short-term memory. *Neural Computation*, 9(8):1735–1780, November.

Sergey Ioffe and Christian Szegedy. 2015. Batch normalization: Accelerating deep network training by reducing internal covariate shift. In David Blei and Francis Bach, editors, *Proceedings of the 32nd International Conference on Machine Learning (ICML-15)*, pages 448–456. JMLR Workshop and Conference Proceedings.

Diederik P. Kingma and Jimmy Ba. 2014. Adam: A method for stochastic optimization. *CoRR*, abs/1412.6980.

Nitish Srivastava, Geoffrey Hinton, Alex Krizhevsky, Ilya Sutskever, and Ruslan Salakhutdinov. 2014. Dropout: A simple way to prevent neural networks from overfitting. *Journal of Machine Learning Research*, 15:1929–1958.

Ilya Sutskever, Oriol Vinyals, and Quoc V. V Le. 2014. Sequence to sequence learning with neural networks. In Z. Ghahramani, M. Welling, C. Cortes, N.D. Lawrence, and K.Q. Weinberger, editors, *Advances in Neural Information Processing Systems 27*, pages 3104–3112. Curran Associates, Inc.

EHU at the SIGMORPHON 2016 Shared Task. A Simple Proposal: Grapheme-to-Phoneme for Inflection

Iñaki Alegria, Izaskun Etxeberria
IXA taldea, UPV-EHU
`{i.alegria,izaskun.etxeberria}@ehu.es`

Abstract

This paper presents a proposal for learning morphological inflections by a grapheme-to-phoneme learning model. No special processing is used for specific languages. The starting point has been our previous research on induction of phonology and morphology for normalization of historical texts. The results show that a very simple method can indeed improve upon some baselines, but does not reach the accuracies of the best systems in the task.

1 Introduction

In our previous work carried out in the context of normalization of historical texts (Etxeberria et al., 2016) we proposed an approach based on the induction of phonology. We obtained good results using only induced phonological weighted finite-state transducers (WFSTs), i.e. by leveraging the phoneme-to-grapheme method to yield a grapheme-to-grapheme model. The research question now is if the grapheme-to-grapheme model can be extended to handle morphological information instead of words or morphological segmentation. To assess this, we test a general solution that works without special processing for specific languages (i.e. we do not focus on special treatment of accents in Spanish and other idiosyncracies).

1.1 Task

We only have taken part in task 1 (Inflection from lemma/citation form) of the SIGMORPHON 2016 Shared Task (Cotterell et al., 2016). Given a lemma with its part-of-speech, the system must generate a target inflected form whose morphosyntactic description is given.[1]

1.2 Corpora and Resources

We use the data provided by the organizers of the task. Our first experiments and tuning were conducted on eight languages before the two additional 'surprise' languages (Maltese and Navajo) were provided.

We also ran experiments using the available bonus-resources (track 3) but after initial results we decided to present only a system using the basic resources.

2 Related work

In our previous work (Etxeberria et al., 2014; Etxeberria et al., 2016) we have used *Phonetisaurus*,[2] a WFST-driven phonology tool (Novak et al., 2012) which learns to map phonological changes using a noisy channel model. It is a solution that works well using a limited amount of training information. The task addressed earlier was the normalization of historical/dialectal texts.

In the same paper we demonstrated that the method is viable for language-independent normalization and we tested the same approach for normalization of Spanish and Slovene historical texts obtaining similar or better results than previous systems reported by Porta et al. (2013) (using hand-written rules) and Scherrer and Erjavec (2015) (using a character-based SMT system).

Because of the model's relative success with historical normalization and its simplicity, we developed the approach further for addressing the shared task problem.

There exist other finite-state transducer-based approaches, generally more complex than what we present, of which two warrant a mention:

(i) Dreyer et al. (2008) develops a model for

---

[1] `http://www.sigmorphon.org/sharedtask`

[2] `https://github.com/AdolfVonKleist/Phonetisaurus`

Proceedings of the 14th Annual SIGMORPHON Workshop on Computational Research in Phonetics, Phonology, and Morphology, pages 27–30,
Berlin, Germany, August 11, 2016. ©2016 Association for Computational Linguistics

string-to-string transduction where results are improved using latent-variables.

(ii) Cotterell et al. (2015) models word-forms using latent underlying morphs and phonology. The system includes finite-state technology (in the form of WFSA and PFSTs) in two of the three steps: concatenation, phonology, and phonetics.

3 Experiments and Evaluation

3.1 Basic Method

We used *Phonetisaurus* to train a WFST-system that learns the changes that occur when going from the citation form to another form. This tool—while not specifically limited to such uses— is widely used for rapid development of high-quality grapheme-to-phoneme (g2p) converters. It is open-source, easy-to-use, and authors report promising results (Novak et al., 2012).

Phonetisaurus uses joint n-gram models and it is based on OpenFST, which learns a mapping of phonological changes using a noisy channel model. The application of the tool includes three major steps:

1. Sequence alignment. The alignment algorithm is based on the algorithm proposed in Jiampojamarn et al. (2007) and includes some minor modifications to it.

2. Model training. An n-gram language model is trained using the aligned data and then converted into a WFST. For producing the language model, we used the Language Model training toolkit *NGramLibrary* for our experiments, although several alternative similar tools exist that all cooperate with *Phonetisaurus*: *mitlm, NGramLibrary,* SRILM, SRILM *MaxEnt extension, CMU-Cambridge SLM.*

3. Decoding. The default decoder used in the WFST-based approach finds the best hypothesis for the input words given the WFST obtained in the previous step. It is also possible to extract a k-best list of output hypotheses for each word.

The alignment algorithm is capable of learning many-to-many relationships and includes three modifications to the basic toolkit: (a) a constraint is imposed such that only many-to-one and one-to-many alignments are considered during training; (b) during initialization, a joint alignment lattice is constructed for each input entry, and any unconnected arcs are deleted;[3] (c) all transitions, including those that model deletions and insertions, are initialized with and constrained to maintaining a non-zero weight.

As the results obtained with this tool were the best ones in our previous scenario, we decided to employ it for this task. Concretely, we have used *Phonetisaurus* to learn a WFST which can translate simplified morphological expressions to words to solve the inflection task. Once the transducer is trained, it can be used to generate correspondences for previously unseen morphological representations and their corresponding word-forms.

3.2 Testing the models

Using the development section for tuning we experimented with different variations in our approach in order to tune a good model for the problem.

First, we compacted the morphological information in a tag (which we consider a pseudo-morpheme) by concatenating the first letter in the category with a consecutive number. For example, the first lines in the training corpus for German

```
aalen pos=V, ... per=1,num=PL    aalen
aalen pos=V, ... per=3,num=PL    aalen
aalen pos=V, ... per=2,num=SG    aaltest
aalen pos=V, ... per=3,num=SG    aalte
aalen pos=V,tense=PRS            aalend
```

are converted into:

```
aalen V0    aalen
aalen V1    aalen
aalen V2    aaltest
aalen V3    aalte
aalen V4    aalend
```

Using this information three experiments were carried out where the morphosyntactic information was

- treated as a suffix.

- treated as a suffix and as a prefix.

- treated as a suffix, as an infix in the center of the lemma, and as a prefix.

---

[3]The topology of the WFST is assigned by the tool and the model is rather large (standard parameters are used: from 1-gram to 7-gram).

The strongest results were obtained using the second model for all languages except Finnish, which yielded the best results using only a suffix-based representation.

To illustrate the encoding, below are the first few entries in the development corpus for German:

N96+Aak+N96	→	*Aak*
V87+aalen+V87	→	*geaalt*
V79+aasen+V79	→	*aaste*
V1+abandonnieren+V1	→	*abandonnieren*
A40+abchasisch+A40	→	*abchasischerem*

In a second step we built different WFSTs depending on the category, but this yielded no improvement. As an alternative, we decided to test if putting only the category information in the prefix (i.e. one character) could help in the task. This produced an improvement only for Finnish.

As a third step we tested the possibility of optimizing the size and the content of the tag (the pseudo-morpheme), attempting to match its length with the length of the corresponding morpheme, as in the following example for German encodings:

N+Aak+N96	→	*Aak*
V87+aalen+V87	→	*geaalt*
V+aasen+V79	→	*aaste*
V+abandonnieren+V1	→	*abandonnieren*
A+abchasisch+A4000	→	*abchasischerem*

This strategy produced no solid improvement in our preliminary experiments.

3.3 Evaluation

We have measured the quality using the metrics and the script provided by the organizers; the baseline figures also originate with the organizers.

In all the languages whole tags were injected as prefixes and suffixes, with the exception of Finnish, where in the prefix tag position only the first character is included. For example, for the wordform *aakkostot* 'alphabets' $N+aakkosto+N9$ is used instead of $N9+aakkosto+N9$.

For the submitted final test we retrained the transducer adding the development section to the training corpus. As can be seen in table 1, a slight improvement was obtained (0.43% on average).

4 Using external information

Trying to take advantage of bonus resources, we used a word list for Spanish, German and Russian available with the *FreeLing* package (Carreras et al., 2004) as a 1-gram language-model of words.

Language	Baseline	Dev	Test
Arabic	**69.40**	67.53	64.68
Finnish	69.80	**86.86**	83.72
Georgian	**91.60**	87.04	83.11
German	89.90	**91.61**	89.86
Hungarian	74.10	**91.04**	85.39
Maltese	36.56	**61.89**	64.80
Navajo	70.30	**93.53**	56.33
Russian	**90.20**	86.74	86.58
Spanish	**95.49**	90.98	91.35
Turkish	59.20	**90.36**	90.84
Mean		**84.76**	79.67

Table 1: Results on the test corpus using 1-best accuracy for evaluation.

Since it is possible to produce multiple outputs from the WFST we train, we also experimented with an approach where the WFST would return several ranked candidates (3, 5, and 10), and selecting the first one found in the word list. If none of the candidates appeared in the list, the first proposal was used.

Using this strategy the results for Spanish improved slightly (by 2%), while the results for German improved slightly less (by 0.2%), and the Russian results worsened (by -0.7%).

Language	Basic	Filtering 3	Filtering 5
German	91.61	**91.80**	91.73
Russian	**86.74**	86.05	84.73
Spanish	90.98	**92.86**	92.86

Table 2: Accuracy when using a word list for filtering the proposals from the WFST. The first column shows the results without any external resources used; in the second column a word list has been used for filtering the top 3 proposals and in the third column for filtering with the top 5 proposals.

Since *FreeLing* is known to produce the highest-quality output for Spanish, we may assume that the results reflect the relative quality of the resources in that package.

Due to this limited improvement, we decided to present only the basic system for track 1.

5 Conclusions and future work

Previous work on lexical normalization on historical and dialectal texts has been extended and applied to a morphological inflection scenario.

While the method is simple and somewhat limited, with results not fully competitive against the best reported systems (Cotterell et al., 2016), some difficult languages saw a relatively good performance (Navajo and Maltese).

In the near future, our aim is to improve the results by trying to place the tags and morphemes in a more congenial configuration for WFST training and to use existing proposals to harness available latent information (Dreyer et al., 2008). In addition to this, we plan to incorporate techniques learned from other participants in the shared task.

References

Xavier Carreras, Isaac Chao, Lluis Padró, and Muntsa Padró. 2004. FreeLing: An open-source suite of language analyzers. In *Proceedings of LREC*.

Ryan Cotterell, Nanyun Peng, and Jason Eisner. 2015. Modeling word forms using latent underlying morphs and phonology. *Transactions of the Association for Computational Linguistics*, 3:433–447.

Ryan Cotterell, Christo Kirov, John Sylak-Glassman, David Yarowsky, Jason Eisner, and Mans Hulden. 2016. The SIGMORPHON 2016 shared task—morphological reinflection. In *Proceedings of the 2016 Meeting of SIGMORPHON*, Berlin, Germany, August. Association for Computational Linguistics.

Markus Dreyer, Jason R Smith, and Jason Eisner. 2008. Latent-variable modeling of string transductions with finite-state methods. In *Proceedings of the conference on empirical methods in natural language processing*, pages 1080–1089. Association for Computational Linguistics.

Izaskun Etxeberria, Inaki Alegria, Mans Hulden, and Larraitz Uria. 2014. Learning to map variation-standard forms using a limited parallel corpus and the standard morphology. *Procesamiento del Lenguaje Natural*, 52:13–20.

Izaskun Etxeberria, Inaki Alegria, Larraitz Uria, and Mans Hulden. 2016. Evaluating the noisy channel model for the normalization of historical texts: Basque, Spanish and Slovene. In *Proceedings of the LREC2016*.

Sittichai Jiampojamarn, Grzegorz Kondrak, and Tarek Sherif. 2007. Applying many-to-many alignments and hidden Markov models to letter-to-phoneme conversion. In *HLT-NAACL*, volume 7, pages 372–379.

Josef R. Novak, Nobuaki Minematsu, and Keikichi Hirose. 2012. WFST-based grapheme-to-phoneme conversion: Open source tools for alignment, model-building and decoding. In *Proceedings of the 10th International Workshop on Finite State Methods and Natural Language Processing*, pages 45–49, Donostia–San Sebastian, July. Association for Computational Linguistics.

Jordi Porta, José-Luis Sancho, and Javier Gómez. 2013. Edit transducers for spelling variation in old Spanish. In *Proc. of the workshop on computational historical linguistics at NODALIDA 2013. NEALT Proc. Series*, volume 18, pages 70–79.

Yves Scherrer and Tomaž Erjavec. 2015. Modernising historical Slovene words. *Natural Language Engineering*, pages 1–25.

Morphological Reinflection via Discriminative String Transduction

Garrett Nicolai, Bradley Hauer, Adam St Arnaud, Grzegorz Kondrak
Department of Computing Science
University of Alberta, Edmonton, Canada
{nicolai,bmhauer,ajstarna,gkondrak}@ualberta.ca

Abstract

We describe our approach and experiments in the context of the SIGMOR-PHON 2016 Shared Task on Morphological Reinflection. The results show that the methods of Nicolai et al. (2015) perform well on typologically diverse languages. We also discuss language-specific heuristics and errors.

1 Introduction

Many languages have complex morphology with dozens of different word-forms for any given lemma. It is often beneficial to reduce the data sparsity introduced by morphological variation in order to improve the applicability of methods that rely on textual regularity. The task of inflection generation (Task 1) is to produce an inflected form given a lemma and desired inflection, which is specified as an abstract tag. The task of labelled reinflection (Task 2) replaces the input lemma with a morphologically-tagged inflected form. Finally, the task of unlabelled reinflection (Task 3) differs from Task 2 in that the input lacks the inflection tag.

In this paper, we describe our system as participants in the SIGMORPHON 2016 Shared Task on Morphological Reinflection (Cotterell et al., 2016). Our approach is based on discriminative string transduction performed with a modified version of the DIRECTL+ program (Jiampojamarn et al., 2008). We perform Task 1 using the inflection generation approach of Nicolai et al. (2015), which we refer to as the *lemma-to-word* model. We also derive a reverse *word-to-lemma* (lemmatization) model from the Task 1 data. We perform Task 3 by composing the *word-to-lemma* and *lemma-to-word* models. We reduce Task 2 to Task 3 by simply ignoring the input inflection tag.

2 Methods

In this section, we describe the application of our string transduction and reranking approaches to the three shared tasks.

2.1 String Transduction

We perform string transduction by adapting DI-RECTL+, a tool originally designed for grapheme-to-phoneme conversion.[1] DIRECTL+ is a feature-rich, discriminative character string transducer that searches for a model-optimal sequence of character transformation rules for its input. The core of the engine is a dynamic programming algorithm capable of transducing many consecutive characters in a single operation. Using a structured version of the MIRA algorithm (McDonald et al., 2005), training attempts to assign weights to each feature so that its linear model separates the gold-standard derivation from all others in its search space.

From aligned source-target pairs, DIRECTL+ extracts statistically-supported feature templates: source context, target n-gram, and joint n-gram features. Context features conjoin the rule with indicators for all source character n-grams within a fixed window of where the rule is being applied. Target n-grams provide indicators on target character sequences, describing the shape of the target as it is being produced, and may also be conjoined with our source context features. Joint n-grams build indicators on rule sequences, combining source and target context, and memorizing frequently-used rule patterns. We train separate models for each part of speech in the training data.

We perform source-target pair alignment with a modified version of the M2M aligner (Jiampojamarn et al., 2007). The program applies the Expectation-Maximization algorithm with the ob-

---

[1] https://code.google.com/p/directl-p

Proceedings of the 14th Annual SIGMORPHON Workshop on Computational Research in Phonetics, Phonology, and Morphology, pages 31–35,
Berlin, Germany, August 11, 2016. ©2016 Association for Computational Linguistics

jective to maximize the joint likelihood of its aligned source and target pairs. In order to encourage alignments between identical characters, we modify the aligner to generalize all identity transformations into a single match operation.

2.2 Task 1: Inflection

For Task 1, we derive a *lemma-to-word* model, which transforms the lemma along with an inflection tag into the inflected form. Our method models affixation with atomic morphological tags. For example, the training instance corresponding to the past participle *dado* of the Spanish verb *dar* "to give" consists of the source `dar+PP` and the target `dado`. The unsupervised M2M aligner matches the `+PP` tag with the `do` suffix on the basis of their frequent co-occurrence in the training data. DIRECTL+ then learns that the `PP` tag should be transduced into `do` when the lemma ends in `ar`. Similarly, prefixes are represented by a tag before the lemma. The transducer can also memorize stem changes that occur within the context of a tag. For example, the training pair `PP+singen+PP` → `gesungen` can inform the transduction `PP+ringen+PP` → `gerungen` at test time.

2.3 Task 2: Labeled Reinflection

Task 2 is to generate a target inflected form, given another inflected form and its tag. Since our current approach is not able to take advantage of the tag information, we disregard this part of the input, effectively reducing Task 2 to Task 3.

2.4 Task 3: Unlabeled Reinflection

In general, Task 3 appears to be harder than Tasks 1 and 2 because it provides neither the lemma nor the inflection tag for the given word-form. In essence, our approach is to first *lemmatize* the source word, and then proceed as with Task 1 as described in Section 2.2. We compose the *lemma-to-word* model from Task 1 with a *word-to-lemma* model, which is derived from the same data, but with the source and target sides swapped. The *word-to-lemma* model transforms the inflected word-forms into sequences of lemmas and tags; e.g. `dado` → `dar+PP`.

The only difference between the two models involves empty affixes (e.g. the plural of *fish* in English). The *lemma-to-word* model can simply delete the tag on the source side, but the *word-to-lemma* model would need to insert it on the target side. In order to avoid the problem of unbounded insertions, we place a dummy *null* character at the boundaries of the word, effectively turning insertion into substitution.

Lemmatization is not the only method of inflection simplification; we experimented with three alternative approaches (Nicolai and Kondrak, 2016):

1. *stem-based* approach, which is composed of the *word-to-stem* and *stem-to-word* models;

2. *stemma-based* approach, which instead pivots on stemmed lemmas;

3. *word-to-word* model, which directly transduces one inflected form into another.

However, as the *lemma-based* method obtained the best accuracy during development, we decided to use it for all following experiments.

2.5 Corpus Reranking

The shared task is divided into three tracks that vary in the amount of information allowed to train reinflection models. Track 1 ("Standard") allows the training data from the corresponding or lower-numbered tasks. We did not participate in Track 2 ("Restricted") because it was formulated after the release of the training data. For Track 3 ("Bonus"), the shared task organizers provided unannotated text corpora for each language.

Our Track 3 approach is to rerank the n-best list of predictions generated by DIRECTL+ for each test word-form using the method of Joachims (2002). For each language, we take the first one million lines from the corresponding Wikipedia dump as our corpus, removing the XML markup with the `html2text` utility. Our reranker contains three features:

1. normalized score of the prediction generated by DIRECTL+;

2. presence in the corpus;

3. normalized log likelihood of the prediction given a 4-gram character language model derived from the corpus.

3 Language-Specific Heuristics

Each language has its own unique properties that affect the accuracy of reinflection. While our approach is designed to be language-independent, we also investigated modifications for improving accuracy on individual languages.

3.1 Spanish Stress Accents

In Spanish, vowels are marked to indicate irregular stress (e.g. *á* in *darás*). This introduces several additional characters that are phonetically related to their unaccented counterparts. In an attempt to generalize unstressed and stressed vowels, we represent each stressed vowel as a pair of an unaccented vowel and the stress mark. (e.g. *darás* becomes *dara's*). After inflecting the test word-forms, we reverse this process: any vowel followed immediately by a stress mark is replaced with the corresponding accented vowel; stress marks not following a vowel are deleted.

3.2 Vowel Harmony

In agglutinative languages such as Finnish, Turkish, and Hungarian, vowels in stems and suffixes often share certain features such as *height, backness*, or *rounding*. We augment DIRECTL+ with features that correspond to vowel harmony violations. Since our development experiments demonstrated a substantial (13%) error reduction only for Turkish verbs, the vowel harmony features were restricted to that subset of the data.

3.3 Georgian Preverbs

Georgian verbs may include *preverb* morphemes, which act more like a derivational affix than an inflectional one. These preverbs primarily distinguish present and future tenses, but can also convey directional meaning. We observed that the Georgian training data contained many preverbs *da* and *ga*, but only some of the instances included the preverb on the lemma. This forced the models to learn two separate sets of rules. Removing these preverbs from the training word-forms and lemmas led to an 8% error reduction on the development set.

3.4 Arabic Sun Letters

In Arabic, consonants are divided into two classes: *sun* letters (i.e. coronal consonants) and *moon* letters (all others). When the definite article *al-* is followed by a sun letter, the letter *lām* assimilates to the following letter. Thus, *al+shams* "the sun" is realized as *ash-shams*. We observed that almost half of the errors on the adjectives could be attributed to this phenomenon. We therefore enforce this type of assimilation with a post-processing script.

4 Experiments

Our transduction models are trained on the pairs of word-forms and their lemmas. The *word-to-lemma* models (Section 2.2), are trained on the Task 1 training dataset, which contains gold-standard lemmas. These models are then employed in Tasks 2 and 3 for lemmatizing the source word-forms. The *lemma-to-word* models (Section 2.4) are derived from the training data of all three tasks, observing the Track 1 stipulations (Section 2.5). For example, the *lemma-to-word* models employed in Task 2 are trained on a combination of the gold-standard lemmas from Task 1, as well as the lemmas generated by the *word-to-lemma* models from the source word-forms in Task 2. Our development experiments showed that this kind of self-training approach can improve the overall accuracy.[2]

4.1 Development Results

Selected development results are shown in Table 1. The Task 1 results are broken down by part-of-speech. Because of an ambiguity in the initial shared task instructions, all development models were trained on a union of the data from all three tasks.

	T1	T2	T3	VB	NN	JJ
ES	98.0	96.3	96.3	96.0	95.9	100
DE	94.4	92.2	92.2	90.5	88.6	97.7
FI	90.0	88.4	88.4	92.1	89.7	63.9
RU	89.5	86.3	86.3	81.9	91.7	96.7
TR	78.6	74.9	74.9	78.8	78.5	n/a
KA	96.8	95.5	95.5	62.9	99.0	99.2
NV	91.3	90.0	90.0	88.5	99.1	n/a
AR	81.1	76.2	76.2	85.7	61.2	84.6

Table 1: Word accuracy on the development sets.

4.2 Test Results

Table 2 shows our test results. In most cases, these results are close to our development results. One exception is Navajo, where the test sets were significantly harder than the development sets. We also note drops in accuracy from Task 1 to Task 2 and 3 that were not evident in development, particularly for Arabic and Turkish. The drops can be attributed to the different training conditions

---

[2]Because of time constraints, we made an exception for Maltese by training on the gold lemmas from Task 1 only.

	Task 1		Task 2		Task 3	
	ST	RR	ST	RR	ST	RR
ES	97.8	98.0	96.2	96.4	96.5	96.6
DE	94.1	93.8	91.1	91.6	91.1	91.6
FI	88.5	88.7	85.6	85.7	85.8	85.9
RU	88.6	89.7	85.5	86.6	85.5	86.6
TR	82.2	87.5	62.5	59.2	63.1	59.2
KA	96.1	96.3	*94.1*	94.2	94.1	94.4
NV	60.3	60.3	50.4	50.8	48.8	49.1
AR	82.1	53.1	71.8	44.1	*72.2*	*58.5*
HU	86.7	89.6	86.3	88.8	86.4	88.9
MT	42.0	42.5	37.5	37.8	37.5	37.8

Table 2: Word accuracy on the test sets.[3]

between development and testing. In Section 5, we describe language specific issues; Arabic and Turkish were particularly affected by less training data.

Table 2 also contains the results for the "Bonus" track (RR). The reranking yields an improvement in almost all cases. Arabic is a clear exception. The data provided for the task was presented in a transliterated Latin script, while the Wikipedia corpus was in the original Arabic text. While a transliterated version of the text was eventually provided, it was not a complete transliteration: certain vowels were omitted, as they are difficult to recover from standard Arabic. This affected our reranker because it depends on correct forms in the corpus and a character language model.

5   Error Analysis

In this section, we discuss a few types of errors that we observed on the development sets for each language.

Spanish   The highest overall accuracy among the tested languages confirms its reputation of morphological regularity. A handful of verb errors are related to the interplay between orthography and phonology. Our models appear to have difficulty generalizing the rigid rules governing the representation of the phonemes [k] and [θ] by the letters q, c and z. For example, the form *crucen*, pronounced [kruθɛn], is incorrectly predicted with z instead of c, even though the bigram *ze* is never observed in Spanish. This demonstrates that the character language model feature of the reranker

is not able to completely prevent orthographically-invalid predictions.

German   Nouns and verbs fall into several different inflectional classes that are difficult to predict from the orthography alone. For example, the plural of *Schnurrbart*, "moustache", is *Schnurrbärte*. Our system incorrectly misses the umlaut, applying the pluralization pattern of the training form *Wart*, "attendant", which is indeed pluralized without the umlaut.

Finnish   A phenomenon known as consonant gradation alternates variants of consonants depending on their context. Given the amount of the training data, our method is unable to learn all of the appropriate gradation contexts.

Russian   The results indicate that verbs are substantially more challenging than nouns and adjectives. Most of the errors involve vowel changes. The reranker reduces the error rate by about 10% on Task 1. In particular, it filters out certain predictions that appear to violate phonotactic constraints, and reduces the number of errors related to lexically-conditioned prefixes in the perfective forms.

Turkish   Occasionally, the forms in crowd-sourced data are incorrect, which can lead to spurious transduction rules both during lemmatization and inflection. For example, the form *çıkaracağım* of the verb *çıkarmak* "to subtract" is erroneously associated in the training data with the lemma *toplamak* "to add", which causes the *word-to-lemma* model to learn a spurious çı → to rule. At test time, this leads to incorrect lemma predictions, which in turn propagate to multiple inflected forms.

Georgian   The highly unpredictable preverbs (Section 3.3) were the cause of a large number of errors on verbs. On the other hand, our system did very well on nouns and adjectives, second only to Spanish.

Arabic   Errors were mainly constrained to irregular forms, such as the nominal *broken plurals*. Unlike *sound plurals* that inflect via suffixation, broken plurals involve consonantal substitution. This is a difficult transduction to learn, given its low frequency in training. Another type of errors involves *weak roots*, which contain semi-vowels rather than full consonants.

---

[3]The results in italics were obtained after the shared task submission deadline.

Navajo In contrast with the test results. our development results were very promising, with near-perfect performance on nouns. After the submission deadline, we were informed that the test set differed in significant ways from the training and development sets, which lead to increased difficulty for this language.

Hungarian As it was one of the surprise languages, we applied no language-specific techniques. Nevertheless, the test results were on par with the other agglutinative languages. We speculate that adding customized vowel harmony features could further improve the results.

Maltese A complicated morphology is represented by an extremely large tag set (3184 distinct tags). For nouns and adjectives, the number of tags is very close to the number of training instances, which precludes any meaningful learning generalization. While many features within tags are repeated, taking advantage of this regularity would require more development time, which was unavailable for the surprise languages. The results highlight a limitation of the atomic tags in our method.

6 Conclusion

Previous work in morphological generation was largely limited to a small number of western European languages. The methods proposed by Nicolai et al. (2015) for the task of inflection generation were originally developed on such languages. The results on the shared task data show that those methods can be adapted to the task of reinflection, and perform well on various morphologically-complex languages. On the other hand, there is room for improvement on languages like Maltese, which provides motivation for future work.

Acknowledgements

We thank Mohammad Salameh for his help with Arabic. We thank the organizers for their hard work preparing the task, their readiness to answer questions, and their flexibility with regards to complications.

This research was supported by the Natural Sciences and Engineering Research Council of Canada, and by Alberta Innovates – Technology Futures and Alberta Innovation & Advanced Education.

References

Ryan Cotterell, Christo Kirov, John Sylak-Glassman, David Yarowsky, Jason Eisner, and Mans Hulden. 2016. The SIGMORPHON 2016 shared task—morphological reinflection. In *SIGMORPHON*.

Sittichai Jiampojamarn, Grzegorz Kondrak, and Tarek Sherif. 2007. Applying many-to-many alignments and hidden markov models to letter-to-phoneme conversion. In *NAACL-HLT*, pages 372–379.

Sittichai Jiampojamarn, Colin Cherry, and Grzegorz Kondrak. 2008. Joint processing and discriminative training for letter-to-phoneme conversion. In *ACL*, pages 905–913.

Thorsten Joachims. 2002. Optimizing search engines using clickthrough data. In *SIGKDD*, pages 133–142. ACM.

Ryan McDonald, Koby Crammer, and Fernando Pereira. 2005. Online large-margin training of dependency parsers. In *ACL*.

Garrett Nicolai and Grzegorz Kondrak. 2016. Leveraging inflection tables for stemming and lemmatization. In *ACL*.

Garrett Nicolai, Colin Cherry, and Grzegorz Kondrak. 2015. Inflection generation as discriminative string transduction. In *NAACL-HLT*, pages 922–931.

Morphological Reinflection with Conditional Random Fields and Unsupervised Features

Ling Liu
Department of Linguistics
University of Colorado
ling.liu@colorado.edu

Lingshuang Jack Mao
Department of Linguistics
University of Colorado
lima4664@colorado.edu

Abstract

This paper describes our participation in the SIGMORPHON 2016 shared task on morphological reinflection. In the task, we use a linear-chain conditional random field model to learn to map sequences of input characters to sequences of output characters and focus on developing features that are useful for predicting inflectional behavior. Since the training data in the task is limited, we also generalize the training data by extracting, in an unsupervised fashion, the types of consonant-vowel sequences that trigger inflectional behavior, and by extending the available training data through inference of unlabeled morphosyntactic descriptions.

1 Introduction

Our approach to the shared task focuses on expanding well-known methods to learning inflections. As our starting point, we assume a discriminative model akin to Durrett and DeNero (2013), Nicolai et al. (2015), and the baseline system provided by the organizers of the shared task, all very similar systems at the core. To improve performance and to address the more difficult reinflection tasks introduced in the shared task, we explore methods of expanding the training data, performing better alignment on the training data for our discriminative sequence classifier, feature development, and using unsupervised features for better generalization from training data.

In what follows, we describe a baseline system we developed, the system we actually participated with, and present the results, together with some analysis.

2 Exploratory experiments: a suffix-based baseline

To assess the difficulty of the task and the variation of inflectional behavior in the data sets, we ran a preliminary test with the data using a simple, suffix-based inflection strategy to complement the SIGMORPHON baseline. The method simply learns to transform input word form suffixes to suffixes of inflected forms. It works as follows: from each Levenshtein-aligned example pair $x \rightarrow y$ belonging to some morphosyntactic description (MSD) $m_{source} \rightarrow m_{target}$, we extract all the possible suffix-based string-to-string mapping rules that describe this mapping. In task 1, where the source MSD is not known, we assume that the source mapping is the lemma form. For example, if we have seen the example Finnish inflection **rakko** $\rightarrow$ **rakoitta**, going from lemma to **pos=N,case=PRIV,num=PL**, we extract the following alignment, with extra start-of-word and end-of-word markers

```
< r a k k o _ _ _ _ >
< r a k _ o i t t a >
```

This allows us to extract rules like the following for inflecting from the lemma form to **pos=N,case=PRIV,num=PL**:

>	$\rightarrow$	**itta>**
o>	$\rightarrow$	**oitta>**
ko>	$\rightarrow$	**oitta>**
kko>	$\rightarrow$	**koitta>**
akko>	$\rightarrow$	**akoitta>**
rakko>	$\rightarrow$	**rakoitta>**

From this, we devise a simple inflection strategy at test time where we always pick the longest matching such rule extracted from all word pairs that pertains to the MSD of the source and the target. The rationale for this baseline is that many

Proceedings of the 14th Annual SIGMORPHON Workshop on Computational Research in Phonetics, Phonology, and Morphology, pages 36–40,
Berlin, Germany, August 11, 2016. ©2016 Association for Computational Linguistics

	Suff baseline	SIGMORPHON baseline
Arabic	48.02 (45.97)	**70.30**
Finnish	**88.36** (88.21)	68.27
Georgian	**94.09** (92.75)	89.83
German	**92.24** (91.99)	90.36
Hungarian	**91.47** (87.76)	74.10
Maltese	**37.69** (36.59)	36.56
Navajo	35.47 (11.33)	**71.90**
Russian	88.94 (88.18)	**90.38**
Spanish	**98.31** (98.25)	96.93
Turkish	**77.65** (76.24)	59.17

Table 1: Results of a simple suffix-based baseline on task 1. Results are on the dev-set, and results in parentheses describe performance on the dev-set duplicates from the training-set removed.

hand-written models of morphology for various languages focus on suffixes to predict morphological behavior (Détrez and Ranta, 2012). As is seen in table 1, this yields comparably strong results for those languages that have largely suffixing inflections in the shared task (Finnish, Georgian, German, Hungarian, Spanish). It also identifies the difficult languages of the task for both——Arabic, Maltese, and Navajo. These are languages that exhibit significant stem-internal alternations and prefixation processes that thus lie outside the scope of this simple method.

3 Sequence labeling

To address the shortcomings of the two baselines tested—that the discriminative classifier-based baseline works well with stem-internal changes but weakly with predominantly suffixing processes, and that the suffix strategy works only with suffixing languages—we develop a discriminative conditional random field (CRF) model and focus on improving the initial alignment of the input and output to better and more consistently capture prefixation and suffixation.

3.1 Alignment

We use the alignment procedure in the baseline provided by the organizers (Cotterell et al., 2016). This is a one-to-one aligner that learns globally optimal costs for aligning a set of word pairs. We first ran all the word pairs as a batch through this aligner, obtaining a one-to-one alignment of each pair in the entire training data. We also experimented with variants on alignment using Levenshtein distance with a bias toward aligning vowels with vowels

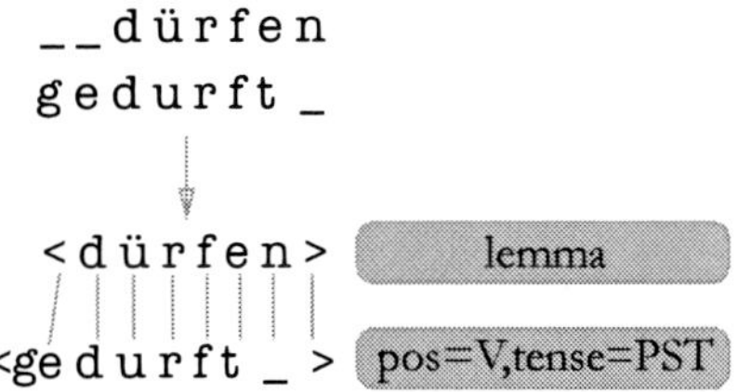

Figure 1: Example of the enforced one-to-many alignment after first aligning input-output pairs one-to-one.

and consonants with consonants, with consistently worse results.

After initial alignment of the input-output pairs, we additionally force a one-to-many alignment of the pairs, with added beginning and end markers < and >. The markers are treated as actual symbols that serve to allow the stems to be entirely aligned on both sides despite possible prefixation and suffixation. In performing the alignment we enforce that the input side of the relation always comes in single characters, each of which alternatively map to the empty string, or a sequence. We bias this alignment in such a way that any initial input side zeroes are collapsed with the <-marker and any final output side zeroes are collapsed together with the >-marker. Stem-internal insertion sequences $x:y\,0:z$ are always greedily associated with the leftmost change and become $x:yz$. This alignment simplifies the labeling process since each input letter is now assigned a label; furthermore, associating prefixes and suffixes with the alignment markers in a predetermined way allows for a consistent model of suffixing and prefixing in the label sequence learning process. This is illustrated in figure 1.

3.2 Labeling

We treat inflection generation as a labeling problem of converting an input sequence $\mathbf{x} = (x_1, \ldots, x_n)$ to an output sequence $\mathbf{y} = (y_1, \ldots, y_n)$. After the forced one-to-many alignment process, we convert the output side to a sequence of decisions $(y_1, \ldots, y_n)$ for use in a sequential labeling process. By default, the output strings, usually single characters, become the labels. However, we do not record a repetition (where the output equals the input) as a unique decision; rather, all repetitions are marked with a special symbol in the label sequence $\mathbf{y}$, i.e. all repetitions are marked alike in the output. Whenever the output differs from the input, however, the output string itself becomes the label. In figure 1, the output sequence $\mathbf{y}$ would be **<-ge-repeat-u-repeat-repeat-t-$\emptyset$-repeat**. Decision sequences thus reflect the possible choices we have for each input symbol (including the boundary markers $<$ and $>$)—we may repeat the symbol, delete the symbol, or output some other sequence of symbols.

Given input words of the form $\mathbf{x} = (x_1, \ldots, x_n)$ and the corresponding decision sequences $\mathbf{y} = (y_1, \ldots, y_n)$ we train a linear-chain CRF (Lafferty et al., 2001) by L-BFGS (Liu and Nocedal, 1989) using *CRFsuite* (Okazaki, 2007).

We model the conditional distribution of the output sequence in the standard way as

$$p(\mathbf{y}|\mathbf{x}) = \frac{1}{Z}\exp\Big(\sum_i^n \phi(y_{i-1}, y_i, \mathbf{x}, i)\Big) \quad (1)$$

where ϕ is a feature function which breaks down into k component functions

$$\phi(y_{i-1}, y_i, \mathbf{x}, i) = \sum_k w_k f_k(y_{i-1}, y_i, \mathbf{x}, i) \quad (2)$$

and where Z is the partition function which normalizes the expression to a proper distribution.

4 Features

We use a number of contextual features that look at variable amounts of context at each x_i point. Apart from standard local contextual features, we also employ features that refer to contexts as sequences of consonants and vowels (C/V).[1] In addition to local contextual C/V-features we also employ non-local features such as the types of vowels seen so far in the word and the last vowel seen at the current position, to better capture harmonic processes and Semitic root-and-pattern morphology. An overview of the most important features retained after ablation analysis is given in table 2.

5 Evaluation

5.1 Outside data

We separately test the feasibility of our approach against the data set published by Durrett and DeNero (2013), five data sets over three languages.

---

[1] We used an off-the-shelf algorithm for this purpose (Hulden, in prep.); there are many highly reliable unsupervised methods for extracting vowels and consonants given a corpus of words in an alphabetic writing system (Guy, 1991; Kim and Snyder, 2013; Moler and Morrison, 1983; Sukhotin, 1962).

That work used a similar approach (a semi-Markov CRF), albeit without the unsupervised features, and we improve upon their results that use a factored model, predicting each inflected word separately, as in the shared task, on three out of five data sets. We expect that with sparser, gappier training data— Durrett and DeNero (2013) used full inflection tables for training—our richer, more generic features will allow for better generalization.

5.2 MSD classification (task 3)

For task 3, where we are asked to inflect a word from an unknown source MSD, we first train a multi-class support vector machine (SVM) classifier (using LIBSVM (Chang and Lin, 2011)) to map the source form to an MSD. Each combination of MSDs is taken to represent a separate class—i.e. we treat each unique MSD-string as a class. As features, we use all substrings starting from the left and right edges of the word form in question, a method used successfully in e.g. morphological paradigm classification (Ahlberg et al., 2015). In track 2 (where only task 3 data is used), we train the classifier on only the given output forms and MSDs in the training data. In track 1, we feed the classifier all seen word forms and MSDs from any task whose data can be used.

5.3 Training method

In track 1, we inflect task 1 forms as described above whereas task 2 (arbitrary form to arbitrary form) is addressed by pivoting in two steps via the lemma form by first mapping the input form to the lemma form, and then mapping that form to the target form. We treat task 3 as a more difficult version of task 2; we first identify the unknown MSD of the task 3 input form, after which the procedure reduces to task 2. In the track 2 tasks 2 and 3, where only task-specific training data can be used, we are unable to pivot since form-to-lemma data is not available, and we train a separate CRF for each MSD to MSD mapping. In track 2 task 3, we first train the SVM classifier to identify MSDs, then classify the unknown MSDs of the input form in the training data, producing training data of the same format as in task 2.

We also experimented with training a single CRF model for each part of speech, using the feature/value pairs of the source/target forms as features. Somewhat surprisingly, this consistently yielded worse results on the development sets compared with training a separate model for each

Feature	Description
`frombeg`	Position counting from left edge
`fromend`	Position counting from right edge
`insymbol`	The current input symbol
`prevsymbol`	The previous input symbol
`prevsymbol2`	The input symbol two to the left
`prevsymbol3`	The input symbol three to the left
`previoustwo`	The previous two input symbols
`nextsymbol`	The next input symbol
`nextsymbol2`	The input symbol two to the right
`nexttwo`	The next two input symbols
`nextgeminate`	1 if the next input equals the current input
`geminate`	1 if the current input equals the previous input
`isC`	Is the current input symbol a consonant
`isV`	Is the current input symbol a vowel
`prevC`	Is the previous input symbol a consonant
`prevV`	Is the previous input symbol a vowel
`nextC`	Is the next input symbol a consonant
`nextV`	Is the next input symbol a vowel
`lastvowel`	What is the last vowel seen to the left of the current position
`allvowels`	The set of vowels in the word
`trigram`	The trigram $x_{i-1}\, x_i\, x_{i+i}$
`trigramCV`	The trigram mapped to C/V symbols

Table 2: The main feature templates used.

	CRF	D&DN13	Suffix-rules
DE-V	**96.14**	94.76	91.29
DE-N	83.75	**88.31**	86.18
ES-V	**99.62**	99.61	63.95
FI-V	97.18	**97.23**	72.00
FI-N	92.30	92.14	**92.62**

Table 3: Our approach on the Durrett and DeNero (2013) dataset, comparing our model with that work (D&DN13) and the simple suffix-replacing model introduced earlier.

lemma-to-MSD (track 1) or MSD-to-MSD (track 2), and we settled for using separate models.

6 Results

The main results on the development data for task 1 are given in tables 4, 5, and 6. We separately list figures with and without the C/V-features, which resulted in an average increase in accuracy of 1.02% (task 1), 1.58% (task 2), and 1.18% (task 3). As the development data includes instances also found in the training data, we separately report the accuracy without such duplicates, given in parentheses, as these results better reflect the performance on the final test data.

7 Discussion

The approach we have used clearly outperforms the baselines provided by the task and our own

	dev		test
	no CV	CV	
Arabic	74.00 (72.13)	**74.63** (72.81)	72.42
Finnish	88.86 (88.71)	**90.05** (89.92)	88.65
Georgian	**94.79** (93.46)	94.59 (93.22)	93.86
German	92.42 (92.05)	**92.61** (92.25)	92.64
Hungarian	91.04 (88.74)	**93.94** (91.28)	91.05
Maltese	**42.03** (40.81)	41.49 (40.22)	43.49
Navajo	88.01 (65.23)	**92.01** (63.67)	53.28
Russian	**90.44** (89.79)	90.13 (89.45)	89.13
Spanish	98.68 (98.63)	**98.74** (98.70)	98.28
Turkish	85.34 (84.15)	**88.91** (88.01)	87.39

Table 4: Main results for track 1, task 1.

	dev		test
	no CV	CV	
Arabic	63.93 (63.93)	**65.62** (65.62)	62.74
Finnish	79.87 (79.87)	**82.00** (82.00)	80.19
Georgian	**92.37** (92.37)	92.25 (92.25)	90.87
German	89.31 (89.31)	**89.43** (89.43)	88.44
Hungarian	87.50 (87.50)	**90.20** (90.20)	87.49
Maltese	**22.66** (22.66)	21.29 (21.79)	22.54
Navajo	70.54 (70.48)	**76.67** (76.62)	46.13
Russian	**87.06** (87.06)	86.93 (86.93)	86.71
Spanish	**97.43** (97.43)	97.12 (97.12)	97.18
Turkish	67.12 (67.12)	**70.37** (70.37)	67.50

Table 5: Main results for track 1, task 2.

	dev		test
	no CV	CV	
Arabic	61.75 (61.75)	**62.62** (62.62)	58.83
Finnish	79.43 (79.43)	**81.68** (81.68)	79.45
Georgian	**91.86** (91.85)	91.80 (91.79)	90.43
German	**87.68** (87.71)	87.62 (87.39)	86.59
Hungarian	87.33 (87.32)	**89.95** (89.94)	87.04
Maltese	**20.54** (20.54)	19.58 (19.58)	20.58
Navajo	71.71 (71.45)	**80.66** (77.54)	47.30
Russian	86.31 (86.29)	**86.37** (86.35)	85.34
Spanish	**96.43** (96.43)	96.18 (96.18)	96.26
Turkish	64.43 (64.41)	**67.50** (67.47)	65.63

Table 6: Main results for track 1, task 3.

baseline. There is room for improvement, however. We attribute the weak performance on the difficult languages of the task (Arabic, Maltese, and Navajo, in particular) to limitations on the linear-chain CRF model. Because of the immediately local dependency on the previous label, the model is unable to accurately capture multiple disjoint changes in going from word form to word form—something that is present in the Semitic languages of the data sets and Navajo. In the future, we want to experiment with more general CRF models to address this shortcoming (Sutton and McCallum, 2011). We also want to explore techniques for training a single model per part-of-speech instead of a separate model for each inflection type. In our experiments of training single models, this produced no improvement, but it seems that such an approach is indispensable in order to be able to generalize beyond the specific training data given. Consider, for example, seeing the Finnish word **talo** ('house') in its *singular* and *plural inessives* **talossa/taloissa** and the *singular abessive*, **talotta**. In a single model, we should be able to infer, without ever seeing an inflection of that type, that the *plural abessive* form is **taloitta**, isolating the plural **i**-morpheme. However, in a model where each complex inflection is learned separately, this cannot be learned without actually seeing an example of the combination *abessive* and *plural*.[2]

References

Malin Ahlberg, Markus Forsberg, and Mans Hulden. 2015. Paradigm classification in supervised learning of morphology. In *Proceedings of NAACL-HLT*, pages 1024–1029, Denver, Colorado, May–June. Association for Computational Linguistics.

Chih-Chung Chang and Chih-Jen Lin. 2011. LIB-SVM: a library for support vector machines. *ACM Transactions on Intelligent Systems and Technology (TIST)*, 2(3):27.

Ryan Cotterell, Christo Kirov, John Sylak-Glassman, David Yarowsky, Jason Eisner, and Mans Hulden. 2016. The SIGMORPHON 2016 shared task—morphological reinflection. In *Proceedings of the 2016 Meeting of SIGMORPHON*, Berlin, Germany, August. Association for Computational Linguistics.

Grégoire Détrez and Aarne Ranta. 2012. Smart paradigms and the predictability and complexity of inflectional morphology. In *Proceedings of the 13th EACL*, pages 645–653. Association for Computational Linguistics.

Greg Durrett and John DeNero. 2013. Supervised learning of complete morphological paradigms. In *Proceedings of NAACL-HLT*, pages 1185–1195.

Jacques B.M. Guy. 1991. Vowel identification: an old (but good) algorithm. *Cryptologia*, 15(3):258–262.

Young-Bum Kim and Benjamin Snyder. 2013. Unsupervised consonant-vowel prediction over hundreds of languages. In *Proceedings of ACL*, pages 1527–1536, Sofia, Bulgaria, August. Association for Computational Linguistics.

John Lafferty, Andrew McCallum, and Fernando C. N. Pereira. 2001. Conditional random fields: Probabilistic models for segmenting and labeling sequence data. In *Proceedings of the Eighteenth International Conference on Machine Learning*, pages 282–289.

Dong C. Liu and Jorge Nocedal. 1989. On the limited memory BFGS method for large scale optimization. *Mathematical Programming*, 45(1-3):503–528.

Cleve Moler and Donald Morrison. 1983. Singular value analysis of cryptograms. *American Mathematical Monthly*, pages 78–87.

Garrett Nicolai, Colin Cherry, and Grzegorz Kondrak. 2015. Inflection generation as discriminative string transduction. In *Proceedings of NAACL-HLT*, pages 922–931, Denver, Colorado, May–June. Association for Computational Linguistics.

Naoaki Okazaki. 2007. CRFsuite: a fast implementation of conditional random fields (CRFs).

Boris V. Sukhotin. 1962. Eksperimental'noe vydelenie klassov bukv s pomoshch'ju EVM. *Problemy strukturnoj lingvistiki*, pages 198–206.

Charles Sutton and Andrew McCallum. 2011. An introduction to conditional random fields. *Machine Learning*, 4(4):267–373.

---

[2]This work has been partly sponsored by DARPA I20 in the program Low Resource Languages for Emergent Incidents (LORELEI) issued by DARPA/I20 under Contract No. HR0011-15-C-0113.

Improving Sequence to Sequence Learning for Morphological Inflection Generation: The BIU-MIT Systems for the SIGMORPHON 2016 Shared Task for Morphological Reinflection

Roee Aharoni and **Yoav Goldberg**
Computer Science Department
Bar Ilan University
`roee.aharoni,yoavgo@gmail.com`

Yonatan Belinkov
CSAIL
MIT
`belinkov@mit.edu`

Abstract

Morphological reinflection is the task of generating a target form given a source form and the morpho-syntactic attributes of the target (and, optionally, of the source). This work presents the submission of Bar Ilan University and the Massachusetts Institute of Technology for the morphological reinflection shared task held at SIGMORPHON 2016. The submission includes two recurrent neural network architectures for learning morphological reinflection from incomplete inflection tables while using several novel ideas for this task: morpho-syntactic attribute embeddings, modeling the concept of templatic morphology, bidirectional input character representations and neural discriminative string transduction. The reported results for the proposed models over the ten languages in the shared task bring this submission to the second/third place (depending on the language) on all three sub-tasks out of eight participating teams, while training only on the Restricted category data.

1 Introduction

Morphological inflection, or reinflection, involves generating a target (surface form) word from a source word (e.g. a lemma), given the morpho-syntactic attributes of the target word. Previous approaches to automatic inflection generation usually make use of manually constructed Finite State Transducers (Koskenniemi, 1983; Kaplan and Kay, 1994), which are theoretically appealing but require expert knowledge, or machine learning methods for string transduction (Yarowsky and Wicentowski, 2000; Dreyer and Eisner, 2011; Durrett and DeNero, 2013; Hulden et al., 2014; Ahlberg et al., 2015; Nicolai et al., 2015). While these studies achieved high accuracies, they also make specific assumptions about the set of possible morphological processes that create the inflection, and require feature engineering over the input.

More recently, Faruqui et al. (2016) used encoder-decoder neural networks for inflection generation inspired by similar approaches for sequence-to-sequence learning for machine translation (Bahdanau et al., 2014; Sutskever et al., 2014). The general idea is to use an encoder-decoder network over characters, that encodes the input lemma into a vector and decodes it one character at a time into the inflected surface word. They factor the data into sets of inflections with identical morpho-syntactic attributes (we refer to each such set as a factor) and try two training approaches: in one they train an individual encoder-decoder RNN per factor, and in the other they train a single encoder RNN over all the lemmas in the dataset and a specific decoder RNN per factor.

An important aspect of previous work on learning inflection generation is the reliance on complete inflection tables – the training data contains all the possible inflections per lemma. In contrast, in the shared task setup (Cotterell et al., 2016) the training is over partial inflection tables that mostly contain only several inflections per lemma, for three different sub-tasks: The first requires morphological inflection generation given a lemma and a set of morpho-syntactic attributes, the second requires morphological re-inflection of an inflected word given the word, its morpho-syntactic attributes and the target inflection's attributes, and the third requires re-inflection of an inflected word given only the target inflection attributes. The datasets for the different tasks are available on the

Proceedings of the 14th Annual SIGMORPHON Workshop on Computational Research in Phonetics, Phonology, and Morphology, pages 41–48,
Berlin, Germany, August 11, 2016. ©2016 Association for Computational Linguistics

shared task's website.[1]

The fact that the data is incomplete makes it problematic to use factored models like the ones introduced in (Faruqui et al., 2016), as there may be insufficient data for training a high-quality model per factor of inflections with identical morpho-syntactic attributes. For example, in the shared task dataset the training data usually contains less than 100 training examples on average per such factor. Moreover, when the data is factored this way, no information is shared between the different factors even though they may have identical inflection rules.

We propose two neural network architectures for the task. The first, detailed in Section 2, departs from the architecture of (Faruqui et al., 2016) by extending it in three novel ways: representing morpho-syntactic attributes, template-inspired modeling, and bidirectional input character representations. The second, described in Section 3, is based on an explicit control mechanism we introduce while also making use of the three extensions mentioned above. Our experimental evaluation over all 10 languages represented in the shared task brings our models to the second or third place, depending on the language.

2 First Approach: Morphological Sequence to Sequence Architecture

Our first proposed architecture is a Morphological Sequence to Sequence (MS2S) architecture, illustrated in Figure 1. It incorporates several novel components in the sequence-to-sequence learning paradigm, as discussed below.

2.1 Morpho-Syntactic Attribute Embeddings

We seek to train models over larger amounts of examples, rather than on factors that strictly contain examples that share all the morpho-syntactic attributes. To do so, instead of factoring the data by the attributes we feed the attributes into the network by creating a dense embedding vector for every possible attribute/value pair (for example, gender=FEM and gender=MASC will each have its own embedding vector). The attribute embeddings for each input are then concatenated and added as parameters to the network while being updated during training similarly to the character embeddings. This way, information can be shared

Figure 1: The Morphological Sequence to Sequence (MS2S) network architecture for predicting an inflection template given the Arabic lemma *tarjama* and a set of morpho-syntactic attributes. A round tip expresses concatenation of the inputs it receives.

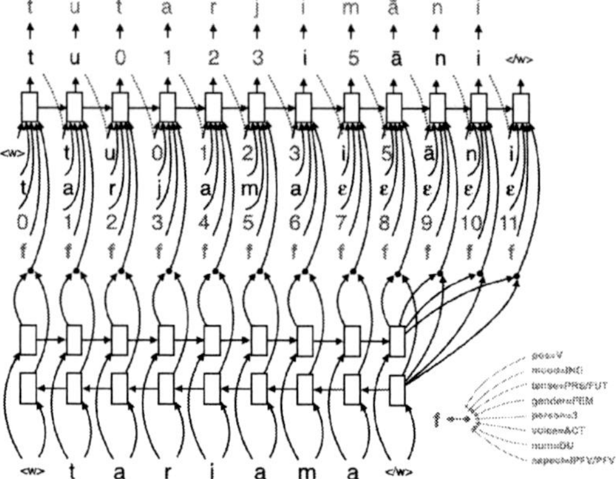

across inflections with different morpho-syntactic attributes, as they are trained jointly, while the attribute embeddings help discriminate between different inflection types when needed. This can be seen in Figure 1, where f is the vector containing a concatenation of the morpho-syntactic attribute embeddings.

While this approach should allow us to train a single neural network over the entire dataset to predict all the different inflection types, in practice we were not able to successfully train such a network. Instead, we found a middle ground in training a network per part-of-speech (POS) type. This resulted in much fewer models than in the factored model, each using much more data, which is essential when training machine learning models and specifically neural networks. For example, on the Arabic dataset of the first sub task (inflection generation from lemma to word) this reduced the amount of trained models from 223 with an average of 91 training examples per model, to only 3 models (one per POS type - verb, noun, adjective) with an average of 3907 training examples per model.

2.2 Morphological Templates

We bring the idea of morphological templates into the model: instead of training the network to predict only a specific inflection character at each step given a lemma and a set of morpho-syntactic features, we train the network to either predict a character from the vocabulary or *to copy* a character at a given position in the input sequence. This enables the network to produce a sequence that resembles a morphological template which can be instantiated with characters from the input to produce the correct inflection. While at train time we encourage the network to perform copy operations when possible, at prediction time the network can decide whether to copy a character from the input by predicting its location in the input or to generate a preferred character from the vocabulary. For example, for the Arabic lemma *tarjama* and a set of morpho-syntactic attributes the network will output the sequence "tu0123i5āni" which can be instantiated with the lemma into the correct inflection, *tutarjimāni*, as depicted in Figure 1.

Intuitively, this method enables the learning process to generalize better as many different examples may share similar templates – which is important when working with relatively small datasets. We saw indeed that adding this component to our implementation of a factored model similar to (Faruqui et al., 2016) gave a significant improvement in accuracy over the Arabic dataset: from 24.04 to 78.35, while the average number of examples per factor was 91.

To implement this, for every given pair of input and output sequences in the training set we need to produce a parameterized sequence which, when instantiated with the input sequence, creates the output sequence. This is achieved by running a character level alignment process on the training data, which enables to easily infer the desired sequence from every input-output sequence alignment. For example, given the input sequences *sabbaba* and output sequence *tusabbibā* with the induced alignment ϵϵsabbaba-tusabbibā, we produce the expected output: tu0123i5ā, as depicted in the next figure:

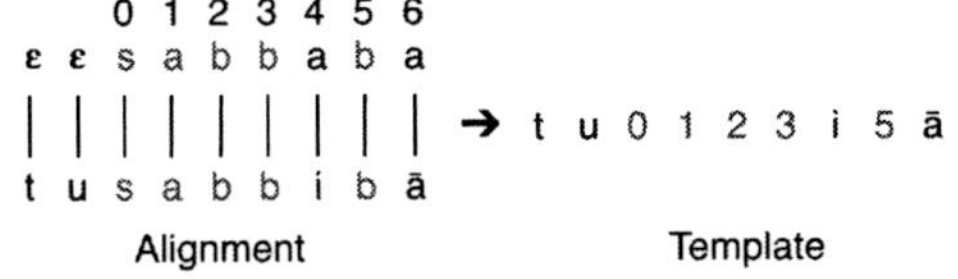

Alignment   Template

We performed the alignment process using a Chinese Restaurant Process character level aligner (Sudoh et al., 2013) as implemented in the shared task baseline system.[2]

---

[2] https://github.com/ryancotterell/ sigmorphon2016/tree/master/src/baseline

2.3 Bidirectional Input Character Representation

Instead of feeding the decoder RNN at each step with a fixed vector that holds the encoded vector for the entire input sequence like Faruqui et. al. (2016), we feed the decoder RNN at each step with a Bi-Directional Long-Short Term Memory (BiLSTM) representation (Graves and Schmidhuber, 2005) per character in the input along with the character embedding learned by the network. The BiLSTM character representation is a concatenation of the outputs of two LSTMs that run over the character sequence up to the current character, from both sides. This adds more focused context when the network predicts the next inflection output, while still including information form the entire sequence due to the bidirectional representation.

2.4 MS2S Decoder Input

For every step i of the decoder RNN for this setup, the input vector is a concatenation of the following:

1. $BiLSTM_i$ – The bidirectional character embedding for the ith input character (if i is larger than the length of the input sequence, the embedding of the last input character is used).

2. c_i – The character embedding for the ith input character. If i is larger than the length of the input sequence, an embedding of a special $\mathcal{E}$ symbol is used, similarly to (Faruqui et al., 2016).

3. i – A character embedding for the current step index in the decoder. In the first step this will be an embedding matching to '0', in the second step it will an embedding matching to '1' etc. These are the same index embeddings used to model copy actions from a specific index.

4. o_{i-1} – The feedback input, containing the embedding of the prediction (either a character or an integer representing an index in the input) from the previous decoder RNN step.

5. f – The vector containing the concatenation of the morpho-syntactic attribute embeddings.

3 Second Approach: The Neural Discriminative String Transducer Architecture

The second approach is based on a Neural Discriminative String Transducer (NDST), a novel neural network architecture that models which specific part of the input sequence is relevant for predicting the next output character at a given time. This is done by maintaining a state consisting of an input sequence position (the input pointer) and an output sequence position (the output pointer), which are controlled by the decoder. This approach can be seen as a more focused replacement to the general attention mechanism of Bahdanau et. al. (2014), tailored to the usually monotonic behavior of the output sequence with respect to the input sequence in the morphological reinflection task. An example for using this architecture is available in Figure 2.

3.1 NDST Decoder Input

For every step i in the NDST decoder RNN, the input vector is a concatenation of the following:

1. p_{input} – The input pointer, holding the embedding that represents the position of the current pointed input sequence element. When $i = 0$, this is initialized with the embedding that stands for the position of the first element in the input. Every time the network outputs the "step" symbol, p_{input} is promoted by setting it with the embedding that represents the next input sequence position.

2. p_{output} – The output pointer, a character embedding representing the next position in the output sequence to be generated. When $i = 0$, this is initialized with the embedding that stands for the position of the first element in the input. Every time the network outputs a symbol other than the "step" symbol, p_{output} is promoted by setting it with the embedding for the next output sequence position.

3. $BiLSTM_{p_{input}}$ – The bidirectional character embedding for the input character currently pointed by p_{input}.

4. o_{i-1} – The feedback input, containing the embedding of the prediction (either a character, an integer representing an index in the input, or the "step" symbol) from the previous decoder RNN step.

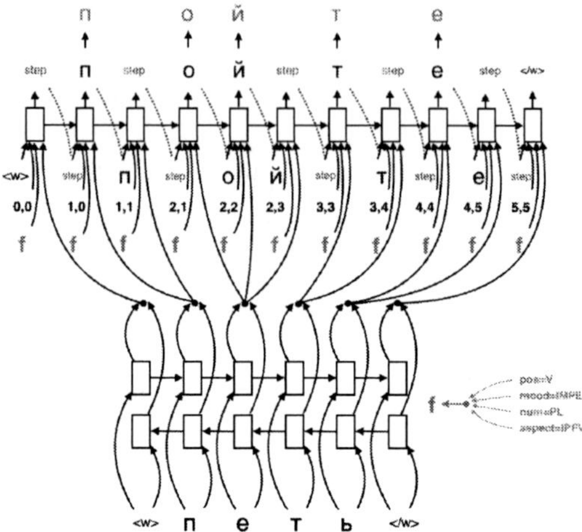

Figure 2: The Neural Discriminative String Transducer (NDST) architecture for predicting an inflection template given a lemma and a set of morpho-syntactic attributes.

5. f – The vector containing the concatenation of the morpho-syntactic attribute embeddings.

To train an NDST network, for every input and output sequence in the training data we should have a sequence of actions (of three types – either a specific character prediction, an index to copy from or a "step" instruction) that when performed on the input sequence, produces the correct output sequence. To get the correct instruction sequences in train time we first run a character level alignment process on the training data, similarly to the MS2S model. Once we have the character level alignment per input-output sequence pair, we deterministically infer the sequence of actions that results in the desired output by going through every pair of aligned input-output characters in the alignment. If the input and output characters in the aligned pair are not identical, we produce the new output character. If the input and output characters in the aligned pair are identical we produce a copy action from the input character location. After that, if the next output character is not the epsilon symbol as seen in the alignment in Figure 2.2 we also produce a "step" action. We train the network to produce this sequence of actions when given the input sequence and the set of morpho-syntactic attributes matching the desired inflection.

44

4 Experimental Details

4.1 Submissions

The shared task allowed submissions in three different tracks: Standard, which enabled using data from lower numbered tasks in addition to the current task data; Restricted, which enabled using only the current task's data; and Bonus, which enabled using the Standard track datasets and an additional monolingual corpus supplied by the organizers.

We submitted two systems to the shared task, both in the Restricted track: The first, named BIU/MIT-1, used the MS2S architecture as described previously and participated in all three sub-tasks. Notice that for the 3rd task, the input is identical to the first task so it does not require changes in the network architecture. To use the MS2S network for the second task we concatenated the source and target morpho-syntactic attribute embeddings and used that vector as the f vector mentioned previously. The output from this system was 5-best lists, meaning 5 predictions for each input. To produce the 5-best list we perform beam search over the MS2S model, which is trained greedily without such search procedure.

The second system, named BIU/MIT-2, used the NDST architecture and participated only in the first and second sub-tasks. This system did not use beam search, producing only one guess per input. Again, to use the NDST architecture for the second task we simply concatenated the input and output morpho-syntactic attribute embeddings.

4.2 Training, Implementation and Hyper Parameters

To train our systems, we used the train portion of the dataset as-is and submitted the model which performed best on the development portion of the dataset, without conducting any specific pre-processing steps on the data. We trained our networks for a maximum of 300 epochs over the entire training set or until no improvement on the development set has been observed for more than 100 epochs. The systems were implemented using pyCNN, the python wrapper for the CNN toolkit.[3] In both architectures we trained the network by optimizing the expected output sequence likelihood using cross-entropy loss. For optimization we used ADAM (Kingma and Ba, 2014) with

no regularization, and the parameters set as $\alpha = 10^{-4}, \beta_1 = 0.9, \beta_2 = 0.999, \epsilon = 10^{-8}$. In all architectures we used the CNN toolkit implementation of an LSTM network with two layers, each having 200 entries. The character embeddings were also vectors with 200 entries, and the morpho-syntactic attribute embeddings were vectors of 20 entries. When using beam search we used a beam width of 5.

5 Results

While developing our systems we measured our performance on the development set with respect to two baselines: the shared task baseline system (ST-Base) inspired by (Nicolai et al., 2015; Durrett and DeNero, 2013), and the factored sequence to sequence baseline (Fact.) similar to the one introduced in (Faruqui et al., 2016). On the test set, our systems ranked second or third out of eight groups in the shared task (depending on the language). The best participating system, LMU-1/2 (Kann and Schütze, 2016) relied on a single encoder-decoder model with attention (Bahdanau et al., 2014) per language, with several improvements like performing prediction using majority voting over an ensemble of five models. In contrast, our first system did not use an explicit attention mechanism and is composed of 3 models per language (one per POS type) without using ensembling. We compare our system to the best system on the test set.

The results for the first task are shown in Table 1, measuring aggregated accuracy across all POS tags. On the development set, our models surpassed both baselines significantly and were competitive with each other, as the MS2S model gained the best aggregated accuracy results on all languages but Russian and Finnish, where the NDST model was better. On the test set, similar results are shown: the MS2S model gives higher accuracies except for Russian, Navajo and Maltese where the NDST model was superior.

For the second task, we measured performance only with respect to ST-Base as can be seen in Table 2. On the development set, the NDST model outperformed the baseline and the MS2S model for all languages but Georgian and Spanish, where the MS2S and ST-Base models were better, respectively, although not with a significant difference. On the test set, the MS2S model gave better results only for Georgian and Hungarian.

Table 1: Results for inflection generation (first sub-task), measuring accuracy on the development set: our models vs. the shared task (ST-Base) and Factored (Fact.) baselines, and mean reciprocal rank (MRR) on the test set: our models vs. the best performing model (Kann and Schütze, 2016).

			Dev		Test		
Language	ST-Base	Fact.	MS2S	NDST	MS2S	NDST	Best
Russian	90.38	84.22	91.57	**93.33**	89.73	90.62	**91.46**
Georgian	89.83	92.37	**98.41**	97.01	97.55	96.54	**98.5**
Finnish	68.27	75.78	**95.8**	94.36	93.81	92.58	**96.8**
Arabic	70.29	24.04	**96.28**	92.95	93.34	89.96	**95.47**
Navajo	71.9	83.47	**98.82**	98.48	80.13	88.43	**91.48**
Spanish	96.92	91.79	98.99	**99.31**	98.41	98.33	**98.84**
Turkish	59.17	64.68	**98.18**	97.8	97.74	96.17	**98.93**
German	89.29	90.35	**96.36**	95.99	95.11	94.87	**95.8**
Hungarian	78.62	65.75	**99.23**	98.76	98.33	97.59	**99.3**
Maltese	36.94	N/A	**87.92**	85.2	82.4	84.78	**88.99**

Table 2: Results for morphological re-inflection with source attributes (second sub-task) measuring accuracy over the development set: our models vs. the shared task (ST-Base) baseline, and mean reciprocal rank (MRR) over the test set: our models vs. the best performing model (Kann and Schütze, 2016)

		Dev		Test		
Language	ST-Base	MS2S	NDST	MS2S	NDST	Best
Russian	85.63	85.06	**86.62**	83.36	85.81	**90.11**
Georgian	91.5	**94.13**	93.81	92.65	92.27	**98.5**
Finnish	64.56	77.13	**84.31**	74.44	80.91	**96.81**
Arabic	58.75	75.25	**78.37**	70.26	73.95	**91.09**
Navajo	60.85	63.85	**75.04**	56.5	67.88	**97.81**
Spanish	**95.63**	93.25	95.37	92.21	94.26	**98.45**
Turkish	54.88	82.56	**87.25**	81.69	83.88	**98.38**
German	87.69	93.13	**94.12**	91.67	92.66	**96.22**
Hungarian	78.33	94.37	**94.87**	92.33	91.16	**99.42**
Maltese	26.2	43.29	**49.7**	41.92	50.13	**86.88**

Table 3: Results for morphological re-inflection without source attributes (third sub-task) measuring accuracy over the development set: our models vs. the shared task (ST-Base) baseline, and mean reciprocal rank (MRR) over the test set: our models vs. the best performing model (Kann and Schütze, 2016)

		Dev		Test	
Language	ST-Base	MS2S	NDST	MS2S	Best
Russian	81.31	**84.56**	84.25	82.81	**87.13**
Georgian	90.68	**93.62**	91.05	92.08	**96.21**
Finnish	61.94	**76.5**	66.25	72.99	**93.18**
Arabic	50	**72.56**	69.31	69.05	**82.8**
Navajo	60.26	**62.7**	54.0	52.85	**83.5**
Spanish	88.94	**92.62**	89.68	92.14	**96.69**
Turkish	52.19	**79.87**	75.25	79.69	**95.0**
German	81.56	**90.93**	89.31	89.58	**92.41**
Hungarian	78	**94.25**	83.83	91.91	**98.37**
Maltese	24.75	**44.04**	3.58	40.79	**84.25**

For the third task we also measured performance with respect to ST-Base as can be seen in Table 3. On the development set, the MS2S model outperformed the others on all languages. Since this was the situation we did not submit the NDST model for this sub-task, thus not showing test results for the NDST model on the test set.

6 Preliminary Analysis

An obvious trend we can see in the results is the MS2S approach giving higher accuracy scores on the first and third tasks, while the NDST approach being significantly better on the second task. While inspecting the data for the second and third tasks we noticed that the datasets only differ in the added morpho-syntactic attributes for the input sequences, and are identical other then that. This is encouraging as it shows how the NDST control mechanism can facilitate the additional data on the input sequence to predict inflections in a better way. We plan to further analyze the results to better understand the cases where the NDST architecture provides added value over the MS2S approach.

7 Discussion and Future Work

Our systems reached the second/third place in the Restricted category in the shared task, depending on the language/sub-task combination. It is also encouraging to see that if we submitted our systems as-is to the Standard and Bonus tracks we would also get similar rankings, even without using the additional training data available there. The winning submission in all tracks, described in (Kann and Schütze, 2016) also used an encoder-decoder approach that incorporated the morpho-syntactic attributes as inputs to the network, but with several differences from our approach like using an attention mechanism similar to (Bahdanau et al., 2014), training a single model for all inflection types rather than one per POS type and performing prediction by using an ensemble of five models with majority voting rather than using a single trained model like we did. Future work may include exploring a hybrid approach that combines the ideas proposed in our work and the latter. Other recent works that propose ideas relevant to explore in future work in this direction are (Gu et al., 2016), which describe a different copying mechanism for encoder-decoder architectures, or (Rastogi et al., 2016), which models the reinflec-

tion task using a finite state transducer weighted with neural context that also takes special care of the character copying issue.

Acknowledgments

We thank Manaal Faruqui for sharing his code with us. This work was supported by the Intel Collaborative Research Institute for Computational Intelligence (ICRI-CI).

References

Malin Ahlberg, Markus Forsberg, and Mans Hulden. 2015. Paradigm classification in supervised learning of morphology. In Rada Mihalcea, Joyce Yue Chai, and Anoop Sarkar, editors, *HLT-NAACL*, pages 1024–1029. The Association for Computational Linguistics.

Dzmitry Bahdanau, Kyunghyun Cho, and Yoshua Bengio. 2014. Neural machine translation by jointly learning to align and translate. *CoRR*, abs/1409.0473.

Ryan Cotterell, Christo Kirov, John Sylak-Glassman, David Yarowsky, Jason Eisner, and Mans Hulden. 2016. The SIGMORPHON 2016 shared task—morphological reinflection. In *Proceedings of the 2016 Meeting of SIGMORPHON*, Berlin, Germany, August. The Association for Computational Linguistics.

Markus Dreyer and Jason Eisner. 2011. Discovering morphological paradigms from plain text using a dirichlet process mixture model. In *EMNLP*, pages 616–627. The Association for Computational Linguistics.

Greg Durrett and John DeNero. 2013. Supervised learning of complete morphological paradigms. In *Proceedings of the 2013 Conference of the North American Chapter of the Association for Computational Linguistics: Human Language Technologies*, pages 1185–1195, Atlanta, Georgia, June. The Association for Computational Linguistics.

Manaal Faruqui, Yulia Tsvetkov, Graham Neubig, and Chris Dyer. 2016. Morphological inflection generation using character sequence to sequence learning. In *NAACL HLT 2016, The 2016 Conference of the North American Chapter of the Association for Computational Linguistics: Human Language Technologies, San Diego, California, USA, June 12 - June 17, 2016*.

A. Graves and J. Schmidhuber. 2005. Framewise phoneme classification with bidirectional LSTM and other neural network architectures. *Neural Networks*, 18(5-6):602–610.

Jiatao Gu, Zhengdong Lu, Hang Li, and Victor OK Li. 2016. Incorporating copying mechanism in sequence-to-sequence learning. *arXiv preprint arXiv:1603.06393*.

Mans Hulden, Markus Forsberg, and Malin Ahlberg. 2014. Semi-supervised learning of morphological paradigms and lexicons. In Gosse Bouma and Yannick Parmentier 0001, editors, *EACL*, pages 569–578. The Association for Computational Linguistics.

Katharina Kann and Hinrich Schütze. 2016. Single-model encoder-decoder with explicit morphological representation for reinflection. In *ACL*, Berlin, Germany, August. The Association for Computational Linguistics.

Ronald M. Kaplan and Martin Kay. 1994. Regular models of phonological rule systems. *Computational Linguistics*, 20(3):331–378.

Diederik Kingma and Jimmy Ba. 2014. Adam: A method for stochastic optimization.

Kimmo Koskenniemi. 1983. Two-level morphology: A general computational model of word-form recognition and production. Technical Report Publication No. 11, Department of General Linguistics, University of Helsinki.

Garrett Nicolai, Colin Cherry, and Grzegorz Kondrak. 2015. Inflection generation as discriminative string transduction. In *Proceedings of the 2015 Conference of the North American Chapter of the Association for Computational Linguistics: Human Language Technologies*, pages 922–931, Denver, Colorado, May–June. The Association for Computational Linguistics.

Pushpendre Rastogi, Ryan Cotterell, and Jason Eisner. 2016. Weighting finite-state transductions with neural context. In *Proc. of NAACL*.

Katsuhito Sudoh, Shinsuke Mori, and Masaaki Nagata. 2013. Noise-aware character alignment for bootstrapping statistical machine transliteration from bilingual corpora. In *EMNLP*, pages 204–209. The Association for Computational Linguistics.

Ilya Sutskever, Oriol Vinyals, and Quoc V. Le. 2014. Sequence to sequence learning with neural networks. In Zoubin Ghahramani, Max Welling, Corinna Cortes, Neil D. Lawrence, and Kilian Q. Weinberger, editors, *NIPS*, pages 3104–3112.

David Yarowsky and Richard Wicentowski. 2000. Minimally supervised morphological analysis by multimodal alignment. In *ACL*. The Association for Computational Linguistics.

Evaluating Sequence Alignment for Learning Inflectional Morphology

David L. King
The Ohio State University
`king.2138@osu.edu`

Abstract

This work examines CRF-based sequence alignment models for learning natural language morphology. Although these systems have performed well for a limited number of languages, this work, as part of the SIGMORPHON 2016 shared task, specifically sets out to determine whether these models handle non-concatenative morphology as well as previous work might suggest. Results, however, indicate a strong preference for simpler, concatenative morphological systems.

Introduction

Morphologically-rich languages pose a challenge for the natural language processing and generation community. Computationally mapping inflected wordforms to a baseform has been standard practice in semantics and generation. Traditionally, hand-coding these as rule-based systems required extensive engineering overhead, but has produced high quality resolution between base and inflected wordforms. This work extends work by Durrett and DeNero (2013) to automatically learn morphological paradigms by comparing edit operations between a lemma and baseform and tests a similar algorithm on other morphologically-rich langauges and those which exhibit more extensive use of non-concatenative morphology.

Background

Morphological reinflection and lemma generation are not trivial tasks, and have been the subject of much research and engineering. Traditionally, rule-based and finite-state methods (Minnen et al., 2001; Koskenniemi, 1984) have been used, particularly when no training data is available. Although these handcrafted systems perform with a high level of accuracy, creating them is difficult and requires a great deal of engineering overhead.

Recently, more automatic, machine learning methods have been utilized. These systems have required far less handcrafting of rules, but also do not perform as well. Specifically, work by Durrett and DeNero (2013) exploits sequence alignment systems across strings, a technique originally developed for DNA analysis. They showed that by computing minimum edit operations between two strings and having a semi-markov conditional random field (CRF) (Sarawagi and Cohen, 2004) predict when wordform edits rules were to be used, a system could achieve state-of-the-art performance in completing morphological paradigms for English and German.

English and German, along with other Germanic languages, have a somewhat rarer tendency towards *ablauting*, that is changing or deleting segments from the lemma of a wordform as part of its inflection. In some circles, morphology is thought of in the purely *concatenative* sense (i.e. *give + -s → gives*). Durrent and DeNero's work shows promise in that they already account for non-concatenative morphonology in English and German. Using a similar system, this work hypothesizes that such an approach will perform well on languages with more prolific non-concatenative morphology, such as Arabic and Maltese.

Shared Task

The 2016 SIGMORPHON (Cotterell et al., 2016) shared task on morphological reinflection consisted of multiple tracks for discerning fully inflected wordforms in ten languages, two of which were surprise languages whose data was not released until a week before the submission deadline. In task 1, participants were given a lemma and a target word's grammatical information with

Proceedings of the 14th Annual SIGMORPHON Workshop on Computational Research in Phonetics, Phonology, and Morphology, pages 49–53,
Berlin, Germany, August 11, 2016. ©2016 Association for Computational Linguistics

Language	Training Items
Arabic	12254
Finnish	12693
Georgian	11576
German	12490
Hungarian	16219
Maltese	18975
Navajo	6012
Russian	12390
Spanish	12575
Turkish	12336

Table 1: Training items available for restricted task 1.

which to guess the fully inflected target wordform. In task 2, participants were supplied with two fully inflected wordforms—one source and one target—and their grammatical features. Task 3 was the same as task 2, except that no source grammatical information was supplied.

Additionally, participants were allowed to choose standard, restricted, or bonus training sets. The standard training allowed for any task to use training data from a task lower than it. Restricted training only allowed for training on data for that given data set (i.e. task 1 can only train on task 1, task 2 on task 2, and task 3 on task 3). A system attempting a certain task number and training on a higher task number (e.g. attempting task 1 and additionally using task 2 training data) constituted using bonus training.

For the purposes of testing this work's hypothesis, task 1 was chosen as being the most analogous and direct means of evaluation. Additionally, restricted training was used to minimize variance between the training sets of the ten languages in question. As seen in table 1, although generally most training sets have about 12,000 items, Navajo, Maltese, and Hungarian are the exceptions.

Implementation

This work exploits string sequence alignment algorithms such as Hirschberg's algorithm (Hirschberg, 1975) and the Ratciff/Obershelp algorithm (Black, 2004) in the same vein as recent work by Durrett and DeNero (2013) and Nicolai et al. (2015). In these frameworks, the fewest number of edits required to convert one string to another are considered to be morphological

give → gave

	g	i	v	e
	g	a	v	e
Rule		-i+a		

kitab → kutub

	k	i	t	a	b
	k	u	t	u	b
Rule		-i+u		-a+u	

springen → gesprungen

		s	p	r	i		n	g	e	n	
	ge	s	p	r	u		n	g	e	n	
Rule	+g+e				-i +u						

Figure 1: Sample edits for English *give → gave*, Arabic *kitab to kutub* ('book' singular → plural), and German *springen → gesprungen* ('to jump' infinitival → past participle). Note that edit rules are applied in a character-by-character manner across the lemma.

rules. As shown in figure 1, source and target words are aligned to minimize edit operations required to make them the same. This minimal list of edit operations is converted into an edit rule at the character level (i.e. this work does not predict word level edit operations). These segment edits are fed with a feature set to be trained on by a linear chain CRF (Sutton and McCallum, 2011) using online passive-aggressive training (Crammer et al., 2006).

Features for the CRF included a mix of data provided by the task data and surface features from the uninflected lemmas. All features were shared across all segments (i.e. at the word level) except for features specific to the the current segment and listed in table 2. Outputs from the CRF were edit operations for each segment of the input lemma. After these operations were carried out on their respective segments within the lemma, a fully inflected wordform was the final output from the system. The feature set was chosen with insight from previous work.

Full feature set:

- Grammatical information – concatenated

- Grammatical information – factored

- Character level bigram information – forwards and backwards

Current	Edit	Affix type	Distance from beginning	Distance from end
start	+g+e	prefixing	0	8
s	empty	infixing	1	7
p	empty	infixing	2	6
r	empty	infixing	3	5
i	-u+i	infixing	4	4
n	empty	infixing	5	3
g	empty	infixing	6	2
e	empty	infixing	7	1
n	empty	suffixing	8	0

spring $\rightarrow$ gesprungen

Table 2: An example of character-specific features as used by the CRF – all other features are shared across the entire edit sequence.

- Character level trigram information – forwards and backwards

- Character indexes from beginning and end

- Distance from the current character to the beginning of the lemma

- Distance from the current character to the end of the lemma

- Affix type (prefixing, infixing, or suffixing – circumfixing was not explicitly encoded into the feature set)

Results

Overall the system performed far better on the development set than the test set. It is easiest to summarize the results from table 6 in terms of the number of edit rules the system had to learn. Languages with under 500 edit rules for the system to learn performed best and only experienced moderate dropoff between the development and test sets. Languages with over 500 edit rules to be learned both performed worse and experienced extreme drop offs in some instances. The exception, Turkish, will be discussed below and in the next section.

Languages traditionally used in these tasks, such as German, performed best, while those less often tested in these systems, such as Maltese, seem to be more difficult for the system to accurately predict. There was a drastic drop in Navajo, which the task organizers claim to be caused by a dialectal shift between the training, development,

Affix Data Set	Dev	Test
Train	-0.764	-0.707
Dev	-0.694	-0.603

Table 3: Correlations of the number of affixes per language in a given data set and the system's accuracy of that language.

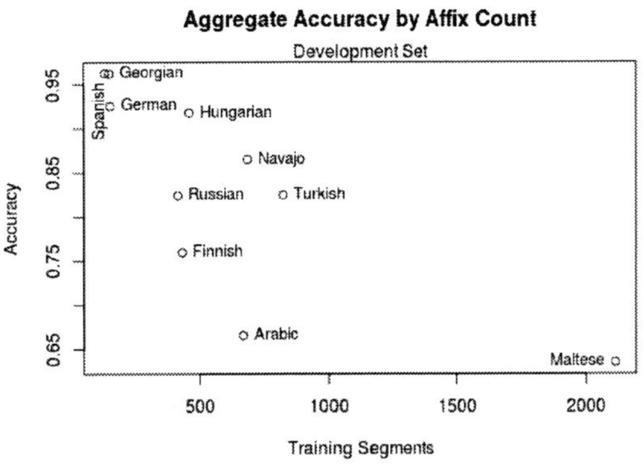

Figure 2: Aggregate Accuracy over the Development Set

and testing data sets, among other reasons. Maltese was not able to be tested since the CRF took 15 days to train, which did not fit within the time allotted for training on the surprise languages. The jump in training time for Maltese was not unexpected, given how many unique affixes the training set had, and taking into account the effect that increasing the number of classes a CRF must predict increases its asymptotic complexity quadratically by some measures (Cohn, 2007). Hungarian, the other surprise language, did not drop as drastically.

Language	Train	Dev
Arabic	3.249	3.170
Finnish	1.835	1.775
Georgian	1.464	1.474
German	1.042	1.035
Hungarian	1.559	1.536
Maltese	3.184	3.103
Navajo	3.260	3.283
Russian	1.803	1.775
Spanish	1.495	1.474
Turkish	2.131	2.058

Table 4: Entropy over affix counts in the training and development data sets.

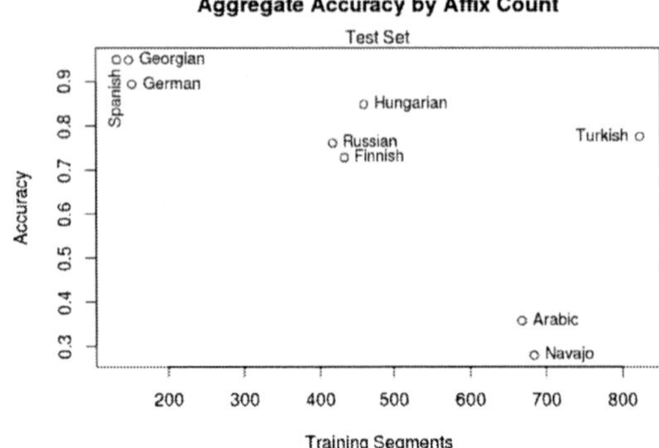

Figure 3: Aggregate Accuracy over the Test Set

Language	Train	Dev
Arabic	668	260
Finnish	433	228
Georgian	149	88
German	153	83
Hungarian	460	279
Maltese	2113	787
Navajo	684	386
Russian	417	170
Spanish	133	88
Turkish	823	438

Table 5: Number of unique affixes in each data set.

Discussion

The difference in system performance between development and testing could be interpreted as overfitting. That said, overfitting to the development set would show a more universal drop in scores from development to testing than is exhibited here. Table 5 shows the number of unique affixes the system had to learn. As expected, languages traditionally thought to have less complex morphological structure had fewer unique affixes in both training and development sets. This is echoed in table 4, where entropy over the unique affix counts was calculated.

In addition to a non-uniform drop in accuracy, a strong negative correlation–as seen in table 3– between the number of affixes in the training set and accuracy seems to indicate that data sparsity might explain this phenomenon more fully. It appears that data sparsity has a greater effect as the number of affixes increases.

Certain languages did appear to drop between development and testing more drastically than others. While Finnish, German, Hungarian, Russian, Spanish, and Turkish fell less that 10%, Navajo and Arabic fell more than 30% each. Navajo's drop can be explained by the lack of training data. In 6012 training items, there were 684 edit rules that the system had to learn. This ratio of edit rules to wordforms is more than 1:10, which is higher than almost any other language in the task, second only to Maltese. What is particularly interesting is the number of affixes between Turkish and Arabic.

Although Arabic fell more drastically, Turkish clearly has more affixes in the data set, both by ratio and sheer count, and should perform worse given the previously-mentioned observations about an overall negative correlation between affix number and system performance. It should be taken into consideration that the kinds of morphology in Arabic and Turkish are not entirely analogous. Turkish, although agglutinative, is also primarily a suffixing language (Lewis, 2000), while Modern Standard Arabic is comparatively more non-concatenative. Arabic and Maltese, both of which have high entropies as seen in table 4 in additional more non-concatenative morphological structures, also performed worse than Turkish in the development results, which had an entropy more akin to Russian and Finnish. This points to the likelihood that non-contatenative morphology is still an issue for sequence alignment algorithms. Whether this problem can be solved by using a different algorithm, increasing training data, or by altering the underlying machine learning is beyond the scope of this task.

It should also be noted that, as far as this work is aware, the data sets were not balanced for frequency. Language learners often rotely memorize irregular forms because they do not fit a productive inflectional pattern. Luckily, irregular forms usually occur more frequently than wordforms subject to productive morphological rules (Bybee and Thompson, 1997; Grabowski and Mindt, 1995). Since the algorithm ostensibly treats productive and lexicalized forms equally, it would be interesting to see if there were any difference in performance between these datasets and others balanced to account for irregular form frequency.

Conclusion

Sequence alignment algorithms have proven useful in automatically learning natural language

Language	Dev	Test
Arabic	0.665	0.358
Finnish	0.759	0.728
Georgian	0.962	0.949
German	0.925	0.894
Hungarian	0.918	0.849
Maltese	0.635	N/A
Navajo	0.865	0.279
Russian	0.824	0.761
Spanish	0.965	0.949
Turkish	0.825	0.776

Table 6: Aggregate Accuracy Across Languages. Maltese required 15 days to train, and was unable to finish before the results were due.

morphology. That said, supervised models require exceptional amounts of training data to overcome data sparsity. Given a lack of training data, more traditional finite-state methods might be preferable given enough time to engineer such systems. This work has shown that CRF-based sequence alignment models do perform well for languages with lower affix to wordform ratios and unique affix count entropy values. Although there is not enough evidence to overtly reject this work's hypothesis, the evidence does indicate a preference for concatenative morphology by CRF-based sequence alignment models.

Acknowledgments

This work acknowledges the contributions of Micha Elsner for advising and assisting both technically and theoretically, without which this would not have come together. This work also thanks the anonymous reviewers for their guidance and insight.

References

Paul E Black. 2004. Ratcliff/Obershelp pattern recognition. *Dictionary of Algorithms and Data Structures*, 17.

Joan Bybee and Sandra Thompson. 1997. Three frequency effects in syntax. In *Annual Meeting of the Berkeley Linguistics Society*, volume 23, pages 378–388.

Trevor A Cohn. 2007. *Scaling conditional random fields for natural language processing*. Ph.D. thesis, Citeseer.

Ryan Cotterell, Christo Kirov, John Sylak-Glassman, David Yarowsky, Jason Eisner, and Mans Hulden.
2016. The SIGMORPHON 2016 Shared Task—Morphological Reinflection. In *Proceedings of the 2016 Meeting of SIGMORPHON*, Berlin, Germany, August. Association for Computational Linguistics.

Koby Crammer, Ofer Dekel, Joseph Keshet, Shai Shalev-Shwartz, and Yoram Singer. 2006. Online passive-aggressive algorithms. *The Journal of Machine Learning Research*, 7:551–585.

Greg Durrett and John DeNero. 2013. Supervised Learning of Complete Morphological Paradigms. In *HLT-NAACL*, pages 1185–1195.

Eva Grabowski and Dieter Mindt. 1995. A corpus-based learning list of irregular verbs in English. *ICAME Journal*, 19(1995):5–22.

Daniel S. Hirschberg. 1975. A linear space algorithm for computing maximal common subsequences. *Communications of the ACM*, 18(6):341–343.

Kimmo Koskenniemi. 1984. A general computational model for word-form recognition and production. In *Proceedings of the 10th International Conference on Computational Linguistics and 22nd annual meeting on Association for Computational Linguistics*, pages 178–181. Association for Computational Linguistics.

G. Lewis. 2000. *Turkish Grammar*. Oxford: Oxford University Press.

Guido Minnen, John Carroll, and Darren Pearce. 2001. Applied morphological processing of English. *Natural Language Engineering*, 7(03):207–223.

Garrett Nicolai, Colin Cherry, and Grzegorz Kondrak. 2015. Inflection generation as discriminative string transduction. In *Proc. of NAACL*.

Sunita Sarawagi and William W Cohen. 2004. Semi-markov conditional random fields for information extraction. In *Advances in neural information processing systems*, pages 1185–1192.

Charles Sutton and Andrew McCallum. 2011. An introduction to conditional random fields. *Machine Learning*, 4(4):267–373.

Using longest common subsequence
and character models to predict word forms

Alexey Sorokin
Moscow State University / GSP-1, Leninskie Gory, 1
Faculty of Mathematics and Mechanics, 119991, Moscow, Russia
Moscow Institute of Physics and Technology / Institutskij per., 9,
Faculty of Innovations and High Technologies, 141701, Dolgoprudny, Russia
alexey.sorokin@list.ru

Abstract

This paper presents an algorithm for automatic word forms inflection. We use the method of longest common subsequence to extract abstract paradigms from given pairs of basic and inflected word forms, as well as suffix and prefix features to predict this paradigm automatically. We elaborate this algorithm using combination of affix feature-based and character ngram models, which substantially enhances performance especially for the languages possessing nonlocal phenomena such as vowel harmony. Our system took part in SIGMORPHON 2016 Shared Task and took 3rd place in 17 of 30 subtasks and 4th place in 7 substasks among 7 participants.

1 Introduction

Automatic paradigm detection has attracted extensive attention in recent years. The most valuable works include (Ahlberg et al., 2014; Ahlberg et al., 2015), which pursue a classification-based approach, encoding every inflection paradigm by a single label, and (Dreyer and Eisner, 2011; Nicolai et al., 2015) applyng transduction-base techniques. The representation of morphological paradigms in (Ahlberg et al., 2014) is based on the *longest common subsequence* (LCS) method, suggesting that the common material in the LCS is the "stem" and the symbols not in the LCS are inflection markers. This approach actually goes back to the 60s and was first applied in the seminal work of Andrey A. Zaliznyak "Russkoe imennoe slovoizmenenie" ("Russian nominal inflection", Zaliznyak (2002)). From the linguistic point of view, transduction-based techniques are more relevant, since when inflection is realised

by several simultaneous modifications (say, prefix and suffix changes and vowel alterations in the stem), it is more natural to represent it by multiple operations, not by a single label. Nevertheless we decide to use the first approach: firstly, machine learning algorithms used for classification are more simple computationally than the ones for string transformations and require less parameter tuning. Secondly, our work was initially conducted for Russian, where most morphological alterations occur in affixes with the exception of several patterns. Our method is based on the one of Ahlberg et al. (2015) with several technical modifications.

Our system participated in SIGMORPHON-2016 Shared Task on morphological inflection (Cotterell et al., 2016). This task required one to guess a single word form of a given category, not the whole paradigm, which is a reverse for one of the standard NLP tasks: lemmatization, where the goal is to predict a basic form of the word (the lemma) given its inflected form. Lemmatization is rarely considered as labeling task, the only exception being Gesmundo and Samardžić (2012). However, the latter work considers only alterations at the edges of the word, while the LCS method allows one to address internal changes as well. A more general method of edit trees used in Chrupala et al. (2008) and Müller et al. (2015) is another realization of the LCS approach. However, lemmatization algorithms extensively exploit context to discriminate between candidate forms which is irrelevant for SIGMORPHON challenge.

Our paper consists of 5 parts, including the introduction. The second part briefly explains how abstract paradigms are induced from data. It also introduces the techniques used for their automatic detection. The third part outlines SIGMORPHON SHARED TASK and the methods we proposed to solve it. The fourth part describes different vari-

Proceedings of the 14th Annual SIGMORPHON Workshop on Computational Research in Phonetics, Phonology, and Morphology, pages 54–61,
Berlin, Germany, August 11, 2016. ©2016 Association for Computational Linguistics

ants of our system and compares their relative performance. We conclude with the error analysis and future work directions.

2 Abstract paradigms

A standard task of paradigm learning is to guess an inflection table given a source form. In the classification approach, this task is solved by encoding the complete table with a label and then predicting this label using standard machine learning technique. The predicted values in our method are *abstract paradigms* introduced in Ahlberg et al. (2014). Informally speaking, an abstract paradigm is a list of patterns, where common parts of word forms are replaced by variables. These variables correspond to maximal contiguous segments of the longest common subsequence of these forms. For example, paradigms *sing-sang* and *drink-drank* both share the same abstract paradigm **1+i+2#1+a+2**. The same approach can be applied not only to complete paradigms, but also to the pairs (source form, inflected form).

Following Ahlberg et al. (2014), we use finite automata to extract LCS. However, our implementation has several technical differences, mentioned below. When several variants of the same length exist, we extract the one with the least total number of gaps and the least total length of these gaps. These two quantities being equal, the number of zero-length gaps is minimized. For example, given Arabic verb *imtāza* "to be distinguished" and its inflected form *tamtaz*, the best LCS is *mt-z* , not *mt-a* since it has two gaps of length 1 instead of one gap of length 2 and one of length 0. We also restrict the maximal length of gaps in the middle and in the beginning of the word to prevent spurious matches. When the language lacks prefix inflection, we simply set the maximal initial gap to 0.

After enumerating all possible abstract paradigms, the task of automatic inflection becomes a standard classification problem. Our basic system uses lemma suffixes and prefixes as features, following the scheme of Ahlberg et al. (2014). We bound their length by some number (usually 5 for suffixes and 3 for prefixes) and encode them as binary features. We also remove frequent affixes before extracting the features, attaching them afterwards. Since the number of possible features can reach several thousands, we perform extensive feature selection. For the

competition we enriched the model by character ngram scores which is our main contribution and significantly boosted performance.   Details are given in Section 4.

3 Sigmorphon Shared Task

First SIGMORPHON SHARED TASK (Cotterell et al., 2016) was held for 10 languages of different genealogy and morphological structure. There were several agglutinative languages (Finnish and Turkish), two Semitic languages (Arabic and Maltese) with "root-and-pattern" morphology, some languages are more difficult to characterize (Navajo). We refer the reader to the organizers' article for a complete description of the task. The competition consisted of 3 parts. In the first participants were asked to construct a word form given its lemma and morphological tag. In the second task the source form was not required to be the lemma, but its tag was also given. In the third task the tag of the source form was unknown.

In the first task our system was trained for each morphological tag separately. Every lemma-form pair was treated as an abstract paradigm containing two cells. Given a lemma at test time, the classifier uses its suffixes and prefixes to detect the most probable abstract paradigm. A paradigm being known, we determine the variable values. Substituting this values for the variables in the second cell of the paradigm, we calculate the target form. The scheme of the process described is presented in Figure 1.

In the second task we first map the form of the source category to its lemma, training on the reverse pairs from the first task, then apply a direct classifier from Task 1. Since our system assigns probabilities, for every source form w_1 of the category c_1 we calculate a set of possible lemmas $l_1, \ldots, l_m$ with their probabilities; afterwards for every lemma we construct its possible forms of target category c_2 and select the forms with the highest total probability $P(w_2|w_1, c_1, c(w_2) = c_2) = \sum_i p(w_2|lem(w_2) = l_i, c(w_2) = c_2)p(lem(w_1) = l_i)$. The algorithm is depicted on Figure 2.

For the third task we learn the transformation from the word form to its lemma, using the reversed training data for Task 1 with target category omitted (only the POS label is known). Then the obtained lemmas were transform to word forms of target category just as in Task 2 using the same

Source form (pos=V,lemma)	features	paradigms (with probs)		variables	target form (pos=V,mood=SBJV, per=3,tense=PRS, num=SG, …)
detentar	^d, ^de	1+ar#1+e	0.82	1=detent	detente
	r$, ar$, tar$	1+e+2+ar#1+ie+2+e	0.13	1=det, 2=nt	detiente
	ntar$, entar$	1+ar#1+ue	0.05	1=detent	detentue

Figure 1: How we model inflection (Task 1). For each lemma in the test set we predict an abstract paradigm, which consists of lemma and target form patterns. Fitting the lemma to its guessed pattern, we find the variables in the paradigm. Using these variables, the target word form is constructed.

Source form pos=V,polar=POS, mood=IMP,per=1,num=PL	Lemmas (with probs)		Target forms (for each lemma)		Target forms (with probs) pos=V,mood=IND,tense=PST, per=1,num=SG,aspect=PFV	
vaguemos	vagar	0.83	vagué	0.90	vagué	0.92
			vagé	0.10	vagé	0.08
	vaguar	0.17	vagué	0.97		
			vaguué	0.03		

Figure 2: How we model reinflection (Task 2). First, for the source form a list of possible lemmas is constructed. Second, for each potential lemma all possible target forms are predicted. The probabilities of these forms are calculated using chain rule.

probability formula. Our system essentially relies on 2 basic components: forward transformation from lemma to its inflected form and the corresponding backward transformation. Therefore in what follows we focus on implementation issues and evaluate performance mainly for these two problems.

We deliberately refrain from using any external sources including linguistic information and corpus statistics. Nevertheless, our method could be easily extended with corpora features, see Ahlberg et al. (2014) and Sorokin and Khomchenkova (2016) for possible strategies.

4 Performing classification

In this section we present some details of our system used to solve Task 1 and its reverse, for the general description see Section 2. Each inflection/lemmatization task was solved without any information about other forms of the given lemma. We applied a logistic regression classifier using suffixes and prefixes as features. Usually the length of suffixes was 5 for inflection and 6 for lemmatization, the maximal length of prefix features was 3. However, prefix features were not used for Turkish and Finnish, while for Navajo we used prefixes of length up to 5 and the length of suffixes was bounded by 3. In all languages words were classified by their last (first for Navajo) letter and a separate classifier was trained for each letter. To avoid data sparsity we performed extensive feature selection, keeping only best 10% of features according to an ambiguity measure (?) and disregarding features observed less than 3 times in the training set. If an affix of length up to 3 unambiguously predicts the paradigm label π, we assign π for any lemma ending by (beginning with) this affix. We also experimented with removing frequent suffixes before extracting features and attaching them afterwards, which slightly improved the results for most of the languages. Language-dependent parameters are given in the Appendix.

We report the results of our system evaluation in Table 1, column SIMPLE. We used the train-dev split provided by the workshop organizers after removing all the duplicates from the development set.[1] For most of the tasks it outperforms the baseline which uses the transductive approach with an averaged perceptron as the classifier. However, for

---

[1]Actually, it was not done in the submission version, which caused slight overfitting for several tasks.

Language	Verbs			Adjectives			Nouns		
	JOINT	SIMPLE	BASE	JOINT	SIMPLE	BASE	JOINT	SIMPLE	BASE
Arabic	80.9	66.0	65.5	94.4	87.2	63.2	76.2	73.4	76.3
Finnish	94.0	93.4	58.4	62.9	62.9	14.3	87.8	87.2	77.9
Georgian	42.3	32.1	48.7	100.0	100.0	100.0	97.6	96.6	95.3
German	90.0	89.3	85.5	97.2	96.7	91.0	91.2	91.2	89.2
Hungarian	92.5	89.8	78.7				75.9	71.4	58.0
Navajo	94.5	93.4	84.6				56.4	47.9	53.9
Russian	83.2	82.8	81.2	95.8	95.8	95.8	91.9	91.5	91.9
Spanish	98.6	98.6	96.2	100.0	100.0	99.1	100.0	100.0	99.5
Turkish	83.5	74.4	61.2				87.3	78.4	56.3

Table 1: Performance quality for inflection (Task 1).

Russian and Arabic there is a marginal gap, while for Georgian and Navajo verbs our results are not satisfying enough.

We try to close this gap using character models. We learn an ngram model on the set of word forms in the train data. Model counts are smoothed using Witten-Bell smoothing. We integrate ngram probabilities in our model via standard reranking scheme: the SIMPLE model is used to generate the n-best list. Then for every form in this list we calculate its log-probability according to SIMPLE model as well as language model logarithmic score normalized by word length. These two features are passed to a logistic regression classifier and the hypothesis with highest decision score is returned. To learn the weights of the scores we apply the following procedure from Joachims (2002): suppose three hypotheses w_1, w_2 and w_3 were generated for the lemma l in the training set , w_2 being the correct word form. If their log probabilities are p_1, p_2, p_3 and n-gram log scores are s_1, s_2, s_3 respectively, we include in the training set vectors $[p_2 - p_1, s_2 - s_1]$ and $[p_2 - p_3, s_2 - s_3]$ as positive instances and $[p_1 - p_2, s_1 - s_2]$ and $[p_3 - p_2, s_3 - s_2]$ as negative. Note that this ranking scheme allows for integration of other task-dependent features as well which might be helpful in lemmatization or POS-tagging.

The results of the improved system are also given in Table 1, column JOINT. We observe that for most of the tasks the combined system confidently beats the baseline, except Georgian verbs. Arabic nouns and Russian nouns and adjectives are on par with the baseline system. Character ngram models are the most helpful for the languages with developed vowel harmony, such as Turkish (the impact for Finnish is more modest since the performance quality of the SIMPLE system was already high). In case of Arabic SIMPLE model often generates about ten forms of approximately the same probability; the character model helps to select the best one and rule out the words which do not satisfy local phonological requirements.

Table 2 contains results for the reverse task of lemmatization used as the first stage in Tasks 2 and 3. There was no baseline available, therefore we compare only performance of the SIMPLE system and the JOINT system using character ngram models. We observe that ngram statistics produce more substantial gain in this task than for inflection. We also provide evaluation results on Tasks 2 and 3 of the Shared Task (Table 3, first line for each language stands for Task 2 and second for Task 3). Since accuracy for these tasks is determined by lemmatization and inflection quality, we will not discuss them further. For the results of the competition itself we refer the reader to organizers' article (Cotterell et al., 2016), we just mention that our system was ranked the 3rd 17 times of 30, 5 times for Task 1 and 6 times for Tasks 2 and 3.

5 Error analysis and discussion

A morphological inflection system may fail to recover a correct form for two reasons: first, it is too restricted to generate a correct paradigm, second, its features are not strong enough to discriminate between correct and incorrect labels. To distinguish these two cases we calculated the recall of our system both for the inflection and lemmatization subtasks, measuring whether a correct word receives probability larger than 1%. Results are collected in Table 4. Interestingly, the ranking precision (which is the percentage of cases when the

Language	Verbs		Adjectives		Nouns	
	JOINT	SIMPLE	JOINT	SIMPLE	JOINT	SIMPLE
Arabic	76.1	56.7	94.5	93.6	83.1	63.6
Finnish	92.7	85.0	62.9	48.7	90.7	84.7
Georgian	51.3	34.6	99.2	98.4	99.4	96.6
German	94.3	92.1	98.1	96.8	94.1	90.7
Hungarian	98.7	96.1			99.1	98.2
Navajo	65.6	44.2			64.2	52.2
Russian	87.5	82.8	97.1	96.8	93.6	89.7
Spanish	98.5	96.5	100.0	99.1	97.2	98.2
Turkish	93.8	91.3			97.0	96.4

Table 2: Performance quality for lemmatization.

Language	Verbs		Adjectives		Nouns	
	JOINT	BASE	JOINT	BASE	JOINT	BASE
Arabic	81.9	55.0	86.9	61.3	71.0	62.8
	84.3	50.9	86.9	49.0	69.2	46.5
Finnish	88.0	74.3	55.6	5.6	89.7	52.5
	88.0	51.1	52.8	5.6	87.5	71.0
Georgian	46.9	37.0	96.0	97.0	97.5	94.2
	44.4	40.6	94.9	92.6	98.1	94.2
German	86.2	81.0	97.8	91.4	91.0	87.2
	85.7	74.4	97.6	87.6	88.8	70.6
Hungarian	95.0	79.9			77.8	63.0
	96.3	78.8			75.0	63.0
Navajo	54.5	47.6			100.0	89.0
	56.6	56.8			100.0	81.1
Russian	78.9	71.7	95.9	96.2	89.5	89.0
	77.1	70.1	96.9	91.6	89.1	83.9
Spanish	98.0	95.5	100.0	96.6	97.2	95.7
	97.9	91.5	100.0	70.3	97.6	84.3
Turkish	85.2	56.0			88.8	54.0
	86.4	55.2			87.7	51.6

Table 3: Performance quality on Tasks 2 and 3.

correct word form was ranked the first provided it was in the candidate list) for the overwhelming majority of tasks is over 90% which shows that affix features and character models are indeed effective in discriminating between candidate paradigms. Omitting Georgian verbs and Finnish adjectives, where the classifier suffers from the lack of training data, we observe two problematic languages: Arabic demonstrates decent recall and moderate precision in both tasks, while results on Navajo degrade mostly due to extremely low recall except the lemmatization of nouns, where precision drops to 66%.

As a key example, consider the *Pres+2+Sg+Masc* form of Arabic verbs, for which the percentage of correctly predicted forms was only 62% (8 of 13). In 4 of 5 erroneous cases the algorithm fails to even suggest the correct transformation (**1+ā+2+a#ta+1+ū+2+u**, e. g. *dāma* "to last" – *tadūmu* "you (Masc) last") because it was never observed in the training set for this particular task and was observed only once at all. The fact that in other forms *ā* was often replaced by *ū* also does not help since transformations are considered "as a whole", not as a sequence of local edits. The remaining mistake (*taḏrag̮iṭṭu* instead of *taḏrig̮aṭṭu* for *iḏrag̮aṭṭa* "to leave") is also frequent: the algo-

Language	Verbs			Adjectives			Nouns		
	Recall	Accur.	Prec.	Recall	Accur.	Prec.	Recall	Accur.	Prec.
Arabic	88.2	80.4	91.16%	95.9	93.6	97.60%	83.9	76.2	90.82%
	85.5	76.1	89.01%	96.1	94.5	98.34%	84.4	83.1	98.46%
Finnish	95.1	94.1	98.95%	63.9	62.9	98.44%	96.0	87.8	91.46%
	96.1	90.6	94.28%	65.7	62.9	95.74%	98.0	92.7	94.59%
Georgian	59.8	42.3	70.74%	100.0	99.2	99.2%	98.5	97.6	98.09%
	62.9	51.3	81.56%	100.0	100.0	100.0%	99.8	99.4	99.60%
German	93.3	90.0	96.46%	98.1	97.2	99.08%	94.8	91.2	96.20%
	94.3	94.3	100.0%	98.4	98.1	99.70%	96.6	94.1	97.41%
Hungarian	97.5	92.5	94.87%				82.1	75.9	92.45%
	99.1	98.7	99.60%				99.1	99.1	100.0%
Navajo	61.8	56.4	91.26%				97.8	94.5	96.63%
	67.9	64.8	95.43%				95.6	63.3	66.21%
Russian	91.4	83.2	91.03%	98.5	95.8	97.26%	98.0	91.9	93.78%
	88.2	86.6	98.19%	97.7	95.2	97.44%	96.8	94.1	97.21%
Spanish	98.8	98.6	99.80%	100.0	100.0	100%	100.0	100.0	100%
	98.6	98.5	99.90%	100.0	100.0	100%	99.5	97.2	97.69%
Turkish	87.7	83.5	95.21%				89.5	87.3	97.54%
	93.8	93.8	100.0%				96.8	96.4	99.59%

Table 4: Recall and precision on inflection (upper) and lemmatization (lower) tasks.

rithm correctly predicts the paradigm description **i+1+a+2+a#ta+1+i+2+u** but erroneously replaces the first root syllable instead of the second. In the case of ambiguity the position of alteration is determined by calculating the probability of "local" transformation **a** $\rightarrow$ **i** in both locations and choosing the most probable according to its immediate context. Since local features cannot distinguish first and second syllables of the root and paradigm description contains no information on the number of vowels in variables, our system cannot avoid such mistakes. However, their percentage can be lowered by allowing the system to predict several surface variants for one abstract paradigm (in current architecture this decision is made before calculating ngram scores).

Another difficult problem for our approach is fusion. Consider the *REAL+Pl+1* form of the Navajo verbs, where only 2 predictions of 7 are correct and in 5 remaining cases the correct paradigm label was not even in the list of possible paradigms. For example, the plural form *deiijįį'* of the verb *yiijįįh* "to stand up" is produced using the pattern **y+1+h#de+1+'** while the training set contained only the transformation **y+1+h#dei+1+'** for *yik'ęęh* $\rightarrow$ *deiik'ęę'*, where the prefix *de-* was fused with initial *y*. That explains the low performance on Navajo inflection in terms of re-

call. The opposite problem holds for lemmatizing Navajo nouns. For example, all 4-th person forms start with *ha-*, however, it can be obtained from the lemma form either by adding initial *h* (*ataa'-hataa'*) or by substitutiing for initial *bi-* (*bijaa'-hajaa'*). This ambiguity cannot be resolved with dictionary or corpus; fortunately, when reinflecting other forms all the potential lemmas generate the same form so the performance on Tasks 2 and 3 is unaffected.

Summarizing, our classification-based approach meets difficulties when faced with 'too local' phenomena like fusion of 'too global' like vowel harmony. Indeed, there is no way to predict vowels in the middle of the word observing only its edges. This difficulty is resolved using character ngrams, which can capture the interdependency between nearby vowels in the word stem. Using models of order up to 6 significantly improves performance on Arabic, Turkish and Finnish. When applying ngram models in the lemmatization stage we observe consistent improvement practically for all languages. Character models cannot help when a correct paradigm was not generated as a candidate

---

[1]Generally, our system was ranked higher on Tasks 2 and 3 which means that lemmatization part works better than inflection partially due to character ngram usage

(recall the discussion on Arabic verbs above). There are two possible strategies in this case: first, a deterministic postprocessing step could be applied to "harmonize" vowels or make other phonetic transformations. Another variant is to create with every abstract paradigm its "phonetic variants" and perform the classification step on the extended set of paradigms. We plan to address this question in future research.

The last thing to say, one of the important merits of our system is its simplicity. It does not require complex techniques for parameter tuning; training the model also relies on well-established algorithms. The features we use are also very simple and they could be easily extended, for example, to capture the context information. Taking into account the solid performance of our system in SIGMORPHON SHARED TASK, we think that classification-based approaches could be useful in a couple of tasks including paradigm induction, morphological parsing and lemmatization for languages of arbitrarily complex morphological structure.

References

Markus Dreyer and Jason Eisner. 2011. Discovering morphological paradigms from plain text using a dirichlet process mixture model. In *Proceedings of the Conference on Empirical Methods in Natural Language Processing*, pages 616–627. Association for Computational Linguistics.

Thomas Müller, Ryan Cotterell, Alexander Fraser, and Hinrich Schütze. 2015. Joint lemmatization and morphological tagging with Lemming. In *Proceedings of the 2015 Conference on Empirical Methods in Natural Language Processing. Association for Computational Linguistics, Lisbon, Portugal*, pages 2268–2274. Association for Computational Linguistics.

Alexey Sorokin and Irina Khomchenkova. 2016. Automatic detection of morphological paradigms using corpora information. In *Dialogue. 22nd International Conference on Computational Linguistics and Intellectual Technologies*, pages 604–616, Moscow, Russia, June. RSUH.

Malin Ahlberg, Markus Forsberg, and Mans Hulden. 2014. Semi-supervised learning of morphological paradigms and lexicons. In *Proceedings of the 14th Conference of the European Chapter of the Association for Computational Linguistics*, pages 569–578, April.

Malin Ahlberg, Markus Forsberg, and Mans Hulden. 2015. Paradigm classification in supervised learning of morphology. In *Proceedings of the Conference of the North American Chapter of the Association for Computational Linguistics Human Language Technologies (NAACL-HLT 2015), Denver, CO*, pages 1024–1029, June.

Garrett Nicolai, Colin Cherry, and Grzegorz Kondrak. 2015. Inflection generation as discriminative string transduction. In *Proceedings of the Conference of the North American Chapter of the Association for Computational Linguistics Human Language Technologies (NAACL-HLT 2015), Denver, CO*, pages 923–931, June.

Andrea Gesmundo and Tanja Samardžić. 2012. Lemmatisation as a tagging task. In *Proceedings of the 50th Annual Meeting of the Association for Computational Linguistics: Short Papers-Volume 2*, pages 368–372. Association for Computational Linguistics.

Grzegorz Chrupala, Georgiana Dinu, and Josef van Genabith. 2008. Learning morphology with Morfette. In *Proceedings of the Sixth International Conference on Language Resources and Evaluation (LREC'08)*, pages 2362–2367, Marrakech, Morocco, May. European Language Resources Association (ELRA).

Ryan Cotterell, Christo Kirov, John Sylak-Glassman, David Yarowsky, Jason Eisner, and Mans Hulden. 2016. The SIGMORPHON 2016 shared task—morphological reinflection. In *Proceedings of the 2016 Meeting of SIGMORPHON*, Berlin, Germany, August. Association for Computational Linguistics.

Thorsten Joachims. 2002. Optimizing search engines using clickthrough data. In *Proceedings of the eighth ACM SIGKDD international conference on Knowledge discovery and data mining*, pages 133–142. ACM.

Andrey A. Zaliznyak. 2002. *Russian nominal inflection*. Yazyki slavyanskoj kultury, Moscow, Russia.

Acknowledgements

The author thanks Irina Khomchenkova for careful assistance during the research. I am also very grateful to anonymous ACL SIGMORPHON reviewers whose detailed comments were very helpful in improving this paper. This work is a part of General Internet Corpus of Russian (`http://www.webcorpora.ru/`) project.

Appendix

Language	Max. gap, initial gap	Max. suffix, prefix length	Affix classifiers	Affix memorization length	ngram model parameters
Arabic	5, 2	4, 4	Suffix	0	6, normalized
	5, 2	4, 4	Suffix, prefix	0	6, unnormalized
Finnish	1, 0	5, 0	Suffix	3	6, normalized
	1, 0	6, 0	Suffix	3	6, normalized
Georgian	5, 1	5, 3	Suffix	0	5, unnormalized
	5 ,1	5, 3	Suffix	0	5, unnormalized
German	2, 2	5, 3	Suffix	3	6, normalized
	2, 2	5, 3	Suffix	3	6, normalized
Hungarian	1, 0	5, 0	Suffix	3	6, normalized
	1, 0	6, 0	Suffix	3	5, normalized
Navajo	3, 7	5, 3	Prefix	3	6, unnormalized
	3, 7	6, 3	Prefix	0	6, unnormalized
Russian	1, 3	5, 0	Suffix	0	3, normalized
	1, 3	6, 3	Suffix	3	6, normalized
Spanish	2, 2	5, 0	Suffix	3	6, normalized
	5, 2	6, 3	Suffix	3	6, normalized
Turkish	1, 0	5, 0	Suffix	3	5, unnormalized
	5, 2	6, 0	Suffix	3	6, normalized

Table 5: System parameters for inflection (upper) and lemmatization (lower) tasks.

MED: The LMU System for the SIGMORPHON 2016 Shared Task on Morphological Reinflection

Katharina Kann and Hinrich Schütze
Center for Information & Language Processing
LMU Munich, Germany
`kann@cis.lmu.de`

Abstract

This paper presents MED, the main system of the LMU team for the SIGMORPHON 2016 Shared Task on Morphological Reinflection as well as an extended analysis of how different design choices contribute to the final performance. We model the task of morphological reinflection using neural encoder-decoder models together with an encoding of the input as a single sequence of the morphological tags of the source and target form as well as the sequence of letters of the source form. The Shared Task consists of three subtasks, three different tracks and covers 10 different languages to encourage the use of language-independent approaches. MED was the system with the overall best performance, demonstrating our method generalizes well for the low-resource setting of the SIGMORPHON 2016 Shared Task.

1 Introduction

In many areas of natural language processing (NLP) it is important that systems are able to correctly analyze and generate different morphological forms, including previously unseen forms. Two examples are machine translation and question answering, where errors in the understanding of morphological forms can seriously harm performance. Accordingly, learning morphological inflection patterns from labeled data is an important challenge.

The task of morphological inflection (MI) consists of generating an inflected form for a given lemma and target tag. Several approaches have been developed for this, including machine learning models and models that exploit the paradigm structure of language (Ahlberg et al., 2015;

Dreyer, 2011; Nicolai et al., 2015). A more complex problem is morphological reinflection (MRI). For this, an inflected form has to be found given another inflected form, a target tag and optionally a source tag.

We use the same approach to both MI and MRI: the character-based and language independent sequence-to-sequence attention model called MED, which stands for *Morphological Encoder-Decoder*. To solve the MRI task, we train one single model on all available source-to-target mappings for each language contained in the training set. This enables the encoder-decoder to learn good parameters for relatively small amounts of training data per target tag already, because most MRI patterns occur in many source-target tag pairs. In our model design, what is learned for one pair can be transferred to others.

The most important point for this is the representation we use for MRI. We encode the input as a single sequence of (i) the morphological tags of the source form, (ii) the morphological tags of the target form and (iii) the sequence of letters of the source form. The output is the sequence of letters of the target form. We train a single generic encoder-decoder per language on this representation that can handle all tag pairs, thus making it possible to make efficient use of the available training data.

The SIGMORPHON 2016 Shared Task on Morphological Reinflection covers both, MI and MRI, for 10 languages as well as different settings and MED outperforms all other systems on all subtasks. The given languages, tracks and tasks will be explained briefly now. For further details on the Shared Task please refer to Cotterell et al. (2016).

Languages. In total, the Shared Task covers 10 languages: Arabic, Finnish, Georgian, German, Hungarian, Maltese, Navajo, Russian, Spanish and Turkish. The training and development datasets

62

Proceedings of the 14th Annual SIGMORPHON Workshop on Computational Research in Phonetics, Phonology, and Morphology, pages 62–70,
Berlin, Germany, August 11, 2016. ©2016 Association for Computational Linguistics

for Hungarian and Maltese were only released at evaluation time.

Tasks. The Shared Task consists of 3 separate tasks with increasing difficulty: task 1 is supposed to be the easiest and task 3 the hardest. The first task consists of mapping a given lemma and target tag to a target form. Task 2 requires the mapping of a given source form, source tag and target tag to a target form. Finally, task 3 consists of finding a target form for a given source form and source tag only.

Tracks. The Shared Task is split into 3 tracks that differ in the information available. The first track is the standard track and requires the solution for each task to use only the training and development data of the current and all lower-numbered tasks, e.g., to use only the data for tasks 1 and 2 for task 2. The restricted track limits the available training and development data to the data belonging to the current task, i.e., data from lower tasks cannot be used, making it impossible to reduce task 2 to task 1 or task 3 to task 2. Track 3 is the bonus track. In this track, all available data per language can be used, including unlabeled corpora which are provided by the task organizers. However, those vary a lot in length, depending on the language. Therefore, we do not make use of them.

In total, there are 90 combinations of languages, tasks and tracks to solve.

The remainder of this paper is organized as follows: In Section 2, our model for the SIGMOR-PHON 2016 Shared Task is presented. Next, our method to preprocess and thus extend the training data is explained in detail. In Section 4 the final results on the test data of the Shared Task are presented and discussed. Afterwards, we analyze the contribution of different settings and components to the overall performance of our system in detail. Finally, in Section 6, we give information about prior work on topics related to our system.

This paper is mainly concerned with the implementation and analysis of the system we submitted to the Shared Task. In (Kann and Schütze, 2016), we instead focus on the novel aspects of our new method MED and compare its performance to prior work on other MRI benchmarks.

2   System description

Our system for the Shared Task is an encoder-decoder recurrent neural network (RNN), called MED, which stands for *Morphological Encoder-Decoder*. It will be described in detail in this Section.

2.1   Neural network model

Our model is based on the network architecture proposed by Bahdanau et al. (2014) for machine translation.[1] The authors describe the model in detail; unless we explicitly say so in the description of our model below, we use the same network configuration as they do.

Bahdanau et al. (2014)'s model is an extension of the recurrent neural network (RNN) encoder-decoder developed by Cho et al. (2014) and Sutskever et al. (2014). The encoder of the latter consists of a gated RNN (GRU) that reads an input sequence of vectors x and encodes it into a fixed-length context vector c, computing hidden states h_t and c by

$$h_t = f(x_t, h_{t-1}) \qquad (1)$$

and

$$c = q(h_1, ..., h_{T_x}) \qquad (2)$$

with nonlinear functions f and q. The decoder uses the context vector to predict the output y:

$$p(y) = \prod_{t=1}^{T_y} p(y_t | \{y_1, ..., y_{t-1}\}, c) \qquad (3)$$

with $y = (y_1, ..., y_{T_y})$ and each conditional probability being modeled with an RNN as

$$p(y_t | \{y_1, ..., y_{t-1}\}, c) = g(y_{t-1}, s_t, c) \qquad (4)$$

where g is a nonlinear function and s_t is the hidden state of the RNN.

Bahdanau et al. (2014) proposed an attention-based version of this model that allows different vectors c_t for each step by automatic learning of an alignment model. They further made the encoder bidirectional. In their model each hidden state h_j at time step j does not only depend on the preceding, but also on the following input:

$$h_j = \left[\overrightarrow{h_j^T}; \overleftarrow{h_j^T} \right]^T \qquad (5)$$

---

[1]Our implementation of MED is based on `https://github.com/mila-udem/blocks-examples/tree/master/machine_translation`.

The formula for $p(y)$ changes accordingly:

$$p(y) = \prod_{t=1}^{T_y} p(y_t|\{y_1, ..., y_{t-1}\}, x) \qquad (6)$$

$$= \prod_{t=1}^{T_y} g(y_{t-1}, s_t, c_t) \qquad (7)$$

with s_t being an RNN hidden state for time t and c_t being the weighted sum of the annotations $(h_1, ..., h_{T_x})$ produced by the encoder:

$$c_i = \sum_{j=1}^{T_x} \alpha_{ij} h_j \qquad (8)$$

The attention weights α_{ij} are calculated for each h_j as

$$\alpha_{ij} = \frac{\exp(e_{ij})}{\sum_{k=1}^{T_x} \exp(e_{ik})} \qquad (9)$$

with

$$e_{ij} = a(s_{i-1}, h_j) \qquad (10)$$

a is parametrized as a feedforward neural network and trained jointly with all other components.

More theoretical background is given in (Bahdanau et al., 2014) and a system overview can be seen in Figure 1.

The final model is a multilayer network with a single maxout (Goodfellow et al., 2013) hidden layer that computes the conditional probability of each element in the output sequence (a character in our case, (Pascanu et al., 2014)). As MRI is less complex than machine translation, we reduce the number of hidden units and the embedding size. After initial experiments, we fixed the hyperparameters of our system and did not further adapt them to a specific task or language. Encoder and decoder RNNs have 100 hidden units each. For training, we use stochastic gradient descent, Adadelta (Zeiler, 2012) and a minibatch size of 20. We initialize all weights in the encoder, decoder and the embeddings except for the GRU weights in the decoder with the identity matrix as well as all biases with zero (Le et al., 2015). We train all models for 20 iterations for all combinations of track and task where we cannot extend the training data with our method described in the next section. Otherwise, we train for 10 epochs.[2] We settled

on this number in early experimentation because training usually converged before that limit.

MED is an ensemble of five RNN encoder-decoders. The final decision is made by majority voting. In case of a tie, the answer is chosen randomly among the most frequent predictions.

2.2 Input and output format

We define the alphabet Σ_{lang} as the set of characters used in the application language. As each tag combination which describes a source or target form consists of one or more subtags, e.g., "number" or "case", we further define Σ_{src} and Σ_{trg} as the set of morphological subtags seen during training as part of the source tag or the target tag, respectively. Finally, we define S_{start} and S_{end} to be a start and an end symbol. Then each input of our system is of the format $S_{start}\Sigma_{src}^+\Sigma_{trg}^+\Sigma_{lang}^+S_{end}$. In the same way, we define the output format as $S_{start}\Sigma_{lang}^+S_{end}$.

For example, a valid input for German would be <w> *IN=pos=ADJ IN=case=GEN IN=num=PL OUT=pos=ADJ OUT=case=ACC OUT=num=PL i s o l i e r t e* </w>. The corresponding system output should be <w> *i s o l i e r t e* </w>.[3]

3 Data and training

3.1 Training data enhancement

Since the Shared Task models a low-resource setting, a way to enhance the given training data is highly desirable. We apply three different methods for this, depending on the track and, therefore, depending on the information available. Even though the training data enhancer could be used to increase the amount of available data for other models as well, we expect it to be especially effective with MED. This is due to the fact that MED is able to reuse information from any combination of input and output tag for any other tag pair.

Restricted track. In the restricted track, only training and development data of the respective task and language can be used. This means that there is less information available than in the other two tracks. Therefore, in this track we can only use a very basic enhancement method and we can

---

[2] For extended data in Maltese we trained only for 6 epochs, due to time constraints.

[3] For task 1 in the restricted and standard track and task 3 throughout all tracks, no source tag is given and we only have one tag combination in the input. Therefore, we do not prepend *IN=* or *OUT=* to the tags. However, internally, this does not make a difference for the model.

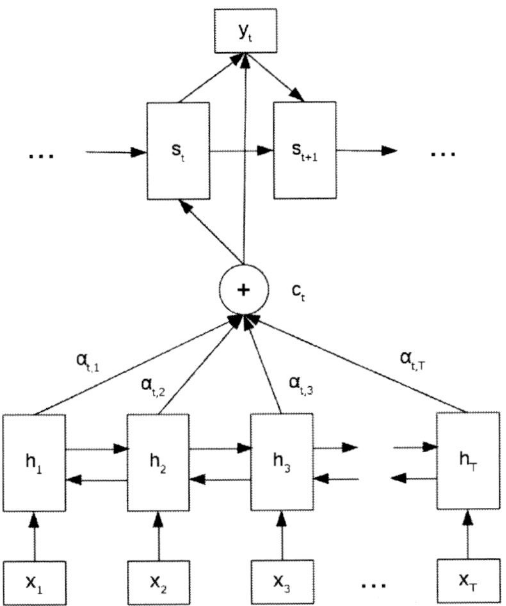

Figure 1: System overview. The input x consists of characters as well as input and output tags. The output y consists of characters only.

only apply it to task 2. The idea the method is based on is that task 2 is symmetric. As described before, the task consists of mapping a triplet of source tag, source form and target tag to a target form. To double the training data it is sufficient to switch the information and thus create a new sample, mapping from target tag, target form and source tag to the source form.

Standard track. The training data enhancement for the standard track combines information from task 1 and task 2 and can therefore, following the Shared Task rules, be used for task 2 and task 3, as only data from lower tasks needs to be accessed. The idea of our enhancement method is that each word form belongs to a certain paradigm which in turn belongs to one single lemma. Therefore, when knowing the lemmas of words, we can group them into paradigms. When having more than one word per paradigm, we can infer the information that all of them can be inflected into each other and thus use them to create new samples. Knowing this, we use task 1 training data to make groups of lemmas and word forms belonging to the same paradigm, keeping the tags. Then, we add all information from task 2 and, knowing that source form and target form always belong to the same lemma, we add both forms with their

tags to a group whenever one of them is already in there.[4] Afterwards, we build all combinations of word pairs of each paradigm and, by doing so, create new training data.

This method could be applied even if there was absolutely no overlap between the lemmas in task 1 and task 2. However, it would then be necessary to train a lemmatizer on task 1 data first and lemmatize all words to sort them into paradigms. When doing this, accuracy could be improved by only accepting predictions with a strong confidence and by only accepting new words for a paradigm if the source and the target form of a sample have the same lemma prediction.

Bonus track. In the bonus track, our training data enhancement can also be used for task 1. In order to do so, we first apply the same method as for the standard track to produce the extended training data. However, we additionally change the input format for task 1 such that it resembles the task 2 input, using *LEMMA* as the input tag. In this way, we can apply the task 2 model to task 1 such that task 1 is able to benefit from the additional data as well.

3.2 Description of the final training data

Depending on the complexity of the language and the structure of the datasets we end up with a different amount of final training samples for each language, even though we start with nearly identical training set sizes. We show the final number of samples for task 2 in different tracks in Table 1. As can be seen, the training data enhancement increases the number of samples by a factor between 10 and 80. Out of all languages, the enhancer has the smallest effect for Finnish. Most additional samples are created for Maltese.

3.3 Training

For each of the 10 languages we train one ensemble for each task of the restricted track as well as for each of tasks 2 and 3 of the bonus track. We do not train a separate model for task 1, due to the fact that the same model can be applied to both task 1 and task 2 of the bonus track. In total, we train 50 ensembles, consisting of 250 single models. For our setting, task 1 of the standard track is the same as for the restricted track, while tasks 2 and 3 are the same as for the bonus track.

---

[4] As for none of the languages task 3 contained new word forms, we did not consider task 3 data here.

Dataset	T2, given no. samples	T2, restricted no. samples	factor	T2, standard no. samples	factor
Arabic	14,400	28,800	2	458,814	32
Finnish	14,400	28,800	2	116,206	8
Georgian	14,400	28,800	2	196,396	14
German	14,400	28,800	2	166,148	12
Hungarian	21,600	43,200	2	643,630	30
Maltese	21,600	43,200	2	1,629,446	75
Navajo	14,385	28,770	2	160,332	11
Russian	14,400	28,800	2	129,302	9
Spanish	14,400	28,800	2	211,030	15
Turkish	14,400	28,800	2	392,136	27

Table 1: Number of training samples for task 2 without (given) and with the training data enhancer (restricted and standard track) together with the factor by which the size of the training set increased. Note that the samples for task 2 in the standard track are the same as the samples for task 1 in the bonus track.

Language	Task 1	Task 2	Task 3
Arabic	95.47%	97.38%	96.52%
Finnish	96.80%	97.40%	96.56%
Georgian	98.50%	99.14%	98.87%
German	95.80%	97.45%	95.60%
Hungarian	99.30%	99.67%	99.50%
Maltese	88.99%	88.17%	87.83%
Navajo	91.48%	96.64%	96.20%
Russian	91.46%	91.00%	89.91%
Spanish	98.84%	98.74%	97.96%
Turkish	98.93%	97.94%	99.31%

Table 2: Exact-match accuracy per language for the standard track of the SIGMORPHON 2016 Shared Task.

Language	Task 1	Task 2	Task 3
Arabic	98.25%	97.38%	96.25%
Finnish	97.30%	97.40%	96.56%
Georgian	99.20%	99.14%	98.87%
German	97.38%	97.45%	95.60%
Hungarian	99.69%	99.67%	99.50%
Maltese	88.53%	88.17%	87.83%
Navajo	98.03%	96.64%	96.20%
Russian	92.15%	91.00%	89.91%
Spanish	99.05%	98.74%	97.96%
Turkish	97.49%	97.94%	99.31%

Table 4: Exact-match accuracy per language for the bonus track of the SIGMORPHON 2016 Shared Task.

Language	Task 1	Task 2	Task 3
Arabic	95.47%	91.09%	82.80%
Finnish	96.80%	96.81%	93.18%
Georgian	98.50%	98.50%	96.21%
German	95.80%	96.22%	92.41%
Hungarian	99.30%	99.42%	98.37%
Maltese	88.99%	86.88%	84.25%
Navajo	91.48%	97.81%	83.50%
Russian	91.46%	90.11%	87.13%
Spanish	98.84%	98.45%	96.69%
Turkish	98.93%	98.38%	95.00%

Table 3: Exact-match accuracy per language for the restricted track of the SIGMORPHON 2016 Shared Task.

For each task of the restricted track we train a separate model for 20 epochs. For the bonus track we reduce the number of epochs to 10, because we have much more training data. For Maltese, we reduce it even further to 6 epochs.

Because we do not tune any hyperparameters, we combine the original training and development sets to one big training set. The numbers reported in Table 1 are considering this big dataset.

4 Results on the Shared Task test data

Tables 2, 3 and 4 list the official final results of MED for the SIGMORPHON 2016 Shared Task. Table 2 shows the results of the standard track for which systems are allowed to access the data of the respective task and all lower numbered tasks. Therefore, we can apply our training data extension to tasks 2 and 3, but not to task 1. Because of this, the two higher tasks have the same scores as in the bonus track: we effectively give the same answers. Task 1, in turn, is the same for the standard and the restricted track, leading to the same numbers in Tables 2 and 3.

For ease of exposition, we will mostly compare the restricted and the bonus track as the standard track can be considered a mixture of those two. For most tasks and languages the accuracy is higher in the bonus than in the restricted track. This is easy to explain as MED has more data to train on (task 1 information for tasks 2 and 3 and task 2 information for task 1). The exception is Navajo: For task 2 the accuracy is higher in the bonus track than in the restricted track. We leave an investigation of this for future work.

Our training data enhancer – which is the only difference between the bonus and the restricted track as we do not use the provided unlabeled corpora – is clearly effective: For Arabic, for example, it leads to 13.72% improvement in performance for task 3. For Turkish, the accuracy for task 3 increases by 4.31%. Those are also the languages for which the training data enhancement was very effective as can be seen in Table 1. That Maltese does not improve so much even though we use a lot more training data is most likely due to the shorter training: we trained only for 6 epochs instead of 10, because of time constraints.

As expected, the scores for task 3 are worse than or at most comparable to the scores for task 2 in all tracks. This is due to the fact that task 3 does not provide a source tag, so less information is available. However, it seems that this information was not much needed as the improvement when adding it is minor. The better result for task 3 for Turkish compared to task 2 in the bonus track may be due to randomness during training – like the order of samples in the training data – as it is below 1.5%.

It may be surprising at first that the results for task 1 are not always better than the results for task 2. This is the case, for example, in the restricted track for Finnish, Georgian, Hungarian and Navajo. As the organizers describe on the Shared Task's homepage, they expect task 1 to be the easiest. Our guess would be that the model has more information in total for task 2 as more forms are given per paradigm. Additionally, task 2 is symmetric; this makes it possible to use twice the training data, as described in Section 3.

5 System Analysis

To analyze which design choices are important and how they influence the performance of MED we conduct several experiments, always keeping all but the investigated design choice fixed to the settings described in Section 2. To make the experiments clearer, we limit them to one combination of task, track and language: Unless mentioned otherwise, we perform all experiments described in this section on task 2 of the restricted track for Russian. For the experiments in this section, the system is trained on training data only and evaluated on the development set. The training data enhancement is not used in this analysis.

5.1 Analysis 1: Number of hidden units in encoder and decoder

In its original configuration MED has 100 hidden units in both the encoder and the decoder. This number was found to be good during initial experiments. However, we want to investigate how the number of hidden units in the RNNs can effect the final accuracy on an MRI task. Therefore, we

Number of hidden units	Exact-match accuracy
50	86.2%
100	88.4%
200	87.2%
400	87.3%

Table 5: Performance of MED for different numbers of hidden units in the encoder and decoder.

Embedding size	Exact-match accuracy
100	86.7%
200	87.3%
300	88.4%
400	90.0%
500	90.3%

Table 6: Performance of MED for different embedding dimensions in the encoder and decoder.

train one ensemble for each of 50, 100, 200 and 400 hidden units. To reduce the number of possible different options and because it agrees with MED's original configuration, we define the numbers of hidden units in encoder and decoder to be equal.

The evaluation in Table 5 shows that the best accuracy is obtained for 100 hidden units. Lower results for fewer hidden units indicate that the model does not have enough capacity to learn the patterns in the data well. Lower results for more hidden units indicate that the model is overfitting the training data.

5.2 Analysis 2: Size of the embeddings

We chose 300 to be the size of the character and tag embeddings in our model for the Shared Task. In this analysis, we want to systematically investigate how MED performs for different embedding sizes for the encoder and decoder embeddings. We train the model with embeddings of the sizes 100, 200, 300, 400 and 500 and report the resulting accuracies in Table 6.

The results show that the bigger the embeddings get the more the perfomance improves. The best accuracy is reached for 500-dimensional embeddings, i.e., the biggest embeddings in this analysis. This suggests that we might have improved our final results in the Shared Task even further by using embeddings of a higher dimensionality. However, this is also a trade-off between a gain in accuracy and longer training time. Keeping in mind that we had to train many single models, 300 was a reasonable choice for the embedding size, with only 1.9% loss of perfomance compared to 500-dimensional embeddings.

Initialization	Exact-match accuracy
Identity	90.5%
Identity + orthogonal	88.4%
Gaussian + orthogonal	89.7%

Table 7: Performance of MED for different initialization types.

5.3 Analysis 3: Initialization

For the Shared Task, most weights of MED are initialized with the identitiy matrix. An exception to this are the weights in the decoder GRU which are initialized using a random orthogonal matrix. All biases are initialized to zero. We now compare how MED's final performance depends on the type of initialization. For this, we train two additional models: (i) we initialize all weights with the identitiy matrix and (ii) we initialize all weights except for the weights in the decoder GRU from a Gaussian distribution. The weights in the decoder GRU are again initialized with a random orthogonal matrix.

The final accuracy of the three models can be seen in Table 7. The random intialization leads to better results than intitializing with the identity matrix together with a random orthogonal matrix. However, the highest accuracy is reached by initializing *all* weights with identity matrices. In fact, the results are 2.1% better than MED's original performance. Thus, we would recommend this initialization for future use of our model.

5.4 Analysis 4: One embedding per tag vs. one embedding per tag combination

To keep the model flexible to handle tag combinations not present in the training set, we split each tag combination into single tags, e.g., *pos=ADJ,case=ACC,gen=FEM,num=SG* becomes *pos=ADJ*, *case=ACC*, *gen=FEM* and *num=SG* with each part having its own embedding which is fed into the model.

We now compare to the performance of a representation in which tags are "fused" and each tag combination has only one single embedding. As this is one of the most important design choices for MED, we do this analysis for several languages and additionally report the number of tag combinations that are not seen during training.

Table 8 shows that unknown tag combinations are generally not a problem with the exception of Maltese. Nevertheless, there is a considerable decrease in performance. The difference is especially big for languages with a lower performance

Language	MED	MED-tag-comb.	Unk.
Arabic	88.8%	83.4%	0
Finnish	95.6%	95.2%	1
Georgian	97.3%	95.6%	0
German	95.1%	93.5%	1
Hungarian	99.3%	99.3%	0
Maltese	85.7%	77.1%	151
Navajo	91.1%	83.4%	1
Russian	88.4%	86.8%	1
Spanish	97.5%	97.0%	0
Turkish	97.6%	95.9%	2

Table 8: Exact match accuracy for the standard representation (MED) as well as the representation with one embedding per tag combination (MED-tag-comb) per language. The last column shows the number of samples that contain tag combinations that appear in dev but not in train, either for the source or the target form.

Tag order type	Exact-match accuracy
MED	88.4%
MED-perm	86.4%

Table 9: Performance of MED when training on samples with tags in always the same order (MED) and samples where the tags are permuted inside each combination (MED-perm).

like Arabic, Maltese, Navajo and Russian. Languages with a general high accuracy do not lose much accuracy when using one embedding per tag combination. We hypothesize that the patterns of these languages are easy enough to even be learned with a harder representation. Overall, it seems that our representation with split-up tag combinations is the better choice for MRI and might even be a key component for MED's success in the Shared Task.

5.5 Analysis 5: The order of tags

In the representation we feed to MED, the order of single tags inside a tag combination is always fixed. We now investigate how much influence this has on the final performance of the model; i.e., we ask: is MRI harder or easier to learn if we permutate the morphological tags? For this analysis, we randomly shuffle the tags of each combination in the training and development data (while still using the development set for testing).

Table 9 shows that learning seems to be easier for non-permuted tags. Indeed, when keeping the order of tags fixed, the system performance is 2% better than for the random tag order. However, the difference is not big. This might actually be different for languages other than Russian as we did not investigate from a linguistic point of view if the order matters contentwise for any of the languages.

6 Related Work

Prior work on morphology includes morphological segmentation (Harris, 1955; Hafer and Weiss, 1974; Déjean, 1998), different approaches for MRI (Ahlberg et al., 2014; Durrett and DeNero, 2013; Eskander et al., 2013; Nicolai et al., 2015). and work on morphological tagging and lemmatization (Müller et al., 2015).

RNN encoder-decoder models, gated RNNs in general as well as LSTMs were applied to several NLP tasks including some on morphology like morphological segmentation (Wang et al., 2016) during the last years. Other tasks they proved to be useful for are machine translation (Cho et al., 2014; Sutskever et al., 2014; Bahdanau et al., 2014), parsing (Vinyals et al., 2015) or speech recognition (Graves and Schmidhuber, 2005; Graves et al., 2013).

The most similar work to ours was probably the one by Faruqui et al. (2015). Indeed, MED's design is very close to their model. However, they trained one network for every tag pair; this can negatively impact performance in a setting with limited training data like the SIGMORPHON 2016 Shared Task. In contrast, we train a single model for each language. This radically reduces the amount of training data needed for the encoder-decoder because most MRI patterns occur in many tag pairs, so what is learned for one can be transferred to others. In order to model all tag pairs of the language together, we introduce an explicit morphological representation that enables the attention mechanism of the encoder-decoder to generalize MRI patterns across tag pairs.

7 Conclusion

In this paper we described MED, our system for the SIGMORPHON 2016 Shared Task on Morphological Reinflection as well as a training data enhancement method based on paradigms. MED is a powerful character-based encoder-decoder RNN and its architecture is completely language-independent, such that we trained the models for all 10 languages of the Shared Task using the same hyperparameters. MED establishes the state of the art for the SIGMORPHON 2016 Shared Task, scoring first in all of the 90 subtasks of the final evaluation.

Furthermore, we presented an extended analysis, evaluating different design choices for MED. The results show that most of our initial settings were good choices, especially the representation of morphological tags. However, it might be possible to further improve MED's performance increasing the size of the used embeddings and choosing another initialization.

Acknowledgments

We are grateful to MILA (`https://mila.umontreal.ca`) for making their neural machine translation model available to us. We further acknowledge the financial support of Siemens for this research.

References

Malin Ahlberg, Markus Forsberg, and Mans Hulden. 2014. Semi-supervised learning of morphological paradigms and lexicons. In *Proc. of EACL*.

Malin Ahlberg, Markus Forsberg, and Mans Hulden. 2015. Paradigm classification in supervised learning of morphology. In *Proc. of NAACL*.

Dzmitry Bahdanau, Kyunghyun Cho, and Yoshua Bengio. 2014. Neural machine translation by jointly learning to align and translate. *arXiv preprint arXiv:1409.0473*.

Kyunghyun Cho, Bart van Merriënboer, Dzmitry Bahdanau, and Yoshua Bengio. 2014. On the properties of neural machine translation: Encoder-decoder approaches. *arXiv preprint arXiv:1409.1259*.

Ryan Cotterell, Christo Kirov, John Sylak-Glassman, David Yarowsky, Jason Eisner, and Mans Hulden. 2016. The SIGMORPHON 2016 shared task—morphological reinflection. In *Proc. of the 2016 Meeting of SIGMORPHON*.

Hervé Déjean. 1998. Morphemes as necessary concept for structures discovery from untagged corpora. In *Proc. of the Joint Conferences on New Methods in Language Processing and CoNLL*.

Markus Dreyer. 2011. *A non-parametric model for the discovery of inflectional paradigms from plain text using graphical models over strings*. Ph.D. thesis, Johns Hopkins University, Baltimore, MD.

Greg Durrett and John DeNero. 2013. Supervised learning of complete morphological paradigms. In *Proc. of HLT-NAACL*.

Ramy Eskander, Nizar Habash, and Owen Rambow. 2013. Automatic extraction of morphological lexicons from morphologically annotated corpora. In *Proc. of EMNLP*.

Manaal Faruqui, Yulia Tsvetkov, Graham Neubig, and Chris Dyer. 2015. Morphological inflection generation using character sequence to sequence learning. *arXiv preprint arXiv:1512.06110*.

Ian Goodfellow, David Warde-farley, Mehdi Mirza, Aaron Courville, and Yoshua Bengio. 2013. Maxout networks. In *Proc. of ICML*.

Alex Graves and Jürgen Schmidhuber. 2005. Framewise phoneme classification with bidirectional LSTM and other neural network architectures. *Neural Networks*, 18(5):602–610.

Alan Graves, Abdel-rahman Mohamed, and Geoffrey Hinton. 2013. Speech recognition with deep recurrent neural networks. In *Proc. of ICASSP*.

Margaret A Hafer and Stephen F Weiss. 1974. Word segmentation by letter successor varieties. *Information storage and retrieval*, 10(11):371–385.

Zellig S Harris. 1955. From phoneme to morpheme. *Language*, 31(2):190–222.

Katharina Kann and Hinrich Schütze. 2016. Single-model encoder-decoder with explicit morphological representation for reinflection. In *Proc. of ACL*.

Quoc V Le, Navdeep Jaitly, and Geoffrey E Hinton. 2015. A simple way to initialize recurrent networks of rectified linear units. *arXiv preprint arXiv:1504.00941*.

Thomas Müller, Ryan Cotterell, Alexander Fraser, and Hinrich Schütze. 2015. Joint lemmatization and morphological tagging with lemming. In *Proc. of EMNLP*.

Garrett Nicolai, Colin Cherry, and Grzegorz Kondrak. 2015. Inflection generation as discriminative string transduction. In *Proc. of NAACL*.

Razvan Pascanu, Caglar Gulcehre, Kyunghyun Cho, and Yoshua Bengio. 2014. How to construct deep recurrent neural networks. In *Proc. of ICLR*.

Ilya Sutskever, Oriol Vinyals, and Quoc V Le. 2014. Sequence to sequence learning with neural networks. In *Proc. of NIPS*.

Oriol Vinyals, Łukasz Kaiser, Terry Koo, Slav Petrov, Ilya Sutskever, and Geoffrey Hinton. 2015. Grammar as a foreign language. In *Proc. of NIPS*.

Linlin Wang, Zhu Cao, Yu Xia, and Gerard de Melo. 2016. Morphological segmentation with window LSTM neural networks. In *Proc. of AAAI*.

Matthew D Zeiler. 2012. Adadelta: An adaptive learning rate method. *arXiv preprint arXiv:1212.5701*.

The Columbia University - New York University Abu Dhabi SIGMORPHON 2016 Morphological Reinflection Shared Task Submission

Dima Taji[†], Ramy Eskander[‡], Nizar Habash[†], Owen Rambow[‡]

[†]Computational Approaches to Modeling Language Lab, New York University Abu Dhabi
{dima.taji,nizar.habash}@nyu.edu
[‡]Center for Computational Learning Systems, Columbia University
{reskander,rambow}@ccls.columbia.edu

Abstract

We present a high-level description and error analysis of the Columbia-NYUAD system for morphological reinflection, which builds on previous work on supervised morphological paradigm completion. Our system improved over the shared task baseline on some of the languages, reaching up to 30% absolute increase. Our ranking on average was 5th in Track 1, 8th in Track 2, and 3rd in Track 3.

1 Introduction

In this paper, we present a high-level description and error analysis of the Columbia University - New York University Abu Dhabi system for morphological reinflection, which was submitted to the SIGMORPHON 2016 shared task on morphological reinflection (Cotterell et al., 2016). The system builds on previous work on supervised morphological paradigm completion (Eskander et al., 2013). Although the core system is the same, additional efforts were needed to preprocess the shared task data in order to make it compatible with our existing approach, as well as to create a new interface that targets morphological reinflection specifically. Our system improved over the baseline on some of the languages, reaching up to 30% absolute increase. Our ranking on average was 5th in Track 1, 8th in Track 2, and 3rd in Track 3.

The rest of this paper is structured as follows. We present some related work in computational morphology in Section 2. We then discuss our approach to the shared task in Section 3. We discuss our performance and insights in Section 4. Finally, we give an outlook on our approach in Section 5.

2 Related Work

The area of computational morphology includes a rich and varied continuum of approaches and techniques. Within it, we find, on one end, systems painstakingly designed by hand (Koskenniemi, 1983; Buckwalter, 2004; Habash and Rambow, 2006; Détrez and Ranta, 2012); and on the other end, unsupervised methods that learn morphology models from unannotated data (Creutz and Lagus, 2007; Dreyer and Eisner, 2011; Rasooli et al., 2014; Monson et al., 2008; Hammarström and Borin, 2011). Closer to the former side of the continuum, we find work on minimally supervised methods for morphology learning that make use of available resources such as parallel data, dictionaries or some additional morphological annotations (Yarowsky and Wicentowski, 2000; Snyder and Barzilay, 2008; Cucerzan and Yarowsky, 2002). Closer to the other end, we find work that focuses on defining morphological models with limited lexicons that are then extended using raw text (Clément et al., 2004; Forsberg et al., 2006). The setting of the shared task on morphological reinflection (Cotterell et al., 2016), which provides a rich partly annotated training data set, encourages methods that are supervised.

Our shared task submission builds on our previously published work on paradigm completion (Eskander et al., 2013), which falls somewhere in the middle of the continuum outlined above. Our approach learns complete morphological models using rich morphological annotations. The match of the requirements for our approach and those for the shared task was far from perfect, but it was interesting to participate since we have always wanted to explore ways to reduce some of the expected input annotations – in particular word segmentations, which are not provided in the shared task.

Proceedings of the 14th Annual SIGMORPHON Workshop on Computational Research in Phonetics, Phonology, and Morphology, pages 71–75,
Berlin, Germany, August 11, 2016. ©2016 Association for Computational Linguistics

3 Approach

Our basic approach is supervised paradigm completion as presented in (Eskander et al., 2013). It was designed to learn a morphological analyzer and generator from data that has been manually segmented and clustered by lexeme. To adapt our approach to the shared task, we added two phases that sandwich the basic paradigm completion in a pipeline architecture: an initial *segmentation* phase to preprocess the shared task data to match our approach's expectations; and a phase to perform reinflection as specified in the various sub-tasks in the shared task.

3.1 Word Segmentation

In the segmentation phase, we segment every word in the training dataset (TRAIN) into prefix, stem, and suffix. For example, the Arabic word *al-muhandisatu* is ideally segmented into *al-+muhandis+atu*. This phase has three steps.

In the first step, we estimate the probability of every possible *affix-feature* and *stem-POS* (Part-of-Speech).[1] This is accomplished by summing over the partial counts of all possible segmentations of every word in TRAIN, constrained only by a minimal stem length parameter, s.[2]

In the second step, we cluster the words in *lemma clusters*, which are groups of words that share the same lemma and only vary in terms of inflectional morphology. For Task 1, lemmas were given in TRAIN, and we clustered all the words that appear with each given lemma. For Task 2 and Task 3, we used cooccurrence evidence to determine the clusters, where if two words appeared together in the same training instance, we assigned them to the same lemma cluster. This may result in under-clustering due to words not appearing together, as well as over-clustering, when the entries consist of derivational rather than inflectional morphology. To normalize the treatment of the different tasks, lemmas in Task 1 were included as words with the feature *feat=lemma*; and words appearing with no features in Task 3 were given the POS of the word they appeared with and the feature *feat=UNK*.

Finally, we decide on the optimal segmentation for each word in the context of its lemma cluster in the following manner. For every word in the cluster, we produce a ranking of top b segmentations[3] as an initial filter. This rank is based on *P(stem-POS)*P(affix-feature)*, which were computed in the first step. We select for each word the segmentation that minimizes the overall number of stems in the lemma cluster, with a bias towards the stem with the highest *prominence score*. A stem prominence score is computed as the probability of the stem-POS multiplied by the number of occurrences it has in the top b segmentation choices (for all words in the cluster). This ensures that, for all the words that have a segmentation including the top stem, this segmentation is selected. For the words that do not have the top stem among their b segmentations, we go for the next stem in the prominence score ranking, and so on.

Two problematic cases are handled exceptionally: words with *feat=UNK*, because it appears very frequently, and features that are infrequent (below a threshold x[4]). Those words are not used as part of determining the prominence score, but the stem is forced upon them.

At the end of this process, we should have a specific segmentation for every word. To assess the algorithm's performance, we ran it on an external data set of Egyptian Arabic (Eskander et al., 2013), for which we had a manually annotated gold standard. Our segmentation algorithm achieves a word segmentation accuracy of 84.7% when tested on this dataset.

3.2 Paradigm Completion

The core of our work is paradigm completion, in which we build complete inflectional classes (ICs) based on corpus annotations. The construction of the ICs follows the technique we presented in (Eskander et al., 2013), where the ICs have all the possible morphosyntactic feature combinations for every lemma in TRAIN.

The paradigm completion step works as follows. First, the entries in TRAIN are converted into paradigms, where each paradigm lists all the inflections of all morphosyntactic feature combinations for a specific lemma seen in the training data. The paradigms are then converted into inflectional classes (ICs), where stem entries are abstracted as templates by extracting out the root letters. We de-

---

[1] For the Arabic word *al-muhandisatu*, the ideal *affix-feature* pairs the affix *al-+ _ +atu*, with the feature set that appears with this word, *pos=ADJ, def=DEF, case=NOM, gen=FEM, num=SG*. The ideal stem-POS pairs the stem *muhandis* with the POS, *pos=ADJ*.

[2] $s = 3$, determined empirically.

[3] $b = 10$, determined empirically.

[4] $x = 5$, determined empirically.

termine which letters should be considered pattern (non-root) letters for each language. These are letters that change between stems in the same IC. For example, in English *sing, sang, sung*, we observe that the vowel *i* can change to *a* or *u*. So these three letters change in this IC. For each letter, we count the number of ICs in which the letter undergoes a change in the IC stems; and we order the letters by this frequency. We then use a small tuning corpus to determine what subset of letters is optimal for the specific language: we repeatedly perform paradigm completion with all initial segments of the ordered list of letters. We choose the subset which results in the best performance on the task. [5] Finally, the generated ICs are merged together into a smaller number of more condensed ICs, where two ICs merge if they share the same inflectional behavior. The ICs are then completed by sharing affix and stem information with each other. We apply the above process to the different POS types in the shared task, independently.

3.3 Morphological Reinflection

The set of ICs created in paradigm completion are used to create a morphological analyzer and generator. In cases in which the input is a previously seen (i.e., in TRAIN) lemma (Task 1) or an inflected form with a tag (Task 2) or without a tag (Task 3), we can match the input against the IC which was created from that item, and then we can just generate the requested form. In cases of unseen lemmas or forms, we run the ICs as a morphological analyzer, which matches it against an IC, and we again proceed to generate the inflected form.

4 Results

4.1 Shared Task

We participated in all the tracks and tasks of the shared task, with a total of nine submissions for almost all languages. Our ranking, on average over all languages and tasks, was 5th (5.4) in Track 1, 8th (7.6) in Track 2, and 3rd (2.6) in Track 3. The best performing systems used neural network models, which have improved performance in many areas of NLP (Manning, 2016).

In Table 1, we present the results for our system (Track 3 Task 3) and baseline together with a number of features of the different language sets and their correlations with the final scores. We do not include the results for Finnish and Russian as our system had many problems and we believe the results are not meaningful.[6] We also do not present any results on the other tasks and tracks, although we participated in all of them, because of limited space. The results across tasks and tracks are comparable to the task we selected here. For some languages, our approach did well, increasing quality over the official baseline for six languages by up to 30% absolute (Turkish).

Given our previous work on Arabic (Eskander et al., 2013), we were dismayed to see the lowish results on Arabic; although this was not unexpected given that the Arabic used in the shared task was not in standard Arabic orthography. Arabic has a morphophonemic orthography that hides some of the allomorphic distinctions made explicit in the shared task, and some of which we do not do well on. For instance, the Arabic definite article morpheme *al-* has a number of allomorphs that assimilate to the consonant that follows the article when the consonant is one of the 14 *sun letters* (see (Habash, 2010) for a discussion), e.g., *al-daftaru* → *ad-daftaru* 'the notebook', and *al-numūru* → *an-numūru* 'the tigers', as opposed to the default *al-'uk̲ti* → *al-'uk̲ti* 'the sister'. In Arabic's morphophonemic orthography, the different allomorphs are written using one form *Al: Ald~aftaru* الدفتر, *Aln~umuwru* النمور, and *AlÂuxti* الأخت.[7]

4.2 Correlation Insights

We present next some insights gained by considering correlations between specific features of the data sets for different languages and the languages' performance in the baseline and our system. We expect some of these insights to be general indicators of the complexity of modeling different languages morphologically.

The first two columns in Table 1, **Stem**$_{allo}$ and **Affix**$_{allo}$, are the stem allomorphy rate and the affix allomorphy rate, respectively. **Stem**$_{allo}$ is computed as the ratio of unique stems divided by the number of lemmas in our training data. The

---

[5] We do this for Task 1 (in which the lemma is available as input), and then use the same set in all task/track combinations. For some task/track combinations we should have used different data, but did not do this for lack of time. We acknowledge the methodological flaw, but we suspect that doing it differently would not have changed our results much.

[6] Our official system's performance on Track 3 Task 3 for Finnish and Russian are 20% (40% below baseline) and 62% (19% below baseline), respectively.

[7] Arabic transliteration is presented in the Habash-Soudi-Buckwalter scheme (Habash et al., 2007).

73

Language	$Stem_{allo}$	$Affix_{allo}$	Features	Lemmas	Examples	log(F)	log(A/S)	log(L/F)	log(E/F)	System	Baseline
Arabic	2.8	8.0	232	5,357	47,298	2.37	0.5	1.36	2.3	59%	51%
Georgian	1.1	5.9	96	9,483	49,813	1.98	0.7	1.99	2.7	90%	87%
German	1.2	6.7	105	10,834	49,633	2.02	0.8	2.01	2.7	79%	82%
Hungarian	2.0	14.3	91	6,936	82,244	1.96	0.9	1.88	3.0	89%	78%
Maltese	4.5	2.6	3,825	3,186	65,597	3.58	-0.2	-0.08	1.2	29%	25%
Navajo	5.9	22.8	58	2,235	41,401	1.76	0.6	1.59	2.9	84%	60%
Spanish	1.2	13.5	90	9,374	48,217	1.95	1.0	2.02	2.7	79%	89%
Turkish	1.8	9.9	195	5,620	46,693	2.29	0.7	1.46	2.4	84%	54%
System$_{correl}$	-0.43	0.54	-0.90	0.45	-0.16	-0.93	0.89	0.91	0.94		
Baseline$_{correl}$	-0.67	0.26	-0.76	0.81	-0.08	-0.82	0.88	0.93	0.85		

Table 1: Results for our system (Track 3 Task 3) and baseline together with a number of features of the different language sets and their correlations with the final scores. In columns 7 through 10: F=Features, L=Lemmas, E=Examples, A=Affixes, and S=Stems.

Affix$_{allo}$ is computed as the ratio of unique affixes divided by the number of features in our training data. Ideally, these two measures would reflect the complexity of the language, as well as how well we model it. The numbers may be larger than or smaller than the ideal model depending on the quality of our segmentation step and the amount of training data. Next in Table 1 are the counts of features, lemmas, and training examples. Finally, we present four metrics that are derived from the previously shown values, e.g. **logE/F** is the log of the ratio of *training examples to features*. In the last two rows, we show the correlation coefficient between each presented value and the final score over all languages.

The languages vary widely in performance in both the baseline and our system. It is immediately evident that among the basic aspects of the training data, the number of features has a very high negative correlation with the results – see Features, and log(F) in Table 1. The number of training examples is not an indicator of performance ranking in this set. However, the log of the ratio of training examples to features is a very strong indicator with very high correlation. This makes sense since we expect languages with richer morphology to require relatively more examples than languages with poorer morphology. We computed the **Stem**$_{allo}$ and **Affix**$_{allo}$ because we thought they may give us insights into how our approach handles different languages and perhaps reflect errors in the segmentation process: we expected segmentation errors to inflate these two values. This hypothesis was not possible to confirm since the number of variant forms is not only dependent on segmentation and number of features in a language, but ultimately the number of train-

ing examples in relation to the number of features. As such, these two values are not well correlated with the results; although, interestingly, the ratio of **Affix**$_{allo}$ to **Stem**$_{allo}$ is. This may simply reflect that languages with less variable stems and more content-heavy affixes may be easier to model. The log of the ratio of lemmas to features, is another interesting measure with very high correlation (particularly in the baseline). This measure reflects that it is harder to model languages with very rich features without providing lots of collections of examples (lemma sets).

4.3 Error Analysis

When analyzing the errors in our output, we observed a number of overlapping phenomena that made the identification of the specific sources of the errors difficult. The following are the three main phenomena we noted.

(1) Stemming errors, where the segmentation process added letters to the stem or ignored letters in the stem. For example, the Arabic word *al-'ajalatu* was stemmed to *l-'ajala* instead of *'ajala*, and the system ended up generating *l-'ajalatay* as the dual possessive noun instead of *'ajalatay*. Similarly, in Maltese the stem of the word *nqtilthomx* was determined to be the word itself, thus generating *nqtilthomxthulhomx* instead of *nqtilthulhomx*.

(2) Paradigm errors, where the system optimized for the wrong pattern because of possible previous stemming errors. In Spanish, for example, the word *curta* was reinflected as *curtéis* instead of *curtáis*, and in Turkish *ortağa* generated *ortağlara* instead of *ortaklara*.

(3) Allomorphy modeling errors, which can be present in affixes or in stems. When one morpheme can have multiple allomorphs, the system might prefer the wrong allomorph. This can be observed in the cases of the Arabic definite article's so-called *sun letters*, where the system generated *al-dafī'i* instead of *ad-dafī'i*, as well as the Turkish vowel harmony issues, where *uğratmiyorsunuz* was generated instead of *uğratmıyorsunuz*. Stem allomorphy happens when the stem slightly changes depending on specific features, for example, in Arabic *qāmūs* and *qawāmīs* are stems for the same noun (one singular and one broken plural), which caused the generation of *al-qāmūsi* instead of *al-qawāmīsi*.

5 Outlook

We built our morphological paradigm completion system for a specific purpose: we are annotating texts by hand in order to develop morphological analyzers and taggers for Arabic dialects. The question now arises whether we can reduce the human annotation work (say, by not requiring human segmentation of the input data) while still maintaining the same quality of morphological resources.

We intend to explore methods to improve the segmentation step in order to reduce the errors produced in it. In particular, we will explore joint segmentation and paradigm completion; better allomorphy modeling, perhaps by introducing new models for allomorphy detection, and for phonological and morphological rewrites; and application of deep learning.

References

Tim Buckwalter. 2004. Buckwalter Arabic Morphological Analyzer Version 2.0. LDC catalog number LDC2004L02, ISBN 1-58563-324-0.

Lionel Clément, Bernard Lang, Benoît Sagot, et al. 2004. Morphology based automatic acquisition of large-coverage lexica. In *LREC 04*, pages 1841–1844.

Ryan Cotterell, Christo Kirov, John Sylak-Glassman, David Yarowsky, Jason Eisner, and Mans Hulden. 2016. The sigmorphon 2016 shared task—morphological reinflection. In *Proceedings of the 2016 Meeting of SIGMORPHON*, Berlin, Germany, August. Association for Computational Linguistics.

Mathias Creutz and Krista Lagus. 2007. Unsupervised models for morpheme segmentation and morphology learning. *ACM Transactions on Speech and Language Processing (TSLP)*, 4(1).

Silviu Cucerzan and David Yarowsky. 2002. Bootstrapping a multilingual part-of-speech tagger in one person-day. In *proceedings of the 6th conference on Natural language learning-Volume 20*, pages 1–7. Association for Computational Linguistics.

Grégoire Détrez and Aarne Ranta. 2012. Smart paradigms and the predictability and complexity of inflectional morphology. *EACL 2012*, page 645.

Markus Dreyer and Jason Eisner. 2011. Discovering morphological paradigms from plain text using a dirichlet process mixture model. In *Proceedings of the Conference on Empirical Methods in Natural Language Processing*, pages 616–627. Association for Computational Linguistics.

Ramy Eskander, Nizar Habash, and Owen Rambow. 2013. Automatic Extraction of Morphological Lexicons from Morphologically Annotated Corpora. In *Proceedings of tenth Conference on Empirical Methods in Natural Language Processing*.

Markus Forsberg, Harald Hammarström, and Aarne Ranta. 2006. Morphological lexicon extraction from raw text data. *Advances in Natural Language Processing*, pages 488–499.

Nizar Habash and Owen Rambow. 2006. MAGEAD: A Morphological Analyzer and Generator for the Arabic Dialects. In *Proceedings of ACL*, pages 681–688, Sydney, Australia.

Nizar Habash, Abdelhadi Soudi, and Tim Buckwalter. 2007. On Arabic Transliteration. In A. van den Bosch and A. Soudi, editors, *Arabic Computational Morphology: Knowledge-based and Empirical Methods*. Springer.

Nizar Habash. 2010. *Introduction to Arabic Natural Language Processing*. Morgan & Claypool Publishers.

Harald Hammarström and Lars Borin. 2011. Unsupervised learning of morphology. *Computational Linguistics*, 37(2):309–350.

Kimmo Koskenniemi. 1983. Two-Level Model for Morphological Analysis. In *Proceedings of the 8th International Joint Conference on Artificial Intelligence*, pages 683–685.

Christopher D Manning. 2016. Computational linguistics and deep learning. *Computational Linguistics*.

Christian Monson, Jaime Carbonell, Alon Lavie, and Lori Levin. 2008. Paramor: Finding paradigms across morphology. *Advances in Multilingual and Multimodal Information Retrieval*, pages 900–907.

Mohammad Sadegh Rasooli, Thomas Lippincott, Nizar Habash, and Owen Rambow. 2014. Unsupervised morphology-based vocabulary expansion. In *ACL (1)*, pages 1349–1359.

Benjamin Snyder and Regina Barzilay. 2008. Unsupervised multilingual learning for morphological segmentation. In *Proceedings of ACL-08: HLT*, pages 737–745, Columbus, Ohio, June.

David Yarowsky and Richard Wicentowski. 2000. Minimally supervised morphological analysis by multimodal alignment. In *Proceedings of the 38th Annual Meeting on Association for Computational Linguistics*, pages 207–216. Association for Computational Linguistics.

Letter Sequence Labeling for Compound Splitting

Jianqiang Ma   Verena Henrich   Erhard Hinrichs
SFB 833 and Department of Linguistics
University of Tübingen, Germany
`{jma,vhenrich,eh}@sfs.uni-tuebingen.de`

Abstract

For languages such as German where compounds occur frequently and are written as single tokens, a wide variety of NLP applications benefits from recognizing and splitting compounds. As the traditional word frequency-based approach to compound splitting has several drawbacks, this paper introduces a letter sequence labeling approach, which can utilize rich word form features to build discriminative learning models that are optimized for splitting. Experiments show that the proposed method significantly outperforms state-of-the-art compound splitters.

1 Introduction

In many languages including German, compounds are written as single word-tokens without word delimiters separating their constituent words. For example, the German term for 'place name' is *Ortsname*, which is formed by *Ort* 'place' and *Name* 'name' together with the linking element 's' between constituents. Given the productive nature of compounding, treating each compound as a unique word would dramatically increase the vocabulary size. Information about the existence of compounds and about their constituent parts is thus helpful to many NLP applications such as machine translation (Koehn and Knight, 2003) and term extraction (Weller and Heid, 2012).

Compound splitting is the NLP task that automatically breaks compounds into their constituent words. As the inputs to compound splitters often include unknown words, which are not necessarily compounds, splitters usually also need to distinguish between compounds and non-compounds.

Many state-of-the-art splitters for German (Popović et al., 2006; Weller and Heid, 2012) mainly implement variants of the following two-step frequency approach first proposed in Koehn and Knight (2003):

1. Matching the input word with known words, generating splitting hypotheses, including the non-splitting hypothesis that predicts the input word to be a non-compound.

2. Choosing the hypothesis with the highest geometric mean of frequencies of constituents as the best splitting. If the frequency of the input word is higher than the geometric mean of all possible splittings, non-splitting is chosen.

The frequency approach is simple and efficient. However, frequency criteria are *not* necessarily optimal for identifying the best splitting decisions. In practice, this often leads to splitting compounds at wrong positions, erroneously splitting non-compounds, and incorrectly predicting frequent compounds to be non-compounds. Parallel corpora (Koehn and Knight, 2003; Popović et al., 2006) and linguistic analysis (Fritzinger and Fraser, 2010) etc. were used to improve the frequency approach, but the above-mentioned issues remain. Moreover, frequencies encode no information about word forms, which hinders knowledge transfer between words with similar forms. In an extreme yet common case, when one or more compound constituents are unknown words, the correct splitting is not even generated in Step 1 of the frequency approach.

To address the above-mentioned problems, this paper proposes a *letter sequence labeling* (LSL) approach (Section 2) to compound splitting. We cast the compound splitting problem as a sequence labeling problem. To predict labels, we train conditional random fields (CRF; Lafferty et al., 2001), which are directly optimized for splitting. Our

Proceedings of the 14th Annual SIGMORPHON Workshop on Computational Research in Phonetics, Phonology, and Morphology, pages 76–81,
Berlin, Germany, August 11, 2016. ©2016 Association for Computational Linguistics

CRF models can leverage rich features of letter n-grams (Section 2.3), such as *ung* (a German nominalization suffix), which are shared among words and applicable to many unknown compounds and constituents. Our method is language independent, although this paper focuses on German.

Evaluated with the compound data from GermaNet (Hamp and Feldweg, 1997; Henrich and Hinrichs, 2010) and Parra Escartín (2014), experiments in Section 3 show that our approach significantly outperforms previously developed splitters. The contributions of this paper are two-fold:

- A novel letter sequence labeling approach to compound splitting

- Empirical evaluations of the proposed approach and developed feature on a large compound list

2 Letter Sequence Labeling (LSL) for Compound Splitting

2.1 Compound splitting as LSL

Before detailing the sequence labeling approach, we first describe the representation of splitting output used for this paper.

Splitting output. The splitting output for the above example *Ortsname* would be *"Orts name"*. In general, we consider the output as string sequences obtained by adding whitespaces between constituent words in the original compound. Linking elements between constituents are attached to the ones before them. Moreover, no lemmatization or morphological analysis is performed. Compound splitting also considers the recognition of non-compounds, the output of which is the word itself. The choice for such representation is to avoid bias to any morphological theory or language-specific property. If needed, however, such output can be mapped to lexemes/lemmas.

Sequence labeling. With the above-mentioned representation, compound splitting can be viewed as a sequence of predictions of what positional role each letter plays in a word/string. Specifically, we label each letter with the **BMES** tag-set. For multi-letter strings, label **B** indicates "the first letter of a string", label **E** indicates "the last letter of a string", and label **M** indicates "a letter in the middle of a string". The rare cases of single-letter strings are labeled as **S**. The label sequence for the example *Ortsname* would be: **B-M-M-E-B-M-M-E**. The splitting output strings can be constructed

by extracting either single letters that are labeled as **S** or the consecutive letters such that (1) the first letter is labeled as **B**; (2) the last letter is labeled as **E**; (3) all the others in between are labeled as **M**.

We call the above formulation of compound splitting *letter sequence labeling*. It falls into the broader category of sequence labeling, which is widely used in various NLP tasks, such as POS tagging (Hovy et al., 2014) and Chinese word segmentation (Ma and Hinrichs, 2015). As many state-of-the-art NLP systems, we build conditional random fields models to conduct sequence labeling, which are detailed in the next subsections.

2.2 Conditional random fields (CRFs)

Conditional random fields (Lafferty et al., 2001) are a discriminative learning framework, which is capable of utilizing a vast amount of arbitrary, interactive features to achieve high accuracy. The probability assigned to a label sequence for a particular letter sequence of length T by a CRF is given by the following equation:

$$p_\theta(\mathbf{Y}|\mathbf{X}) = \frac{1}{Z_\theta(\mathbf{X})} \exp \left\{ \sum_{t=1}^{T} \sum_{k=1}^{K} \theta_k f_k(y_{t-1}, y_t, x_t) \right\}$$

(1)

In the above formula, X is the sequence of letters in the input compound (or non-compound), Y is the label sequence for the letters in the input and $Z(X)$ is a normalization term. Inside the formula, θ_k is the corresponding weight for the *feature function f_k*, where K is the total number of features and k is the index. The letters in the word being labeled is indexed by t: each individual x_t and y_t represent the current letter and label, while y_{t-1} represents the label of the previous letter.

For the experiments in this paper, we use the open-sourced CRF implementation *Wapiti*, as described in Lavergne et al. (2010).

2.3 Feature templates

A feature function $f_k(y_{i-1}, y_i, x_i)$ for the letters x_i under consideration is an indicator function that can describe previous and current labels, as well as a complete letter sequence in the input word. For example, one feature function can have value **1** only when the previous label is **E**, the current label is **B** and the previous three letters are *rts*. Its value is **0** otherwise. This function describes a possible feature for labeling the letter *n* in *Ortsname*.

In our models, we mainly consider functions of *context features*, which include *n*-grams that appear in the local window of h characters that centers at letter x_i. In this paper, we use $1 \leq n \leq 5$ for n-grams and $h = 7$ for window size, as we found that smaller windows or only low order n-grams lead to inferior results. The contexts are automatically generated from the input words using feature templates by enumerating the corresponding n-grams, the index of which is relative to the current letter (i.e. x_i). Table 1 shows the templates for the context features used in this work.

Type	Context features
unigram	$x_{i-3}, x_{i-2}, x_{i-1}, x_i, x_{i+1}, x_{i+2}, x_{i+3}$
bigram	$x_{i-3}x_{i-2}, x_{i-2}x_{i-1}, ..., x_{i+2}x_{i+3}$
trigram	$x_{i-3}x_{i-2}x_{i-1}, ..., x_{i+1}x_{i+2}x_{i+3}$
4-gram	$x_{i-3}x_{i-2}x_{i-1}x_i, ..., x_ix_{i+1}x_{i+2}x_{i+3}$
5-gram	$x_{i-3}x_{i-2}x_{i-1}x_ix_{i+1}, ...$

Table 1: Context feature templates.

Besides context features, we also consider *transition features* for current letter x_i, each of which describes the current letter itself in conjunction with a possible transition between the previous and the current labels, i.e. (x_i, y_{i-1}, y_i) tuples.

3 Experiments

3.1 Gold-standard data

The training of CRFs requires gold-standard labels that are generated from the gold-standard splittings (non-splittings) of compounds (non-compounds). We use GermaNet (GN) for this purpose, as it has a large amount of available, high-quality annotated compounds (Henrich and Hinrichs, 2011). We have extracted a total of 51,667 unique compounds from GermaNet 9.0. The compounds have 2 to 5 constituents, with an average of 2.1 constituents per compound. The remaining words are, nevertheless, not necessarily non-compounds, as not all the compounds are annotated in GN. So we extract 31,076 words as non-compounds, by choosing words that have less than 10 letters and are not known compounds. The heuristic here is that compounds tend to be longer than simplex words. The resulting non-compound list still contains some compounds, which adversly affects modeling.

We also employ the Parra Escartín (2014; henceforth PE) data to allow a fair comparison of our approach with existing compound splitters. The PE dataset has altogether 342 compound tokens and 3,009 non-compounds. PE's compounds have 2 to 5 constituents, with an average amount of 2.3 constituents.

3.2 Evaluation metrics

In our experiments, we use evaluation metrics proposed in Koehn and Knight (2003), which are widely used in the compound splitting literature. Each compound splitting result falls into one of the following categories: **correct split**: words that should be split (i.e. compounds) and are correctly split; **correct non-split**: words that should not be split (i.e. non-compounds) and are not split; **wrong non-split**: words that should be split but are not split; **wrong faulty split**: words that should be split and are split, but at wrong position(s); **wrong split**: words that should not be split but are split. As in Koehn and Knight (2003), the following scores are calculated from the above counts to summarize the results that only concern compounds:

- **precision**: (correct split) / (correct split + wrong faulty split + wrong split)
- **recall**: (correct split) / (correct split + wrong faulty split + wrong non-split)
- **accuracy**: (correct) / (correct + wrong)

3.3 Experiments on GermaNet data

In the experiments of this subsection, a random set of 70% of the GN data is used for training the LSL model and another 10% is used as a development set for choosing hyper parameters of the model. The remaining 20% is the test set, which is put aside during training and only used for evaluation.

Model	Precision	Recall	Accurracy
uni- & bigrams	0.873	0.833	0.857
+ trigrams	0.937	0.920	0.925
+ 4-grams	0.952	0.940	0.942
+ 5-grams	**0.955**	**0.941**	**0.943**

Table 2: Results of models with different context features on GermaNet. Best results in **bold face**.

Since our models predict splittings solely based on the information about the input word, different tokens of the same word type appearing in various sentences would result in exactly the same prediction. Therefore the learning and evaluation with the GN data is based on *types* rather than tokens. As shown in Table 2, the model performance improves steadily by adding higher-order letter n-gram features.

Models	Correct		Wrong			Scores		
	split	non	non	faulty	split	precision	recall	accuracy
Popović et al. (2006)	248	**3009**	84	10	**0**	0.961	0.725	0.972
Weller and Heid (2012)	259	3008	82	**1**	1	**0.992**	0.757	0.975
Letter sequence labeling (this work)	**319**	2964	**14**	10	44	0.855	**0.930**	**0.980**

Table 3: Comparison with the state-of-the-art. Best results are marked in **bold face**.

The best overall accuracy of 0.943 is achieved by the model that uses features of n-grams up to order 5. No further improvement is gained by even higher order n-grams in our experiments, as the model would overfit to the training data. The high accuracy on the GN data is a reliable indicator for performance in real-life scenario, due to its rigid non-overlapping division of large training and test sets.

3.4 Experiments on Parra Escartín's data

When comparing our method with frequency-based ones, it would be ideal if each method was trained and tested (on disjoint partitions of) the same benchmark data, which provides *both* gold-standard splitting and frequency information. Unfortunately, GermaNet provides no frequency information and most large-scale word frequency lists have no gold-standard splits, which makes neither suitable benchmarks. Another practical difficulty is that many splitters are not publicly available. We plan to complement the GN data with frequency information extracted from large corpora to construct such benchmark data in the future. For the present work, we evaluate our model on the test data that other methods have been evaluated on. For this purpose, we use the PE data, as two state-of-the-art splitters, namely Popović et al. (2006) and Weller and Heid (2012)[1], have been evaluated on it.

We train the best model from the last subsection using modified GN data, which has longer non-compounds up to 15 letters in length and excludes words that also appear in the PE data. The model is evaluated on the PE data using the same metrics as described in Section 3.2, except that the evaluation is by *token* rather than by type, to be compatible with the original PE results. Table 3 shows the results, which are analyzed in the remainder of this section.

Splitting compounds. *Accuracy* and *precision*

consider both non-compounds and compounds and are influenced by the ratio of the two, which is 8.8:1 for the PE data. It means that both metrics are mostly influenced by how well the systems distinguish compounds from non-compounds. By contrast, *recall* depends solely on compounds and is thus the best indicator for splitting performance. The recall of our model is significantly higher than that of previous methods, which shows that it generalizes well to splitting unknown compounds.

Recognizing non-compounds. The relatively low *precision* of our model is mainly caused by the high *wrong split* count. We found that almost half of these "non-compounds" that our model "wrongly" splits *are* compounds, as the PE annotation skips all adjectival and verbal compounds and also ignores certain nominal compounds. The remaining of wrong split errors can be reduced by using higher quality training cases of non-compounds, as the current gold-standard non-compounds were chosen by the word length heuristic, which introduced noise in learning.

4 Discussion and Related Work

Work on compound splitting emerged in the context of machine translation (Alfonseca et al., 2008b; Stymne, 2008; El-Kahlout and Yvon, 2010) and speech recognition (Larson et al., 2000) for German, Turkish (Bisazza and Federico, 2009), Finnish (Virpioja et al., 2007) and other languages (Alfonseca et al., 2008a; Stymne and Holmqvist, 2008). Most works, including discriminative learning methods (Alfonseca et al., 2008a; Dyer, 2009), follow the frequency approach. A few exceptions include, for example, Macherey et al. (2011) and Geyken and Hanneforth (2005), the latter of which builds finite-state morphological analyzer for German, where compound splitting is also covered. In contrast to most previous work, this paper models compound splitting on the lower level of letters, which can better generalize to unknown compounds and constituents. Moreover, it is possible to integrate word-level knowledge into

---

[1] Parra Escartín (2014) evaluated Weller and Heid (2012) 'as is', using a model pre-trained on unknown data, which might have overlaps with the test data.

the proposed sequence labeling model, by adding features such as "the current letter starts a letter sequence that matches a known word in the lexicon".

The basic idea of letter or phoneme sequence-based analysis goes back to early structural linguistics work. Harris (1955) studies the distribution of distinct phoneme unigrams and bigrams before or after a particular phoneme, i.e. *predecessor/successor variety*. The change of these variety scores in an utterance is used to determine the word boundaries. That idea has been adopted and further developed in the context of word segmentation of child-directed speech (Çöltekin and Nerbonne, 2014), where all the intra-utterance word boundaries are absent. Another instance of such sentence-wise word segmentation is Chinese word segmentation (Peng et al., 2004), where it is a standard solution to conduct CRF-based sequence labeling, using ngrams of orthographic units as features. To some extent, compound splitting can be seen as a special case of the above two word segmentation tasks. In particular, our method is clearly inspired by that of Chinese word segmentation, such as Peng et al. (2004). Although it might seem obvious to model compound splitting as letter sequence labeling in hindsight, it is not really so in foresight. Both the dominance of word frequency-based approach and the extra challenges in morphology makes is less natural to think in terms of letter operation and labeling.

5 Conclusion and Future Work

Conclusion. This paper has introduced a novel, effective way of utilizing manually split compounds, which are now available for many languages, to boost the performance of automatic compound splitting. The proposed approach is language independent, as it only uses letter n-gram features that are automatically generated from word forms. Such features capture morphological and orthographic regularities without explicitly encoding linguistic knowledge. Moreover, our approach requires no external NLP modules such as lemmatizers, morphological analyzers or POS taggers, which prevents error propagation and makes it easy to be used in other NLP systems. The proposed approach significantly outperforms existing methods.

Future work. We would like to conduct extrinsic evaluations on tasks such as machine translation to investigate how compound splitting impacts the performance of NLP applications. It is interesting to study how new features and alternative sets of labels for letters would influence the results and to test our approach on other languages such as Dutch and Swedish.

Acknowledgments

The authors would like to thank Daniël de Kok and the anonymous reviewers for their helpful comments and suggestions. The financial support for the research reported in this paper was provided by the German Research Foundation (DFG) as part of the Collaborative Research Center "The Construction of Meaning" (SFB 833), project A3.

References

Enrique Alfonseca, Slaven Bilac, and Stefan Pharies. 2008a. Decompounding query keywords from compounding languages. In *Proceedings of ACL: Short Papers*, pages 253–256.

Enrique Alfonseca, Slaven Bilac, and Stefan Pharies. 2008b. German decompounding in a difficult corpus. In *Computational Linguistics and Intelligent Text Processing*, pages 128–139. Springer.

Arianna Bisazza and Marcello Federico. 2009. Morphological pre-processing for Turkish to English statistical machine translation. In *Proceedings of the International Workshop on Spoken Language Translation*, pages 129–135.

Çağrı Çöltekin and John Nerbonne. 2014. An explicit statistical model of learning lexical segmentation using multiple cues. In *Proceedings of EACL 2014 Workshop on Cognitive Aspects of Computational Language Learning*.

Chris Dyer. 2009. Using a maximum entropy model to build segmentation lattices for MT. In *Proceedings of NAACL*, pages 406–414.

Ilknur Durgar El-Kahlout and François Yvon. 2010. The pay-offs of preprocessing for German-English statistical machine translation. In *Proceedings of International Workshop of Spoken Language Translation*, pages 251–258.

Fabienne Fritzinger and Alexander Fraser. 2010. How to avoid burning ducks: combining linguistic analysis and corpus statistics for German compound processing. In *Proceedings of the Joint Fifth Workshop on Statistical Machine Translation and MetricsMATR*, pages 224–234.

Alexander Geyken and Thomas Hanneforth. 2005. Tagh: A complete morphology for german based on weighted finite state automata. In *Finite-State Methods and Natural Language Processing*, pages 55–66. Springer.

Birgit Hamp and Helmut Feldweg. 1997. GermaNet –
a lexical-semantic net for German. In *Proceedings
of ACL workshop Automatic Information Extraction
and Building of Lexical Semantic Resources for NLP
Applications*, Madrid.

Zellig S Harris. 1955. From phoneme to morpheme.
Language.

Verena Henrich and Erhard Hinrichs. 2010. GernEdiT
– the GermaNet editing tool. In *Proceedings of
LREC*, pages 2228–2235, Valletta, Malta, May.

Verena Henrich and Erhard Hinrichs. 2011. Determining immediate constituents of compounds in GermaNet. In *Proceedings of the International Conference Recent Advances in Natural Language Processing 2011*, pages 420–426.

Dirk Hovy, Barbara Plank, and Anders Søgaard. 2014.
Experiments with crowdsourced re-annotation of a
POS tagging data set. In *Proceedings of ACL*, pages
377–382.

Philipp Koehn and Kevin Knight. 2003. Empirical
Methods for Compound Splitting. In *EACL*, page 8.

John Lafferty, A. McCallum, and F. Pereira. 2001.
Conditional random fields: probabilistic models for
segmenting and labeling sequence data. In *Proceedings of International Conference on Machine Learning*, pages 282–289.

Martha Larson, Daniel Willett, Joachim Köhler, and
Gerhard Rigoll. 2000. Compound splitting and lexical unit recombination for improved performance of
a speech recognition system for german parliamen-
tary speeches. In *Proceedings of INTERSPEECH*,
pages 945–948.

Thomas Lavergne, Olivier Cappé, and François Yvon.
2010. Practical very large scale CRFs. In *Proceedings of ACL*, pages 504–513.

Jianqiang Ma and Erhard Hinrichs. 2015. Accurate
linear-time Chinese word segmentation via embedding matching. In *Proceedings of ACL-IJCNLP
(Volume 1: Long Papers)*, pages 1733–1743, Beijing, China, July.

Klaus Macherey, Andrew M Dai, David Talbot,
Ashok C Popat, and Franz Och. 2011. Language-
independent compound splitting with morphological
operations. In *Proceedings of ACL*, pages 1395–
1404.

Carla Parra Escartín. 2014. Chasing the perfect split-
ter: a comparison of different compound splitting
tools. In *LREC*, pages 3340–3347.

Fuchun Peng, Fangfang Feng, and Andrew McCallum.
2004. Chinese segmentation and new word detection using conditional random fields. In *Proceedings
of COLING*, pages 562–568.

Maja Popović, Daniel Stein, and Hermann Ney. 2006.
Statistical machine translation of German compound
words. In *Advances in Natural Language Processing*, pages 616–624. Springer.

Sara Stymne and Maria Holmqvist. 2008. Processing of Swedish compounds for phrase-based statistical machine translation. In *Proceedings of the 12th
Annual Conference of the European Association for
Machine Translation*, pages 180–189.

Sara Stymne. 2008. German compounds in factored
statistical machine translation. In *Advances in Natural Language Processing*, pages 464–475. Springer.

Sami Virpioja, Jaakko J Väyrynen, Mathias Creutz,
and Markus Sadeniemi. 2007. Morphology-aware
statistical machine translation based on morphs induced in an unsupervised manner. *Machine Translation Summit XI*, 2007:491–498.

Marion Weller and Ulrich Heid. 2012. Analyzing and
Aligning German Compound Nouns. In *Proceedings of LREC*, pages 2–7.

Automatic Detection of Intra-Word Code-Switching

Dong Nguyen[12]   **Leonie Cornips**[23]
[1]Human Media Interaction, University of Twente, Enschede, The Netherlands
[2] Meertens Institute, Amsterdam, The Netherlands
[3]Maastricht University, Maastricht, The Netherlands
`d.nguyen@utwente.nl, leonie.cornips@meertens.knaw.nl`

Abstract

Many people are multilingual and they may draw from multiple language varieties when writing their messages. This paper is a first step towards analyzing and detecting code-switching within words. We first segment words into smaller units. Then, words are identified that are composed of sequences of subunits associated with different languages. We demonstrate our method on Twitter data in which both Dutch and dialect varieties labeled as Limburgish, a minority language, are used.

1   Introduction

Individuals have their own linguistic repertoire from which they can draw elements or codes (e.g., language varieties). In both spoken and written communication, multilingual speakers may use multiple languages in a single conversation, for example within a turn or even within a syntactic unit, often referred to as intra- and extra-sentential code-switching.

In online communication the usage of multiple languages is also prevalent. Over 10% of the Twitter users tweet in more than one language (Hale, 2014) and code-switching has been observed on various social media platforms as well (Androutsopoulos, 2013; Johnson, 2013; Jurgens et al., 2014; Nguyen et al., 2015). The occurrence of code-switching in online communication has sparked interest in two research directions.

First, the presence of code-switching in text introduces new challenges for NLP tools, since these tools are usually designed for texts written in a single language. Recently, various studies have focused on automatic language identification at a more-fine grained level, such as words instead of documents (Solorio et al., 2014), to facilitate the processing of such texts. Several studies have adapted NLP tools for code-switched texts (e.g., Solorio and Liu (2008) and Peng et al. (2014)).

Second, the availability of social media data has enabled studying code-switching patterns in a multitude of social situations and on a larger scale than datasets collected using more traditional methods. To fully leverage these large amounts of data, several recent studies have employed automatic language identification to study code-switching patterns in social media (Kim et al., 2014; Nguyen et al., 2015).

Research in both these directions has so far studied code-switching by assigning concrete languages to messages or individual words. However, the notion of *languages* or *a language* implies that languages are concrete, stable, countable identities that can be distinguished unproblematically from each other. In reality, however, people use *language*: linguistic resources (features, items, nouns, morphemes, etc.) that are recognized by the speakers or others as belonging to two or more sets of resources (Jørgensen and Juffermans, 2011). From this perspective, code-switching can thus occur *within* words. For example, in *oetverkocht* 'sold out', the particle *oet* 'out' is used that is associated with Limburgish whereas *verkocht* 'sold' is associated with Dutch.

This study is a first step towards detecting code-switching within words using computational methods, which could support the processing of code-switched texts and support sociolinguists in their study of code-switching patterns. We focus on tweets from a province in the Netherlands where a minority language is spoken alongside Dutch (see Section 3). We automatically segment the words into smaller units using the Morfessor tool (Section 4). We then identify words with subunits that are associated with different languages (Section 5).

Proceedings of the 14th Annual SIGMORPHON Workshop on Computational Research in Phonetics, Phonology, and Morphology, pages 82–86,
Berlin, Germany, August 11, 2016. ©2016 Association for Computational Linguistics

2 Related Work

This paper builds on research on morphology and automatic language identification.

Morphology We focus on tweets written in Limburg, a province in the Netherlands. Morphological analysis for Dutch using computational approaches has been the focus in several studies. Van den Bosch and Daelemans (1999) proposed a memory-based learning approach. Cast as a classification problem, morpheme boundaries were detected based on letter sequences. De Pauw et al. (2004) built on this work and compared a memory-based learning method with a finite state method. One of the characteristic features of Dutch is diminutive formation (Trommelen, 1983) and computational approaches have been explored to predict the correct diminutive suffix in Dutch (Daelemans et al., 1996; Kool et al., 2000).

McArthur (1998) identified four major types of code-switching, ranging from tag-switching (tags and set of phrases) to intra-word switching, where a change occurs within a word boundary. The occurrence of intra-word switching has only been rarely addressed in computational linguistics research. Habash et al. (2005) developed a morphological analyzer and generator for the Arabic language family. The tool allows combining morphemes from different dialects.

Language Identification The prevalence of code-switching in online textual data has generated a renewed interest in automatic language identification. Instead of focusing on document level classification, recent studies have focused on language identification on a word level to support the analysis and processing of code-switched texts (Nguyen and Doğruöz, 2013). In the First Shared Task on Language Identification in Code-Switched Data (Solorio et al., 2014), a small fraction of the words were labeled as '*mixed*', indicating that these words were composed of morphemes from different languages. However, many participating systems had very low performance, i.e., zero F-scores, on this particular category (Chittaranjan et al., 2014; Jain and Bhat, 2014; Bar and Dershowitz, 2014; Shrestha, 2014). Oco and Roxas (2012) focused on detecting code-switching points and noted that intra-word code-switching caused difficulties to a dictionary based approach. In this study, we segment words into smaller units to detect intra-word code-switching.

3 Dataset

We confine our analysis to tweets from users in the Dutch province of Limburg, the southernmost province in the Netherlands. The 'dialects' of Limburg were extended minor recognition in 1997 under the label 'Limburgish' by The Netherlands, a signatory of the 1992 European Charter for Regional and Minority Languages (cf. Cornips (2013)). To collect users located in Limburg, seed users were identified based on geotagged tweets and manual identification. The set was then expanded based on the social network of the users. Users were then mapped to locations based on their provided profile location to create the final set. Tweets are labeled with languages, such as Dutch, Limburgish, and English, using an in-house language identification tool. The dataset is described in more detail in Nguyen et al. (2015).

4 Morphological Segmentation

The first step in our analysis is to segment the words into smaller units. We use the Morfessor Baseline implementation (Virpioja et al., 2013) to learn a model for what is called morphological segmentation in an unsupervised manner. Morfessor segments the words into *morphs* (usually 'morpheme-like' units), such that words in the data can be formed by concatenation of such morphs.

Training We experiment with two different sources to train Morfessor: tweets and Wikipedia texts. The tweets come from the data described in Section 3. We also downloaded the Dutch and Limburgish Wikipedia versions. More specifically, we have the following datasets:

- Dutch Wikipedia (**NL_WIKI**)

- Limburgish Wikipedia (**LIM_WIKI**)

- Dutch tweets (**NL_TWEETS**)

- Limburgish tweets (**LIM_TWEETS**)

We exclude words that only occur once. Following Creutz and Lagus (2005), we explore two different ways for training Morfessor: based on word tokens (such that the frequencies of words are taken into account) and based on word types. Creutz and Lagus (2005) suggest using word types, which in their experiments led to a higher recall.

Data	#types	Dutch				Limburgish			
		Word tokens		Word Types		Word tokens		Word Types	
		P	R	P	R	P	R	P	R
NL_WIKI	1,377,658	0.976	0.681	0.842	0.765	0.805	0.745	0.662	0.812
LIM_WIKI	68,255	0.743	0.806	0.559	0.867	0.752	**0.788**	0.586	**0.839**
NL_TWEETS	115,319	0.968	0.685	0.833	0.779	0.893	0.745	0.627	0.818
LIM_TWEETS	37,054	0.867	**0.757**	0.648	**0.874**	**0.956**	0.711	0.665	0.826
TWEETS + WIKI	1,460,724	**0.985**	0.674	**0.871**	0.747	0.955	0.689	**0.827**	0.771

Table 1: Results of morphological segmentation using Morfessor, reporting Precision (P) and Recall (R)

Evaluation To evaluate the performance of Morfessor on the Twitter data we randomly annotated a set of tweets attributed to either Dutch or Limburgish, resulting in 330 words from Dutch tweets and 312 words from Limburgish tweets. Table 1 reports the precision and recall as calculated by the Morfessor tool. Overall, the performance differences are small. The best performance is obtained when Limburgish data is part of the training data. Furthermore, training on word tokens results in a higher precision, while training on word types results in a higher recall, matching the findings of Creutz and Lagus (2005).

An analysis of the resulting segmentations in the Twitter data illustrates this even more. We consider models trained on both the Wikipedia and Twitter data. A model trained on word tokens segments only 23.5% of the words, while a model trained on word types segments 71.4% of the words. For our application, a higher recall is preferred, and thus following Creutz and Lagus (2005) we use a model trained on word types in the remaining part of this paper. Example segmentations using this model are *rogstaekersoptocht* as *rogstaeker+s+optocht* 'carnivalsname+s+parade', *leedjesaovend* as *leedjes+aovend* 'songs+evening' and *zoemetein* as *zoe+metein* 'immediately'.

5 Detection of Intra-Word Code-Switching

We now identify code-switching within words based on the extracted morphs (e.g., morphemes, particles, bare nouns and character sequences).

5.1 Language Identification

To identify code-switching within words, we first compute the association of the morphs with Dutch and Limburgish. For illustration, we separate

3	LIM	*roë,wêr, sjw, lië, pke*
	NL	*pje, ful, cre, ary, ica*
4	LIM	*wari, ônne, blié, gesj, tere*
	NL	*isme, tttt, pppp, gggg, oool*
5	LIM	*oetge, raods, telik, erlik, aafge*
	NL	*uitge, erweg, eloos, logie, zwerf*

Table 2: Most distinguishing morphs with lengths 3-5 that do not occur on their own, for Dutch (NL) and Limburgish (LIM) according to the odds ratio.

morphs that occur on their own in the data from morphs that only occur in combination with other morphs. For each morph, we compute its probability in each language (Dutch and Limburgish) and apply Laplace smoothing. For each morph, the odds ratio is then computed as follows (Mladenic and Grobelnik, 1999), with m being the morph:

$$log(\frac{P(m|NL)(1 - P(m|LIM))}{(1 - P(m|NL))(P(m|LIM)}) \quad (1)$$

Since the odds ratio is sensitive to infrequent words, only morphs were considered that occur in at least 5 words. Table 2 displays the most distinguishing morphs that do not occur on their own. While some of the extracted morphs are not strictly morphemes but grapheme sequences, they do seem to reflect the differences between the Dutch and Limburgish language. One example is reflected in *pje* and *pke*. The diminutive *je* is associated with Dutch, while *ke* is associated with Limburgish. We also see the frequent use of diacritics, characteristic of Limburgish orthography. The results are also affected by the informal nature of social media, such as the use of lengthening in the extracted morphs (e.g., *oool*). Furthermore, the occurrence of English words has led to morphs like *ary* (from, e.g., *anniversary*) and *ful*. We also

| 3 | LIM | *oèt, veu, iér, vuu, ôch* |
| | NL | *gro, hor, cal, tec, ish* |

| 4 | LIM | *hoëg, kaup, roop, stök, zurg* |
| | NL | *rook, rouw, uuuu, ship, doek* |

| 5 | LIM | *slaop, sjaol, paort, hoeëg, rieje* |
| | NL | *fonds, dorps, kruis, kraam, keten* |

Table 3: Most distinguishing morphs with lengths 3-5 that do occur on their own, for Dutch (NL) and Limburgish (LIM) according to the odds ratio.

see *oetge* and *uitge* where *oet* 'out' is associated with Limburgish. Table 3 shows the distinguishing morphs that do occur on their own. In this table we find many units that are bare nouns, like *rook* ('smoke'), *rouw* ('mourning'), etc.

5.2 Identified Words

Since many words are cognates in Dutch and Limburgish, we apply a strict threshold to assign the extracted units to a single language (1.5 and -1.5 odds ratio). We then extract all words that are composed of sequences of units that are associated with different languages.

Results In total 50 words were identified. We manually checked whether they were correct, and if not, the type of error that was made (Table 4). Since Limburgish is a label for various dialect varieties, we consulted several sources to determine the Limburgish form(s).[1]

Type	Freq	%
Correct	17	34%
Error: name	15	30%
Error: concatenation	2	4%
Error: English	2	4%
Error: spelling mistake	2	4%
Error: other	12	24%

Table 4: Evaluation of the identified words.

An example of an identified word with code-switching is *cijfer* + *kes* 'small numbers'. The Limburgish plural diminutive *kes* is combined with the Dutch noun *cijfer* 'number' whereas /ˈsiːfəʀ/ is associated with Limburgish. As another example, in *sjlaag* + *boom* ('crossing gate') Limburgish *sjlaag* (palatized /s/) is combined with Dutch *boom* (instead of /boːm/).

[1] eWND (www.meertens.knaw.nl/dialectwoordenboeken/), WLD (dialect.ruhosting.nl/wld/zoeken_materiaalbases.html) and Limburghuis (www.limburghuis.nl/).

Error analysis Manual inspection of the identified words shows that the informal nature of the Twitter data makes the task challenging. In particular, spelling mistakes (e.g., *woendag* 'Wednesday' instead of *woensdag*), the occurrence of English words (e.g., *wearable*), and concatenated words (e.g., *kleiduivenschieten* instead of *kleiduiven schieten*) were sometimes incorrectly identified as words containing code-switching. Furthermore, most of the errors were names that were incorrectly identified (*prinsestraat, kleistekerstraat*). We therefore expect that more preprocessing, like removing named entities, would improve the system.

6 Conclusion

Research using automatic language identification to study code-switching patterns has so far focused on assigning languages to messages or individual words (Nguyen et al., 2016). This study is a first step towards automatic language identification and analysis of code-switching patterns within words. Our experiments demonstrate that Twitter users do code-switch within words and are creative in their language use by combining elements from both the standard language (Dutch) and the minority language (Limburgish).

The precision of the system could be improved by applying more preprocessing steps, such as filtering named entities. Evaluation was challenging due to the difficulty of labeling languages on such a fine-grained level as the extracted morphs. In particular, when focusing on minority languages such as Limburgish for which no standard exists and which shares many cognates with Dutch, it is not always clear whether a certain variant is associated with Dutch, Limburgish, or both. A future study could focus on a more extensive evaluation of the system.

Acknowledgements

This research was supported by the Netherlands Organization for Scientific Research (NWO), grants 314-98-008 (Twidentity) and 640.005.002 (FACT).

References

Jannis Androutsopoulos. 2013. Code-switching in computer-mediated communication. In *Pragmatics of Computer-Mediated Communication*. De Gruyter Mouton.

Kfir Bar and Nachum Dershowitz. 2014. The Tel Aviv university system for the code-switching workshop shared task. In *Proceedings of the First Workshop on Computational Approaches to Code Switching.*

Gokul Chittaranjan, Yogarshi Vyas, Kalika Bali, and Monojit Choudhury. 2014. Word-level language identification using CRF: Code-switching shared task report of MSR India system. In *Proceedings of the First Workshop on Computational Approaches to Code Switching.*

Leonie Cornips. 2013. Recent developments in the Limburg dialect region. In Frans Hinskens and Johan Taeldeman, editors, *Language and Place. An International Handbook of Linguistic Variation.* De Gruyter Mouton.

Mathias Creutz and Krista Lagus. 2005. *Unsupervised morpheme segmentation and morphology induction from text corpora using Morfessor 1.0.* Helsinki University of Technology.

Walter Daelemans, Peter Berck, and Steven Gillis. 1996. Unsupervised discovery of phonological categories through supervised learning of morphological rules. In *Proceedings of COLING 1996.*

Guy De Pauw, Tom Laureys, Walter Daelemans, and Hugo Van hamme. 2004. A comparison of two different approaches to morphological analysis of Dutch. In *Proceedings of the Seventh Meeting of the ACL Special Interest Group in Computational Phonology.*

Nizar Habash, Owen Rambow, and George Kiraz. 2005. Morphological analysis and generation for Arabic dialects. In *Proceedings of the ACL Workshop on Computational Approaches to Semitic Languages.*

Scott A. Hale. 2014. Global connectivity and multilinguals in the Twitter network. In *CHI '14.*

Naman Jain and Riyaz Ahmad Bhat. 2014. Language identification in code-switching scenario. In *Proceedings of the First Workshop on Computational Approaches to Code Switching.*

Ian Johnson. 2013. Audience design and communication accommodation theory: Use of Twitter by Welsh-English biliterates. In *Social Media and Minority Languages: Convergence and the Creative Industries.* Multilingual Matters.

J. Normann Jørgensen and Kasper Juffermans. 2011. Languaging.

David Jurgens, Stefan Dimitrov, and Derek Ruths. 2014. Twitter users #codeswitch hashtags! #moltoimportante #wow. In *Proceedings of the First Workshop on Computational Approaches to Code Switching.*

Suin Kim, Ingmar Weber, Li Wei, and Alice Oh. 2014. Sociolinguistic analysis of Twitter in multilingual societies. In *Proceedings of the 25th ACM conference on Hypertext and social media.*

Anne Kool, Walter Daelemans, and Jakub Zavrel. 2000. Genetic algorithms for feature relevance assignment in memory-based language processing. In *Proceedings of CoNLL-2000 and LLL-2000.*

Tom McArthur. 1998. Code-mixing and code-switching. Concise Oxford companion to the English language.

Dunja Mladenic and Marko Grobelnik. 1999. Feature selection for unbalanced class distribution and Naive Bayes. In *Proceedings of ICML '99.*

Dong Nguyen and A. Seza Doğruöz. 2013. Word level language identification in online multilingual communication. In *Proceedings of EMNLP 2013.*

Dong Nguyen, Dolf Trieschnigg, and Leonie Cornips. 2015. Audience and the use of minority languages on Twitter. In *Proceedings of ICWSM 2015.*

Dong Nguyen, A. Seza Doğruöz, Carolyn P. Rosé, and Franciska de Jong. 2016. Computational sociolinguistics: A survey. *To appear in Computational Linguistics.*

Nathaniel Oco and Rachel Edita Roxas. 2012. Pattern matching refinements to dictionary-based code-switching point detection. In *PACLIC 26.*

Nanyun Peng, Yiming Wang, and Mark Dredze. 2014. Learning polylingual topic models from code-switched social media documents. In *ACL 2014.*

Prajwol Shrestha. 2014. Incremental n-gram approach for language identification in code-switched text. In *Proceedings of the First Workshop on Computational Approaches to Code Switching.*

Thamar Solorio and Yang Liu. 2008. Part-of-speech tagging for English-Spanish code-switched text. In *Proceedings of EMNLP 2008.*

Thamar Solorio, Elizabeth Blair, Suraj Maharjan, Steven Bethard, Mona Diab, Mahmoud Ghoneim, Abdelati Hawwari, Fahad AlGhamdi, Julia Hirschberg, Alison Chang, and Pascale Fung. 2014. Overview for the first shared task on language identification in code-switched data. In *Proceedings of the First Workshop on Computational Approaches to Code Switching.*

Mieke Trommelen. 1983. *The Syllable in Dutch.* Walter de Gruyter.

Antal Van den Bosch and Walter Daelemans. 1999. Memory-based morphological analysis. In *Proceedings of ACL 1999.*

Sami Virpioja, Peter Smit, Stig-Arne Grönroos, Mikko Kurimo, et al. 2013. Morfessor 2.0: Python implementation and extensions for Morfessor baseline.

Read my points: Effect of animation type when speech-reading from EMA data

Kristy James
University of Groningen
Saarland University
kristyj@coli.uni-saarland.de

Martijn Wieling
University of Groningen
The Netherlands
m.b.wieling@rug.nl

Abstract

Three popular vocal-tract animation paradigms were tested for intelligibility when displaying videos of pre-recorded Electromagnetic Articulography (EMA) data in an online experiment. EMA tracks the position of sensors attached to the tongue. The conditions were dots with tails (where only the coil location is presented), 2D animation (where the dots are connected to form 2D representations of the lips, tongue surface and chin), and a 3D model with coil locations driving facial and tongue rigs. The 2D animation (recorded in VisArtico) showed the highest identification of the prompts.

1 Introduction

Electromagnetic Articulography (EMA) is a popular vocal-tract motion capture technique used increasingly for second language learning and speech therapy purposes. In this situation, an instructor aids the subject to reach a targeted vocal tract configuration by showing them a live augmented visualization of the trajectories of (some of) the subject's articulators, alongside a targeted configuration.

Current research into how subjects respond to this training uses a variety of different visualizations: Katz et al. (2010) and Levitt et al. (2010) used a 'mouse-controlled drawing tool' to indicate target areas as circles on the screen, with the former displaying an 'image of [the] current tongue position', the latter displaying a 'tongue trace'. Suemitsu et al. (2013) displayed a mid-sagittal representation of the tongue surface as a spline between three sensors along the tongue, as well as showing a palate trace and lip coil positions and targets as circles. Katz and Mehta (2015) used a 3D avatar with a transparent face mesh, pink tongue rig, including colored shapes that lit when touched as targets.

For audiovisual feedback scenarios the optimal manner of presenting the stimuli has not yet been explicitly studied, but rather the experiments have reflected recent software developments. Meanwhile, different tools (Tiede, 2010; Ouni et al., 2012) have emerged as state of the art software for offline processing and visualization. The claim that subjects make gains in tongue gesture awareness only after a practice period with the visualization (Ouni, 2011) underlies the need for research into how EMA visualizations can best be presented to subjects in speech therapy or L2-learning settings.

The main inspiration for this work is the finding of Badin et al. (2010) that showing normally-obscured articulators (as opposed to a full face, with and without the tongue) has a positive effect on the identification of VCV stimuli. An established body of research already focuses on quantifying the intelligibility-benefit or realism of animated talking heads, ideally as compared to a video-realistic standard (Ouni et al., 2007; Cosker et al., 2005). However, as the articulators that researchers/teachers wish to present to their subjects in the aforementioned scenario are generally outside the line of sight, these evaluation methods cannot be directly applied to intra-oral visualizations. We aim to fill this gap by comparing commonly-used EMA visualizations to determine which is most intelligible,[1] hoping this may guide future research into the presentation of EMA data in a visual feedback setting.

---

[1]This word-identification task differs from the most common speech-training usage whereby a learner's attention is drawn to the difference between a live animation of their movements and some reference placement or movement.

Proceedings of the 14th Annual SIGMORPHON Workshop on Computational Research in Phonetics, Phonology, and Morphology, pages 87–92,
Berlin, Germany, August 11, 2016. ©2016 Association for Computational Linguistics

2 Method

In this experiment, animations of eighteen CVC English words were presented in silent conditions to participants of differing familiarity levels with vocal tract animations in an online survey; subjects were asked to identify the word in a forced-choice paradigm (a minimal pair of the prompt could also be chosen) and later give qualitative feedback about their experience speech-reading from the different systems.[2]

2.1 Participants

Participants were recruited through promotion on social media, university mailing lists, on the internet forum *Reddit* and on *Language Log*. In sum, 136 complete responses were collected, with three of these excluded for breaking the experiment over several days. We analyze the results of all 84 native English speakers. Participants had varying levels of previous exposure to vocal tract animations: of those analysed 43% had seen such animations before, 25% had no exposure, 25% had studied some linguistics but not seen such animations, and 6% considered themselves experts in the topic.

2.2 Stimuli

The prompts presented were nine minimal pairs of mono-syllabic CVC words spoken by a single British female speaker recorded for the study of Wieling et al. (2015).

Three of the pairs differed in the onset consonant, three in the vowel, and three in the coda consonant. Care was taken that the pairs had a significant difference in place or manner that would be visible in the EMA visualization.

In order to compare the animations, they were standardized as follows: a frontal view was presented on the left half of the screen, a mid-sagittal

---

[2]The experimental design also collected data about whether subjects could perceive differences between the competing animation paradigms, for a separate research question.

Onset	Nucleus	Coda
sad/bad	bet/bit	time/ties
mess/yes	mat/mitt	sum/sun
bale/tale	whale/wheel	maid/male

Table 1: Prompt minimal pairs, by location of difference.

view with the lips to the left on the right half. No waveform or labeling information was displayed. Lip coils were green, tongue coils red and chin/incisor coils blue. Where surfaces were shown, lips were pink, and tongues were red. A palate trace, made using each tool's internal construction method, was displayed in black. A white or light grey background was used.

The animations were produced as follows: **Dots with tails** were produced using functions from Mark Tiede's MVIEW package (Tiede, 2010), with an adapted video-production script for the standardizations mentioned above. **2D animations** were produced from VisArtico (Ouni et al., 2012), using the internal video-production processes. **3D animations** were produced using a simulated real-time animation of the data in Ematoblender (James, 2016), which manipulates an adapted facial rig from MakeHuman in the Blender Game Engine. See Figure 1 for examples of the three types of visualizations.

2.3 Procedure

This experiment was hosted on the platform SurveyGizmo. Firstly the EMA data was explained and participant background information was collected. This included information about previous exposure to linguistics studies and vocal tract visualizations. A brief training session followed, in which participants saw four prompts covering a wide range of onset and coda consonants in all three animation systems. They were free to play these animations as many times as they wished.

Subsequently, subjects were presented with two silent animations. The animations were either matching or non-matching (minimal pair) stimuli, which were displayed as HTML5 videos in web-friendly formats. They were controlled only by separate 'Play' buttons below each video. For each of these animations the subject was presented with four multiple choice options (one correct, one minimal pair, one randomly chosen pair, with the items and order retained across both questions). They were also asked to rate whether they believed the two stimuli to be the same word or not.

Upon submitting their answers, the subject was asked to view the videos again (as often as they liked) with sound, allowing them to check their answers and learn the mapping between animation and sound. The time that they spent viewing each prompt (for identification and after the an-

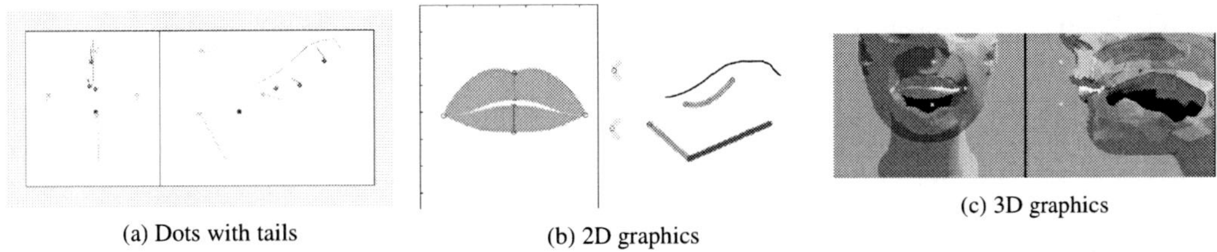

(a) Dots with tails   (b) 2D graphics   (c) 3D graphics

Figure 1: Different animation paradigms tested.

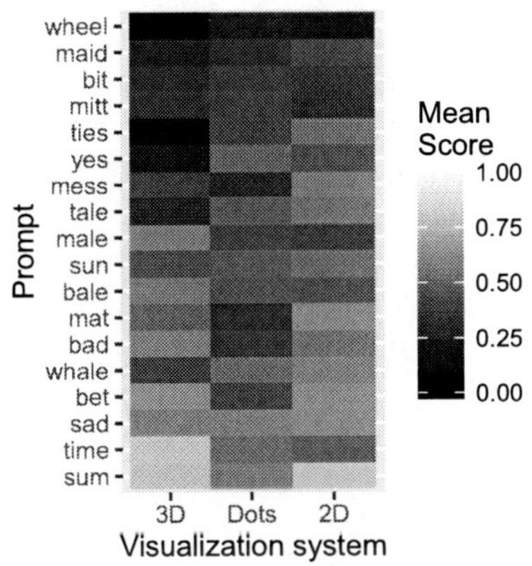

Figure 2: Prompt variability by animation type. Lighter colors indicate a better response.

	ID model
(Intercept)	$-0.26(0.14)$
SYSM	$-0.08(0.11)$
SYSV	$0.27(0.11)^{*}$
AIC	3261.90
Num. obs.	2486
Num. groups: RESPID	83
Num. groups: PROMPT	18

$^{***}p < 0.001, ^{**}p < 0.01, ^{*}p < 0.05$

Table 2: Coefficient, standard error and significance and of fixed effects for the mixed model of the identification dataset. 2D animations (SYSV) improve identification significantly over the baseline (3D animations). Table created with texreg (Leifeld, 2013).

swer was revealed) was also measured. After each three questions they were asked to rate their confidence at guessing the prompts' identities. Then after twelve questions they were asked to comment about their strategies. Finally, they could complete another six questions, or skip to the concluding qualitative questions.

3 Data Analysis

The prompt identification task yielded a binomial dataset based on the correctness of the identification. The random assignment of prompt pairs to system combinations led to an unbalanced dataset, which motivated the use of generalized linear mixed-effects regression models (GLMMs) for analysis (Bates et al., 2015). Random intercepts and slopes were included if they improved the model in a model comparison procedure.

In order to take into account the variability in subject responses, random intercepts for subject were included. Similarly, random intercepts were included for each prompt. The prompt variability was quite extensive and is visualized in Figure 2.

4 Results

The resulting model for the identification data included random intercepts for the subject, random intercepts for the prompt (with a random slope for the match-mismatched condition), and a fixed effect for the system, shown in Table 2. The 2D animation was significantly better-identified than the 3D animation. The Dots animation was slightly (but not significantly) less well-performing than the 3D animation.

Even within the most intelligible system (2D graphics), it is evident that there is much variability in how well participants are able to identify the various prompts (see Figure 2). A generalized logistic mixed-effects regression model was fitted to analyze the effects of onset and coda consonants and the nuclear vowel in the prompts.

When assessing the effect of either onset, coda or nucleus on how well people were able to detect the correct utterance, we found that the type of nucleus (i.e. the vowel) was most important. For example, whenever a stimulus contained the vowel /a/ its recognition was better than with a different vowel. In contrast, a stimulus with the vowel /i/ was much less well recognized. As the vowel necessitates greater movements of especially the lips than consonants, it makes sense that the type of vowel is an important predictor. Given that we only had a limited number of stimuli, including the onset or coda together with the nucleus did not help predict the recognition of the stimulus.

The hypothesized effect on the identification score of question number and time spent watching the videos (a learning effect was expected) was not borne out in the results. Though many subjects improved over time, others worsened, which could be attributed to fatigue or boredom during the long experiment. Similarly, including the subjects' previous experience with linguistics and vocal tract visualizations did not significantly improve the model.

5 Discussion

5.1 Identification strategies

The model's identification of the ease of interpreting 2D animations was reflected in participants' comments about the strategies they used for speech-reading. The frequency with which these strategies were mentioned is shown in Table 3.

Strategy	Frequency
Lip aperture/shape	71
Mimic the animation	56
Tongue placement/movement	48
Tongue-palate contact/distance	25
Knowledge of phonetics	21
Deduce using answer options	15
Tongue timing	7
Start/end position	5
Counting syllables/gestures	3
Vowel length	2
Visualize someone else	1

Table 3: Identification strategy frequency by number of mentions over all participants.

One participant (ID 1233) summed up the particular difficulty of the 'dots with tails' system succinctly: "In the ones with lips and tongue, I spoke each of the possible answers myself and tried to envision how closely my own lips and tongue resembled the videos. In the one with just dots, I was purely guessing."

5.2 Pitfalls of the 3D animation

Whereas it might seem somewhat surprising that the 3D animation did not result in (significantly) better recognition over the simplest representation (dots with tails), participants' comments highlight some possible causes.

Firstly, the colors of the lips and tongue were similar, which was especially problematic in the front view of this experiment. Though the color choices were made based on VisArtico's color scheme, the 2D animation avoids this problem by excluding the tongue from the frontal view.

Secondly, participants expressed that they would have liked to see teeth and a facial expression in the 3D animation. They also commented that they expected more lip-rolling movement. Indeed, seeing a more realistic avatar with these crucial elements missing may have been somewhat unnatural-looking.

Some linguistically-experienced participants also indicated that they expected a detailed 3D avatar to also indicate nasality, the place where the soft and hard palates meet, or 'what the throat is doing'. Unfortunately, this information is not available using EMA data.

Finally, many subjects commented that they found the 3D animation 'too-noisy' and preferred the 'clean' and 'clearer' 2D option.[3] Subjects' descriptions of their personal identification strategies indicates that they often used lip-reading strategies, and that this was easier in 2D where the lip shape was clear, and there was no difficulty with any color contrasts from the tongue. While the graphics quality of the 3D system was not as clear as for the other systems, the setup is similar to the 3D state of the art such as reported in Katz et al. (2014).[4]

5.3 Additional observations

Though the speaker and analyzed participants all identified themselves as English native speakers, two American participants noted that they

---

[3]Due to a combination of video capture technique and data streaming rate (the 3D system was recorded with real-time processing) the frame rate of the 3D system was lower than the other systems. Consequently, some participants also commented they wished for smoother 3D animations.

[4]The shapes of the tongue and lips in the 3D animation are controlled by internal constraints within the Blender Game Engine, and are dependent on the mesh shape. The performance of the 3D graphics could be improved by using a more-detailed facial rig and mesh and allowing a slower rendering (or using a faster game engine).

perceived the British speaker as having a foreign/German accent. Several participants mentioned that their main tactic was mimicking the speaker saying the answer options (and in doing so mimicking their interpretation of the speaker's accent), which they on occasion found difficult. This underlines the usefulness of using dialect-appropriate trajectories for the speech-reader.

In this experiment, all animations were based on EMA recordings from a single speaker in one recording session. In general usage however, the differing coil placement for each subject and recording session may also affect the identification ability. Other visualization methods (e.g., cineradiography or MRI) give a high-dimensional picture of the vocal tract and avoid these problems. However, these technologies are not practical for real-time speech training due to their health-risk and cost, respectively. One strategy to compensate for this problem when creating the animations is to use photos of the coil placement during recording to manually specify the offset from the intended placement on the articulator. For example, VisArtico allows the user to specify whether the lip coils were placed close to or above/below the lip opening.

6 Conclusion

In sum, the simplicity and clarity of 2D graphical animations is preferable for subjects to identify silent animations of EMA data. The features of the most successful animation paradigm suggest that future EMA-animations should include both indications of lip and tongue surface shape. If used, 3D models should ensure that they provide clear and clean demonstrations, in which the edges of the articulators (particularly in the frontal view) can easily be distinguished.

References

Pierre Badin, Yuliya Tarabalka, Frédéric Elisei, and Gérard Bailly. 2010. Can you 'read' tongue movements? Evaluation of the contribution of tongue display to speech understanding. *Speech Communication*, 52(6):493–503.

Douglas Bates, Martin Mächler, Ben Bolker, and Steve Walker. 2015. Fitting linear mixed-effects models using lme4. *Journal of Statistical Software*, 67(1):1–48.

Blender. https://www.blender.org/. Accessed: 2016-04-14.

Darren Cosker, Susan Paddock, David Marshall, Paul L Rosin, and Simon Rushton. 2005. Toward perceptually realistic talking heads: Models, methods, and mcgurk. *ACM Transactions on Applied Perception (TAP)*, 2(3):270–285.

Kristy James. 2016. Watch your tongue and read my lips: a real-time, multi-modal visualisation of articulatory data. Master's thesis, Saarland University/University of Groningen.

William F Katz and Sonya Mehta. 2015. Visual feedback of tongue movement for novel speech sound learning. *Frontiers in human neuroscience*, 9.

William F Katz, Malcolm R McNeil, and Diane M Garst. 2010. Treating apraxia of speech (AOS) with EMA-supplied visual augmented feedback. *Aphasiology*, 24(6-8):826–837.

WF Katz, Thomas F Campbell, Jun Wang, Eric Farrar, J Coleman Eubanks, Arvind Balasubramanian, Balakrishnan Prabhakaran, and Rob Rennaker. 2014. Opti-speech: A real-time, 3D visual feedback system for speech training. In *Proc. Interspeech*.

r/languagelearning. https://www.reddit.com/r/languagelearning/. Accessed: 2016-04-14.

Philip Leifeld. 2013. texreg: Conversion of statistical model output in R to LaTeX and HTML tables. *Journal of Statistical Software*, 55(8):1–24.

June S Levitt and William F Katz. 2010. The effects of EMA-based augmented visual feedback on the English speakersácquisition of the Japanese flap: a perceptual study. *stroke*, 4:5.

Mark Liberman. 2016. Language Log. http://languagelog.ldc.upenn.edu/nll/?p=24223. Accessed: 2016-04-14.

MakeHuman Open Source tool for making 3D characters. http://www.makehuman.org/download.php. Accessed: 2016-02-09.

Slim Ouni, Michael M Cohen, Hope Ishak, and Dominic W Massaro. 2007. Visual contribution to speech perception: measuring the intelligibility of animated talking heads. *EURASIP Journal on Audio, Speech, and Music Processing*, 2007(1):3–3.

Slim Ouni, Loïc Mangeonjean, and Ingmar Steiner. 2012. VisArtico: a visualization tool for articulatory data. In *13th Annual Conference of the International Speech Communication Association-InterSpeech 2012*.

Slim Ouni. 2011. Tongue Gestures Awareness and Pronunciation Training. In ISCA, editor, *12th Annual Conference of the International Speech Communication Association - Interspeech 2011*, Florence, Italy, August. (accepted).

r/samplesize. https://www.reddit.com/r/SampleSize. Accessed: 2016-04-14.

SurveyGizmo. `http://www.surveygizmo.com/`. Accessed: 2015-11-13.

Atsuo Suemitsu, Takayuki Ito, and Mark Tiede. 2013. An electromagnetic articulography-based articulatory feedback approach to facilitate second language speech production learning. In *Proceedings of Meetings on Acoustics*, volume 19, page 060063. Acoustical Society of America.

Mark Tiede. 2010. MVIEW: Multi-channel visualization application for displaying dynamic sensor movements. *unpublished*.

Martijn Wieling, Pauline Veenstra, Patti Adank, Andrea Weber, and Mark Tiede. 2015. Comparing L1 and L2 speakers using articulography. In *Proceedings of the 18th International Congress of Phonetic Sciences*. University of Glasgow, August.

Predicting the Direction of Derivation in English Conversion

Max Kisselew[*]**, Laura Rimell**[†]**, Alexis Palmer**[‡]**, and Sebastian Padó**[*]
[*] IMS, Stuttgart University, Germany
{pado,kisselmx}@ims.uni-stuttgart.de
[†] Computer Laboratory, University of Cambridge, UK
laura.rimell@cl.cam.ac.uk
[‡] Leibniz ScienceCampus, ICL, Heidelberg University, Germany
palmer@cl.uni-heidelberg.de

Abstract

Conversion is a word formation operation that changes the grammatical category of a word in the absence of overt morphology. Conversion is extremely productive in English (e.g., *tunnel, talk*). This paper investigates whether distributional information can be used to predict the diachronic direction of conversion for homophonous noun–verb pairs. We aim to predict, for example, that *tunnel* was used as a noun prior to its use as a verb. We test two hypotheses: (1) that derived forms are less frequent than their bases, and (2) that derived forms are more semantically specific than their bases, as approximated by information theoretic measures. We find that hypothesis (1) holds for N-to-V conversion, while hypothesis (2) holds for V-to-N conversion. We achieve the best overall account of the historical data by taking both frequency and semantic specificity into account. These results provide a new perspective on linguistic theories regarding the semantic specificity of derivational morphemes, and on the morphosyntactic status of conversion.

1 The Morphology of Conversion

Word formation operations that change the grammatical category of a word in the absence of overt morphology pose interesting linguistic challenges. Such operations are highly productive in English, especially between the categories of noun and verb (consider examples such as *tunnel* or *walk*, also more recent examples such as *email*). This phenomenon is also observed in other languages, for example German (Vogel, 1996), Dutch (Don, 1993), Hungarian (Kiefer, 2005), and Bulgarian (Manova and Dressler, 2005). We call these cases

"conversion", without any theoretical commitment.

Conversion in English, especially N-to-V conversion, has been extensively studied within morphology and syntax. Historically, accounts for this phenomenon involved (a) *conversion* (proper), a category-changing word-formation operation assumed to be different from other types of derivational morphology (Koziol, 1937; Bauer, 1983; Plag, 1999), or (b) *zero-derivation*, involving a derivational affix akin to *-ize, -ify, -er*, etc., but which happens to be phonologically null (Bloomfield, 1933; Marchand, 1969; Kiparsky, 1982). Most current syntactic theories of conversion, though, are based on *underspecification*. This is the idea that meaning-sound correspondences are stored in the lexicon as uncategorized roots and obtain a grammatical category when combined with syntactic heads, which may be phonologically null or overt (Halle and Marantz, 1993; Pesetsky, 1995; Hale and Keyser, 2002; Borer, 2005a; Arad, 2005).

The range of meanings resulting from conversion has been a key source of evidence for various theoretical approaches. Verbs derived via N-to-V conversion can have a wide variety of meanings, seemingly constrained only by the template 'action having to do with the noun', such as in the phrase *celluloid the door open*, meaning 'use a credit card to spring the lock open' (Clark and Clark, 1979). V-to-N conversion has a narrower semantic range. It is likely to result in a noun referring to the event described by the verb or to its result, e.g. *talk* (Grimshaw, 1990).

This paper presents a computational study of conversion: we study which factors are able to account for *diachronic* precedence in cases of English V-to-N and N-to-V conversion. The goal is to predict, e.g., that *tunnel* was originally used as a noun and *walk* as a verb. Historical precedence provides a theory-neutral ground truth which we treat as a proxy for the actual direction of conversion.

Proceedings of the 14th Annual SIGMORPHON Workshop on Computational Research in Phonetics, Phonology, and Morphology, pages 93–98,
Berlin, Germany, August 11, 2016. ©2016 Association for Computational Linguistics

We use methods from distributional semantics to test two morphological hypotheses: (1) that derived forms are less frequent than their bases, and (2) that derived forms are more semantically specific than their bases. We use information theoretic measures to gauge semantic specificity, applying these measures for the first time to theoretical questions regarding derivational morphology.

2 The Direction of Derivation

We analyze corpus data as a source of evidence for the direction of derivation in lemmas attested in both nominal and verbal contexts. We take historical precedence as the gold standard for the grammatical category of the base. For example, the lemma *tunnel* was first attested in English as a noun around the year 1440, and as a verb in 1577, according to the Oxford English Dictionary. The gold standard direction of derivation is therefore N-to-V. On the other hand, the lemma *drive* was first attested as a verb around 900 and as a noun in 1697, so the gold standard direction is V-to-N.

The idea of predicting a direction of derivation is not uncontroversial from a theoretical perspective. According to underspecification accounts of conversion, there is no direction to predict, since both nominal and verbal uses result from syntactic categorization of a root which is unspecified for category. Nevertheless, even underspecification allows for the fact that some roots seem to be used primarily in one category or another (Harley and Noyer, 1999; Arad, 2005; Borer, 2005b). Moreover, historical precedence provides an objective ground truth, regardless of any particular theory of word formation (Rimell, 2012).

Gold Standard. Our gold standard consists of 1,044 English lemmas which have undergone N-to-V conversion and 948 lemmas which have undergone V-to-N conversion. We obtained the historical precedence data from CELEX (Baayen et al., 1995) using the WebCelex interface.[1] N-to-V lemmas are coded in CELEX as monomorphemic nouns and also conversion verbs; V-to-N lemmas are monomorphemic verbs and also conversion nouns.[2] We limited the dataset to lemmas which are monomorphemic in their base grammatical cat-

egory in order to avoid root compounds and denominal verbs formed from already-derived nouns, such as *leverage* and *commission*, which we believed would complicate the analysis. We manually excluded a handful of lemmas which appeared in both CELEX searches due to polysemy.

3 Methods

3.1 Hypotheses

We advance two main hypotheses which can be investigated in a corpus-based fashion.

1. Derived forms are *less frequent* than their base words.

2. Derived forms are *semantically more specific* than their base words.

The first hypothesis is not entirely straightforward, since some derived forms are in fact more frequent than their bases, especially when the base is frequent (Hay, 2001). However, derived forms have been found to have lower frequency than their bases in general (Harwood and Wright, 1956; Hay, 2001); therefore, while the hypothesis as stated may be an oversimplification, we use it as a first approximation to a frequency-related analysis of conversion.

The second hypothesis corresponds to the Monotonicity Hypothesis of Koontz-Garboden (2007), which states that derivational morphemes always add content to their bases, in the form of compositional lexical semantic operators. Linguistic support for this proposal comes from cross-linguistic examination of word-formation operations, such as causative and anticausative operations on verbs. If conversion is the result of a phonologically null derivational affix, we would expect the Monotonicity Hypothesis to hold. Semantic specificity, or complexity – with a derived word assumed to have a more complex, or narrower, meaning because it has more semantic subcomponents – has also been used as a diagnostic for the direction of derivation in conversion (Plag, 2003), but based on linguistic judgments rather than distributional semantics.

The rest of this section is concerned with operationalizing these two hypotheses. We first describe the corpus that we are using, then the semantic representations that we construct from it to pursue the second hypothesis, and finally the concrete predictors that instantiate the hypotheses.

---

[1] `http://celex.mpi.nl`

[2] N-to-V lemmas have a CELEX entry with Class=N (part of speech) and MorphStatus=M (monomorphemic), and a second entry with Class=V and MorphStatus=Z (conversion). The converse holds for V-to-N lemmas.

3.2 Corpus

Our corpus is a concatenation of the lemmatized and part-of-speech (PoS) tagged BNC[3] and ukWaC corpora[4], containing 2.36 billion tokens. Both corpora are widely used for building distributional spaces. Together, they cover a large range of text types both in terms of genres and of domains.

Since we will use this corpus to extract information about the noun and verb usages of morphologically unmarked conversion cases, it is a pertinent question how well standard part-of-speech taggers recognize this distinction. To test this, we carried out a manual annotation study.

From each corpus we extracted 33 examples each of 100 lemmas, chosen randomly from the lemmas in the gold standard, half on the N-to-V conversion list and the other half on the V-to-N list. Two of the authors, both native English speakers, annotated the PoS tags for correctness. Inter-annotator agreement was κ=0.68. Overall, the accuracy of the PoS tags was 85%, which we considered sufficiently reliable for good quality category-specific representations.[5]

While many lemmas and their instances were straightforward to annotate as either noun or verb, some examples presented difficulties. Two prominent cases were gerunds and adjectival forms (**forked** *tongue, fuselage was* **skinned** *with aluminum*), although there were a variety of other, less frequent cases. In these instances we used the overt inflectional morphology as a guide; for example, *-ing* or *-ed* endings indicated a verb. This strategy is based on the fact that inflectional morphology strictly selects for the part of speech of its base.

3.3 Vector Representations

To measure semantic specificity, we perform a distributional analysis which represents each conversion case with two 10,000-dimensional bag-of-words vectors: one for the verb and one for the noun, relying on automatic PoS tags (cf. Section 3.2). The dimensions correspond to the most frequent content words in the corpus. The context window size is set to 5 words on either side of the target. Following standard practice, we apply a Positive Pointwise Mutual Information (PPMI) transformation and L1-normalize each vector.[6]

Downsampling. The use of vectors based on co-occurrence counts poses a methodological difficulty, because word frequency is a potential confounder for the information-theoretic measures with which we operationalize the specificity hypothesis (Section 3.4). The potential difficulty arises because more frequent words might have denser vectors (more non-zero values), which could lead to observing spurious increases in specificity that are merely correlates of frequency rather than the result of a conceptual shift. To avoid this danger, we balance the frequencies of bases and derived forms by *downsampling*. For each verb-noun conversion pair, both vectors are constructed from the same number of occurrences, namely $min(f_N, f_V)$, by skipping instances of the more frequent category uniformly at random. For example, *tunnel (n.)* occurs 38,967 times in the corpus and *tunnel (v.)* 2,949 times. Through downsampling, the vectors both for *tunnel (n.)* and for *tunnel (v.)* are constructed from 2,949 instances.

3.4 Operationalizing the Hypotheses

Frequency. We assess the frequency hypothesis by directly comparing the number of nominal and verbal corpus occurrences of a target lemma.

Semantic Specificity. We operationalize the semantic specificity hypothesis by applying measures of information content to distributional representations. This follows the example of two recent studies. In the context of hyponymy identification, Santus et al. (2014) proposed *entropy* as a measure of the semantic specificity $S(w)$ of a word w, via its distributional, L1-normalized vector $\vec{w}$. Entropy is supposed to be inversely correlated with semantic specificity, since higher specificity corresponds to more restrictions on context, which means lower entropy, defined as

$$S(w) = H(\vec{w}) = -\sum_i \vec{w}_i \cdot \log \vec{w}_i \qquad (1)$$

---

[3]http://www.natcorp.ox.ac.uk, tagged with the CLAWS4 tagger and the C5 tagset

[4]http://wacky.sslmit.unibo.it, tagged with Tree-Tagger and the Penn Treebank tagset

[5]We performed the same annotation on Wikipedia data, tagged with TreeTagger and the Penn Treebank tagset, but found the automatic PoS tagging to be less reliable. Therefore, we excluded it from consideration.

[6]Much recent work in distributional semantics has made use of low-dimensional, dense vectors, obtained either by dimensionality reduction of co-occurrence vectors, or as word embeddings from a neural network trained to optimize context prediction. Although reduced vectors and embeddings perform well on a variety of Natural Language Processing tasks, they are not suitable for our approach, because their feature weights are not interpretable probabilistically, which information-theoretic measures rely on.

Predictor	N-to-V	V-to-N	all
Most Freq. Class	100%	0%	52.4%
Entropy H	50.1%	75.5%	62.2%
KL divergence	53.8%	**76.7%**	64.6%
Frequency	**84.7%**	58.7%	72.3%
Freq + H + KL	77.4%	76.0%	**76.8%**

Table 1: Accuracies for predicting the direction of derivation, presented by gold standard direction (all results on downsampled space)

Predictor	Estimate	Std. Err.	Sig.
Intercept	0.15	0.06	**
Δ entropy	-2.08	0.18	***
Δ KL divergence	-2.22	0.18	***
Δ log frequency	1.74	0.09	***

Table 2: Logistic regression model (Δ always denotes noun value minus verb value)

The second study (Herbelot and Ganesalingam, 2013) was directly interested in measuring specificity and proposed to equate it with the Kullback-Leibler (KL) divergence D between a word vector $\vec{w}$ and the "neutral" vector $\vec{n}$:

$$S(w) = D(\vec{w}||\vec{n}) = \sum_i \vec{w}_i \cdot \log \frac{\vec{w}_i}{\vec{n}_i} \qquad (2)$$

where $\vec{n}$ is the prior distribution over all words. We compute $\vec{n}$ as the centroid of approximately 28,000 word vectors in our vector space; the vectors are computed according to the procedure in Section 3.3. In this approach, higher KL divergence corresponds to higher semantic specificity. We note that the entropy and KL divergence values are closely related mathematically and highly correlated in practice ($\rho = 0.91$).

Combined Model. Finally, we combine the individual indicators (standardized differences in log frequency, entropy, and KL divergence within each pair) as features in a logistic regression model. We also experimented with including an interaction between the information-theoretic terms and frequency, but did not obtain a better model fit.

4 Results and Discussion

Assessing the Hypotheses. The quantitative results of our experiments are shown in Table 1.

Compared against the most frequent class baseline, which assigns the most frequent direction in the gold standard — that is, N-to-V— to all cases, both our hypotheses are substantially, and significantly, more successful in predicting the direction of derivation (at a significance level of $\alpha = 0.05$).

Furthermore, the frequency hypothesis is more successful than the semantic specificity hypothesis on the complete conversion dataset. However, there is a striking complementarity between the frequency and specificity hypotheses with respect to the gold standard direction (N-to-V vs. V-to-N). Among the N-to-V cases, frequency excels with almost 85% accuracy, while the specificity predictors are at baseline level. V-to-N shows the opposite behavior, with above 75% accuracy for the specificity predictors and a sharp drop for frequency.

This complementarity among the predictors also enables the regression model to combine their respective strengths. It yields accuracies of 76%+ for both N-to-V and V-to-N conversion, with an overall accuracy of 76.8%, significantly better than frequency only. Table 2 shows normalized coefficients obtained for the four predictors in the model, all of which contribute highly significantly. Positive coefficients increase the log odds for the class N-to-V. As expected, the frequency difference between noun and verb comes with a positive coefficient: a higher noun frequency indicates N-to-V. According to hypothesis (2), we would expect a negative coefficient for the KL divergence difference between noun and verb and and a positive one for entropy. While this expectation is met for KL divergence, we also see a negative coefficient for entropy. This is due to the very strong correlation between the two predictors: the regression model uses the weaker one, entropy, as a "correction factor" for the stronger one, KL divergence.

Table 3 shows some examples (taken from the top of the alphabetically-ordered list of conversion cases), cross-classified by whether two complementary predictors (frequency and KL divergence) both make the correct prediction, disagree, or both fail, together with the number of conversion instances for each class. The two predictors agree more often than they disagree, but among the disagreements, the strong asymmetry between N-to-V (top) and V-to-N (below) is readily visible.

Part-of-speech Differences as a Confounder. A possible criticism of our results is that they arise primarily from distributional differences between

correct direction: N-to-V			
wrong in both size=112	wrong in f size=48	wrong in KL size=370	correct in both size=514
augur	*balk*	*age*	*air*
biff	*calk*	*alarm*	*alloy*
correct direction: V-to-N			
wrong in both size=132	wrong in f size=259	wrong in KL size=91	correct in both size=466
ally	*account*	*act*	*accord*
answer	*address*	*babble*	*ache*

Table 3: Conversion examples cross-classified according to the frequency (f) and KL divergence (KL) predictors, with sizes of various classes.

the two parts of speech (nouns and verbs) and are not specifically related to conversion. To test this hypothesis, we first inspected the means of entropy, KL divergence and log frequency in our sample and found that downsampling was successful in largely eliminating differences at the part-of-speech level (e.g., $\bar{H}_N = 6.57$, $\bar{H}_V = 6.62$). We tested the importance of the remaining differences by re-running our experiments with predictors that were normalized by part-of-speech (i.e., either subtracting the part-of-speech mean or dividing by it). The performance of the individual predictors hardly changed, nor did the performance of the logistic regression model (slight increase in accuracy from 76.8% to 77.0%). Our conclusion is that the patterns that we observe are indeed reflections of semantic shifts due to conversion, rather than inherent differences between parts of speech.

Consequences of Asymmetry for Theory. The asymmetry observed between N-to-V and V-to-N conversion in Table 1 suggests that different theoretical accounts of conversion may be appropriate for the two directions. The failure of the specificity hypothesis to predict the direction of N-to-V conversion at better than chance level is consistent with an underspecification approach, rather than a derivational one (cf. Section 1). The theoretical justification for our hypothesis (2), namely that derived forms are more semantically specific than their bases, assumes that the input to N-to-V conversion is a noun, to which semantic content is added in the form of a phonologically null operator. If, instead, an uncategorized root merges with a categorizing head to form both the noun and the verb, there is no reason why one would be more semantically specific than the other. On the other

hand, the high accuracy of the information theoretic measures on V-to-N conversion are consistent with a derivational approach.

There is an interesting positive correlation between semantic regularity and (gain in) frequency. As often noted in the literature, the semantics of N-to-V conversion is irregular, with conversion verbs exhibiting a wide range of meanings – for example, *age*, meaning something like 'increase in age'. In N-to-V conversion, the derived word often occurs less frequently than its base, possibly because the high level of semantic flexibility encourages nonce formations. On the other hand, V-to-N conversion has much more regular semantics, where the noun typically names the event or its result – for example, an *address* involves the act of *addressing*. In V-to-N conversion, frequency is a poor predictor of the direction of derivation, indicating that the derived word often occurs more frequently than its base, possibly because semantic regularity allows usages to become entrenched.

5 Conclusion

In this paper, we have analyzed the phenomenon of diachronic direction of derivation in English conversion. An initial experiment has shown a striking complementarity in the ability of frequency and semantic specificity to account for the direction of conversion in N-to-V and V-to-N cases, as well as good overall accuracy for a combined model. This opens up interesting avenues for future exploration. We believe corpus-based, distributional measures can yield useful insights for theoretical approaches to morphology and syntax. Finally, we note that Herbelot and Ganesalingam (2013) found a frequency-based measure and KL divergence to perform about equally well on the task of predicting lexical specificity, e.g. that *cat* is more specific than *animal*. The relationship between various corpus-based measures remains to be fully explored.

Acknowledgments. We thank the reviewers for their valuable comments and student assistant Olga Chumakova for her support. MK and SP acknowledge partial funding by Deutsche Forschungsgemeinschaft (SFB 732, Project B9). LR acknowledges EPSRC grant EP/I037512/1 and ERC Starting Grant DisCoTex (306920). AP acknowledges Leibniz Association grant SAS-2015-IDS-LWC and the Ministry of Science, Research, and Art of Baden-Württemberg.

References

Maya Arad. 2005. *Roots and patterns: Hebrew morpho-syntax*. Springer, Dordrecht.

Harald R. Baayen, Richard Piepenbrock, and Leon Gulikers. 1995. *The CELEX lexical database. Release 2. LDC96L14*. Linguistic Data Consortium, University of Pennsylvania, Philadelphia, PA.

Laurie Bauer. 1983. *English word-formation*. Cambridge University Press, Cambridge.

Leonard Bloomfield. 1933. *Language*. Henry Holt, New York.

Hagit Borer. 2005a. *In name only: Structuring sense, Volume I*. Oxford University Press, Oxford.

Hagit Borer. 2005b. *The normal course of events: Structuring sense, Volume II*. Oxford University Press, Oxford.

Eve V. Clark and Herbert H. Clark. 1979. When nouns surface as verbs. *Language*, 55:767–811.

Jan Don. 1993. *Morphological conversion*. Ph.D. thesis, Utrecht University.

Jane Grimshaw. 1990. *Argument Structure*. MIT Press, Cambridge.

Ken Hale and Samuel Jay Keyser. 2002. *Prolegomenon to a theory of argument structure*. MIT Press, Cambridge.

Morris Halle and Alec Marantz. 1993. Distributed morphology and the pieces of inflection. In S.J. Keyser and K. Hale, editors, *The view from Building 20*, pages 111–176. MIT Press, Cambridge.

Heidi Harley and Rolf Noyer. 1999. State-of-the-article: Distributed Morphology. *GLOT*, 4:3–9.

Frank W. Harwood and Alison M. Wright. 1956. Statistical study of English word formation. *Language*, 32(2):260–273.

Jennifer Hay. 2001. Lexical frequency in morphology: Is everything relative? *Linguistics*, 39:1041–70.

Aurélie Herbelot and Mohan Ganesalingam. 2013. Measuring semantic content in distributional vectors. In *Proceedings of ACL*, pages 440–445, Sofia, Bulgaria.

Ferenc Kiefer. 2005. Types of conversion in hungarian. In *Approaches to Conversion/Zero-Derivation*. Waxmann, Münster.

Paul Kiparsky. 1982. Word formation and the lexicon. In Fred Ingeman, editor, *Proceedings of the Mid-America Linguistics Conference*, page 3–29. University of Kansas.

Andrew Koontz-Garboden. 2007. *States, changes of state, and the Monotonicity Hypothesis*. Ph.D. thesis, Stanford University.

Herbert Koziol. 1937. *Handbuch der englischen Wortbildungslehre*. C. Winter, Heidelberg.

Stela Manova and Wolfgang U. Dressler. 2005. The morphological technique of conversion in the inflecting-fusional type. In *Approaches to Conversion/Zero-Derivation*. Waxmann, Münster.

Hans Marchand. 1969. *The categories and types of present-day English word-formation: A synchronic-diachronic approach, 2nd edition*. C.H. Becksche Verlagsbuchhandlung, München.

David Pesetsky. 1995. *Zero syntax: Experiencers and cascades*. MIT Press, Cambridge.

Ingo Plag. 1999. *Morphological productivity: Structural constraints in English derivation*. Mouton de Gruyter, Berlin and New York.

Ingo Plag. 2003. *Word-Formation in English*. Cambridge University Press, Cambridge.

Laura Rimell. 2012. *Nominal Roots as Event Predicates in English Denominal Conversion Verbs*. Ph.D. thesis, New York University.

Enrico Santus, Alessandro Lenci, Qin Lu, and Sabine Schulte im Walde. 2014. Chasing hypernyms in vector spaces with entropy. In *Proceedings of EACL*, pages 38–42, Gothenburg, Sweden.

Petra Maria Vogel. 1996. *Wortarten und Wortartenwechsel. Zu Konversion und verwandten Erscheinungen im Deutschen und in anderen Sprachen*. Mouton de Gruyter, Berlin and New York.

Morphological Segmentation Can Improve Syllabification

Garrett Nicolai   **Lei Yao**   **Grzegorz Kondrak**
Department of Computing Science
University of Alberta
`{nicolai,lyao1,gkondrak}@ualberta.ca`

Abstract

Syllabification is sometimes influenced by morphological boundaries. We show that incorporating morphological information can improve the accuracy of orthographic syllabification in English and German. Surprisingly, unsupervised segmenters, such as Morfessor, can be more useful for this purpose than the supervised ones.

1 Introduction

Syllabification is the process of dividing a word into syllables. Although in the strict linguistic sense syllables are composed of phonemes rather than letters, due to practical considerations we focus here on orthographic syllabification, which is also referred to as *hyphenation*. Some dictionaries include hyphenation information to indicate where words may be broken for end-of-line divisions, and to assist the reader in recovering the correct pronunciation. In many languages the orthographic and phonological representations of a word are closely related.

Orthographic syllabification has a number of computational applications. Incorporation of the syllable boundaries between letters benefits grapheme-to-phoneme conversion (Damper et al., 2005), and respelling generation (Hauer and Kondrak, 2013). Hyphenation of out-of-dictionary words is also important in text processing (Trogkanis and Elkan, 2010). Because of the productive nature of language, a dictionary look-up process for syllabification is inadequate. Rule-based systems are generally outperformed on out-of-dictionary words by data-driven methods, such as those of Daelemans et al. (1997), Demberg (2006), Marchand and Damper (2007), and Trogkanis and Elkan (2010).

Morphological segmentation is the task of dividing words into morphemes, the smallest meaning-bearing units in the word (Goldsmith, 2001). For example the morpheme *over* occurs in words like *hold+over*, *lay+over*, and *skip+over*.[1] Roots combine with derivational (e.g. *refut+able*) and inflectional affixes (e.g. *hold+ing*). Computational segmentation approaches can be divided into rule-based (Porter, 1980), supervised (Ruokolainen et al., 2013), semi-supervised (Grönroos et al., 2014), and unsupervised (Creutz and Lagus, 2002). Bartlett et al. (2008) observe that some of the errors made by their otherwise highly-accurate system, such as *hol-dov-er* and *coad-ju-tors*, can be attributed to the lack of awareness of morphological boundaries, which influence syllabification.

In this paper, we demonstrate that the accuracy of orthographic syllabification can be improved by considering morphology. We augment the syllabification approach of Bartlett et al. (2008), with features encoding morphological segmentation of words. We investigate the degree of overlap between the morphological and syllable boundaries. The results of our experiments on English and German show that the incorporation of expert-annotated (*gold*) morphological boundaries extracted from lexical databases substantially reduces the syllabification error rate, particularly in low-resource settings. We find that the accuracy gains tend to be preserved when unsupervised segmentation is used instead. On the other hand, relying on a fully-supervised system appears to be much less robust, even though it generates more accurate morphological segmentations than the unsupervised systems. We propose an explanation for this surprising result.

---

[1] We denote syllable boundaries with '-', and morpheme boundaries with '+'.

Proceedings of the 14th Annual SIGMORPHON Workshop on Computational Research in Phonetics, Phonology, and Morphology, pages 99–103,
Berlin, Germany, August 11, 2016. ©2016 Association for Computational Linguistics

2   Methods

In this section, we describe the original syllabification method of Bartlett et al. (2008), which serves as our baseline system, and discuss various approaches to incorporating morphological information.

2.1   Base system

Bartlett et al. (2008) present a discriminative approach to automatic syllabification. They formulate syllabification as a tagging problem, and learn a Structured SVM tagger from labeled data (Tsochantaridis et al., 2005). Under the Markov assumption that each tag is dependent on its previous n tags, the tagger predicts the optimal tag sequence (Altun et al., 2003). A large-margin training objective is applied to learn a weight vector to separate the correct tag sequence from other possible sequences for each training instance. The test instances are tagged using the Viterbi decoding algorithm on the basis of the weighted features.

Each training instance is represented as a sequence of feature vectors, with the tags following the "Numbered NB" tagging scheme, which was found to produce the best results. In the scheme, the B tags signal that a boundary occurs after the current character, while the N tags indicate the distance from the previous boundary. For example, the word *syl-lab-i-fy* is annotated as: N1 N2 B N1 N2 B B N1 N2. The feature vectors consist of all n-grams around the current focus character, up to size 5. These n-grams are composed of context letters, and word-boundary markers that are added at the beginning and end of each word.

2.2   Morphological information

We incorporate available morphological information by adding morpheme boundary markers into the input words. The extracted features belong to two categories: orthographic and morphological. The orthographic features are identical to the ones described in Section 2.1. The morphological features are also contextual n-grams, but may contain morphological breaks, which can potentially help identify the correct syllabification of words. Manually-annotated morphological lexicons sometimes distinguish between inflectional, derivational, and compound boundaries. We can pass this information to the syllabification system by marking the respective boundaries with different symbols.

Since morphologically annotated lexicons are expensive to create, and available only for well-studied languages, we investigate the idea of replacing them with annotations generated by fully-supervised, distantly-supervised, and unsupervised segmentation algorithms.

2.2.1   Fully-supervised

While supervised methods typically require large amounts of annotated training data, they can perform segmentation of unseen (out-of-dictionary) words. As our fully-supervised segmenter, we use the discriminative string transducer of Jiampojamarn et al. (2010). The transducer is trained on aligned source-target pairs, one pair per word; the target is identical to the source except that it includes characters that represent morphological breaks. Using source and target context, the transducer learns to insert these breaks into words.

2.2.2   Distantly-supervised

Whereas morphologically-annotated lexicons are rare, websites such as Wiktionary contain crowd-generated inflection tables for many languages. A distantly-supervised segmenter can be trained on semi-structured inflection tables to divide words into stems and affixes without explicit segmentation annotation. We adopt the approach of Nicolai and Kondrak (2016), which combines unsupervised alignment with a discriminative string transduction algorithm, An important limitation of this approach is that it can only identify inflectional morpheme boundaries.

2.2.3   Unsupervised

Unsupervised methods have the advantage of requiring no training data. We investigate the applicability of two unsupervised segmenters: Morfessor (Creutz and Lagus, 2005) and Morpheme++ (Dasgupta and Ng, 2007). Morfessor uses the minimum description length (MDL) principle to predict a word as a likely sequence of morphemes. Since the baseline version of Morfessor tends to over-segment rare words, we instead apply Morfessor FlatCat (Grönroos et al., 2014), which reduces over-segmentation through the use of a hidden Markov model. Morpheme++ is another system that is capable of distinguishing between prefixes, suffixes, and stems by taking advantage of the regularity of affixes.

3 Experiments

In this section, we introduce our data sets, and discuss the overlap between morphological and syllabic boundaries. We investigate the quality of the morphological segmentations of produced by various methods, and replicate the syllabification results of Bartlett et al. (2008). Finally, we discuss the results of incorporating morphological information into the syllabification system.

3.1 Data

Our data comes from the English and German sections of the CELEX lexical database (Baayen et al., 1995). The English and German training sets contain 43,212 and 41,382 instances, with corresponding development sets of 8,735 and 5,173 instances, and test sets of 8,608 and 5,173 instances. The distantly-supervised and fully-supervised segmenters were trained on the union of the training and development sets, while the unsupervised segmenters were applied to the union of the training, development and test sets. The distantly-supervised system had no access to the gold morphological segmentations.

The annotation in CELEX distinguishes between inflectional vs. derivational affixes, as well as derivational vs. compound breaks. The latter distinction did not help in our development experiments, so we disregard it. We refer to the two subsets of the morpheme boundary annotations as "Gold Inflectional" and "Gold Derivational".

3.2 Quality of morphological segmentation

Table 1 shows the word accuracy (entire words segmented correctly) of various segmentation methods on the test sets. Unsurprisingly, the fully-supervised segmenter is substantially more accurate than the other systems. The distantly-supervised system can only identify inflectional boundaries. so its overall accuracy is rather low;

	EN	DE
Morfessor 1.0	59.4	39.8
Morfessor FlatCat	59.6	40.8
Morpheme++	66.3	39.1
Distantly-supervised	63.5	21.3
Fully-supervised	95.4	71.3

Table 1: Morphological segmentation word accuracy on the test set.

however, its accuracy on the inflectional boundaries is 96.0% for English, and 82.6% for German. Among the unsupervised systems, Morfessor FlatCat is only slightly better than Morfessor 1.0, while Morpheme++ is comparable on German, and significantly better on English. It should be noted that since our focus is on syllabification, no careful parameter tuning was performed, and our data excludes word frequency information.

	EN	DE
Morfessor	38.2	61.4
Morfessor FlatCat	39.1	66.7
Morpheme++	46.4	67.1
Distantly-supervised	24.8	7.9
Fully-supervised	44.5	51.5
Gold	45.1	49.7
Gold Inflectional	24.4	4.5
Gold Derivational	68.6	57.6

Table 2: Overlap between syllabic and morphological boundaries on the test set.

Table 2 shows the percentage of the predicted morphological breaks that match gold syllable boundaries. We observe that the inflectional boundaries are far less likely than the derivational ones to correspond to syllable breaks. We also note that on German the unsupervised segmenters exhibit much higher syllabification overlap than the gold annotation. We attribute this to the tendency of the unsupervised methods to oversegment.

3.3 Baseline syllabification

As a baseline, we replicate the experiments of Bartlett et al. (2008), and extend them to low-resource settings. Since the training sets are of slightly different sizes, we label each training size point as specified in Table 3. We see that correct syllabification of approximately half of the words is achieved with as few as 100 English and 50 German training examples.

3.4 Morphologically-informed syllabification

Our main set of experiments concerns the incorporation of the morphological information obtained from methods described in Section 2.2 into the baseline syllabification system. As seen in Table 3, the accuracy of the baseline syllabification system trained on a large number of instances is already very high, so the gains introduced by mor-

Label	Training Size		Error Rate	
	EN	DE	EN	DE
A	51	45	61.27	52.97
B	101	91	51.25	44.08
C	203	182	43.05	35.37
D	406	364	34.00	25.32
E	812	727	27.23	19.01
F	1623	1455	21.50	12.74
G	3247	2910	16.96	9.24
H	6493	5819	10.50	6.27
I	12987	11639	6.61	4.64
J	25974	23278	3.73	3.19
K	51947	46555	2.18	2.04

Table 3: Absolute error rate for the baseline with varying amounts of the training data.

phology are necessarily small. In Figures 1 and 2, we show the relative error reduction at various training sizes. The absolute error rate can be obtained by multiplying the values from the table and the figures.

For the sake of clarity, we omit some of the methods from the graphs. The unsupervised methods are represented by Morfessor FlatCat. The distantly-supervised system is generally successful at predicting the inflectional boundaries, but fails to improve on the baseline, as they are less important for syllabification than the derivational boundaries.

3.5 Discussion

Overall, the results confirm that morphology can help syllabification. The incorporation of gold segmentation boundaries consistently leads to the reduction of the syllabification error rate; the only exception occurs on the full English training set. While the fully-supervised system provides a benefit at lower training thresholds, it actually hurts the accuracy at larger training sizes. Notably, unsupervised segmentation appears to outperform fully-supervised segmentation as the amount of the training data increases; the corresponding error rate reduction approaches 25% on German.

One explanation for the strong performance of the unsupervised systems is their high accuracy on compound words. Consider the German compound *Toppflagge* "masthead flag". An unsupervised system is able to guess that the word is composed of the words *Topp* and *Flagge* that exist in the lexicon on their own. To produce the same

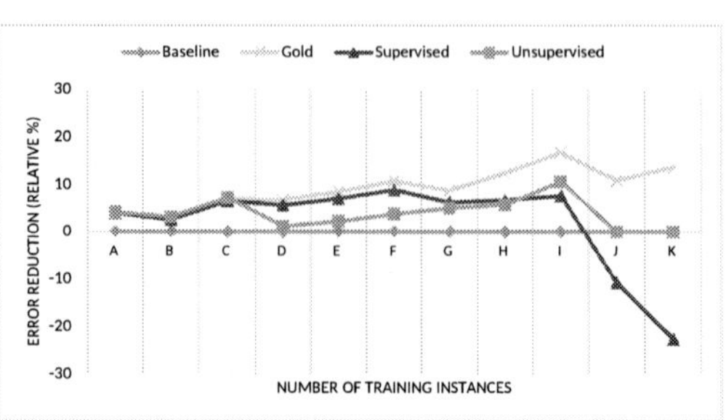

Figure 1: Syllabification error rate reduction on English.

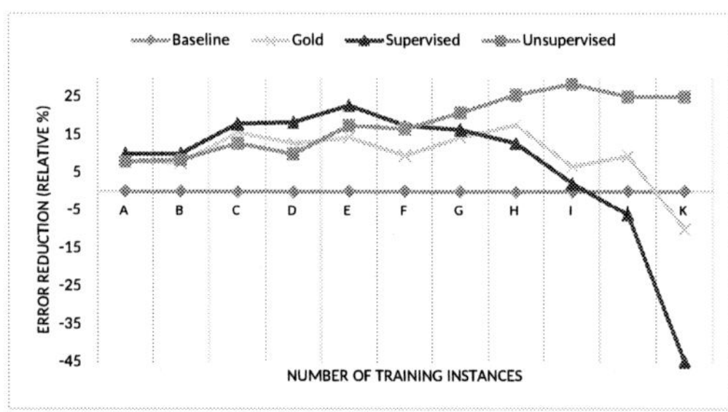

Figure 2: Syllabification error rate reduction on German.

segmentation, the fully-supervised system must be trained on a number of compound words that include either *topp* or *flagge*. Since compound boundaries are almost always syllable breaks as well, they have a strong effect on syllabification.

Sometimes even a linguistically incorrect segmentation proposed by an unsupervised segmenter may work better for the purposes of syllabification. Many words of Latin origin contain affixes that are no longer productive in English. Thus, an unsupervised system over-segments the word *ob+literate*, which allows it to produce the correct syllabification *ob-lit-er-ate*, as opposed to *o-blit-er-ate* predicted by the gold-informed system. This phenomenon appears to be particularly frequent in German.

4 Conclusion

We have demonstrated that morphological information can improve the accuracy of orthographic syllabification. We have found that unsupervised segmentation methods often perform better than supervised methods, and can rival gold human annotation. We have proposed two explanations for this counter-intuitive phenomenon. We hope that this work will contribute a computational perspective on the issue of interaction between syllabification and morphology.

Acknowledgments

This research was supported by the Natural Sciences and Engineering Research Council of Canada, and the Alberta Innovates Technology Futures.

References

Yasemin Altun, Ioannis Tsochantaridis, and Thomas Hofmann. 2003. Hidden Markov support vector machines. In *ICML*, pages 3–10.

Harald R. Baayen, Richard Piepenbrock, and Leon Gulikers. 1995. *The CELEX Lexical Database. Release 2 (CD-ROM)*. Linguistic Data Consortium, University of Pennsylvania.

Susan Bartlett, Grzegorz Kondrak, and Colin Cherry. 2008. Automatic syllabification with structured SVMs for letter-to-phoneme conversion. In *ACL*, pages 568–576.

Mathias Creutz and Krista Lagus. 2002. Unsupervised discovery of morphemes. In *Proceedings of the ACL-02 workshop on Morphological and phonological learning-Volume 6*, pages 21–30.

Mathias Creutz and Krista Lagus. 2005. Inducing the morphological lexicon of a natural language from unannotated text. In *Conference on Adaptive Knowledge Representation and Reasoning (AKRR)*, pages 51–59.

Walter Daelemans, Antal van den Bosch, and Ton Weijters. 1997. Igtree: Using trees for compression and classification in lazy learning algorithms. *Artificial Intellegence Review*, 11(1-5):407–423.

Robert I Damper, Yannick Marchand, J-DS Marsters, and Alexander I Bazin. 2005. Aligning text and phonemes for speech technology applications using an em-like algorithm. *International Journal of Speech Technology*, 8(2):147–160.

Sajib Dasgupta and Vincent Ng. 2007. High-performance, language-independent morphological segmentation. In *HLT-NAACL*, pages 155–163.

Vera Demberg. 2006. Letter-to-phoneme conversion for a german text-to-speech system.

John Goldsmith. 2001. Unsupervised learning of the morphology of a natural language. *Computational Linguisitics*, 27(2), June.

Stig-Arne Grönroos, Sami Virpioja, Peter Smit, and Mikko Kurimo. 2014. Morfessor FlatCat: An HMM-based method for unsupervised and semi-supervised learning of morphology. In *COLING*, pages 1177–1185.

Bradley Hauer and Grzegorz Kondrak. 2013. Automatic generation of English respellings. In *NAACL*, pages 634–643.

Sittichai Jiampojamarn, Colin Cherry, and Grzegorz Kondrak. 2010. Integrating joint n-gram features into a discriminative training network. In *NAACL*.

Yannick Marchand and Robert I. Damper. 2007. Can syllabification improve pronunciation by analogy of English? *Natural Language Engineering*, 13(1):1–24.

Garrett Nicolai and Grzegorz Kondrak. 2016. Leveraging inflection tables for stemming and lemmatization. In *ACL*.

Martin F Porter. 1980. An algorithm for suffix stripping. *Program*, 14(3):130–137.

Teemu Ruokolainen, Oskar Kohonen, Sami Virpioja, and Mikko Kurimo. 2013. Supervised morphological segmentation in a low-resource learning setting using conditional random fields. In *CoNLL*.

Nikolaos Trogkanis and Charles Elkan. 2010. Conditional random fields for word hyphenation. In *ACL*, pages 366–374.

Ioannis Tsochantaridis, Thorsten Joachims, Thomas Hofmann, and Yasemin Altun. 2005. Large margin methods for structured and interdependent output variables. In *Journal of Machine Learning Research*, pages 1453–1484.

Towards a Formal Representation of Components of German Compounds

Thierry Declerck
DFKI GmbH
D-66123 Saarbrücken, Germany
&
Austrian Centre for Digital Humanities
A-1010 Vienna, Austria
`declerck@dfki.de`

Piroska Lendvai
Dept. of Computational Linguistics
Saarland University
D-66123 Saarbrücken, Germany
`piroska.r@gmail.com`

Abstract

This paper presents an approach for the formal representation of components in German compounds. We assume that such a formal representation will support the segmentation and analysis of unseen compounds that feature components already seen in other compounds. An extensive language resource that explicitly codes components of compounds is GermaNet, a lexical semantic network for German. We summarize the GermaNet approach to the description of compounds, discussing some of its shortcomings. Our proposed extension of this representation builds on the *lemon* lexicon model for ontologies, established by the W3C Ontology Lexicon Community Group.

1 Introduction

The motivation for our study is the assumption that the availability of a formal representation of components in German compound words can help in the detection, processing and analysis of new unseen compounds. Compounding in German is a productive process to create (new) words, and these typically consist of lexical items partly seen in other compounds already. Our aim is to create a formal repre-

sentation of such components in German, in order to facilitate the segmentation and possibly the generation of compound words.

Several German lexical resources feature designated elements to mark up entries as compounds, whereas they typically lack elements that would represent the components of compounds.

One of the most fully-fledged resource of German compound nouns is GermaNet (Hamp and Feldweg, 1997; Kunze and Lemnitzer, 2002), a lexical semantic net for German following the principles of the Princeton WordNet (Fellbaum, 1998). The approach of GermaNet to the encoding of elements of compounds within the lexical-semantic net is described in (Henrich and Hinrichs, 2011). Additionally to this representation of compounds, GermaNet offers a freely available list of 66,047 nominal compounds split to their modifier(s) and head, in a tab-delimited (tsv) format[1]. Table 1 shows few examples taken from this list, while Example ?? shows the encoding of the compound *Rotsperre* ('red card suspension') within the XML representation of the GermaNet lexical semantic network.

Based on the GermaNet description of compounds, several studies on annotating and sys-

---

[1] `http://www.sfs.uni-tuebingen.de/`
`GermaNet/documents/compounds/split_` ·
`compounds_from_GermaNet11.0.txt`

Proceedings of the 14th Annual SIGMORPHON Workshop on Computational Research in Phonetics, Phonology, and Morphology, pages 104–109,
Berlin, Germany, August 11, 2016. ©2016 Association for Computational Linguistics

tems on processing compounds have been proposed (Hinrichs et al., 2013; Santos, 2014; Dima et al., 2014; Dima and Hinrichs, 2015).

Compound	Modifier(s)	Head
Rotschopf	rot	Schopf
Rotschwanz	rot	Schwanz
Rotschwingel	rot	Schwingel
Rotspecht	rot	Specht
Rotsperre	rot	Sperre
Rotstich	rot|Rot	Stich
Rotstift	rot	Stift
Rotstiftaktion	Rotstift	Aktion

Table 1: Examples from the GermaNet list of nominal compounds.

The few examples listed in Table 1 show that GermaNet describes explicitly only immediate constituents of compounds, but is also reflecting the recursive nature of compounds that have more than two constituent parts, as can be seen with the words *Rotstift* ('red pencil') and *Rotstiftaktion* ('cutback', 'reduce spending'). In this case a tool can easily split *Rotstiftaktion* into *rot*, *Stift* and *Aktion*, on the basis of the segmentation of *Rotstift*.

We note also that one compound can have more than one modifier, as in the case of *Rotstich* ('tinge of red'), where we have both an adjectival (*rot*) and a nominal (*Rot*) modifier. GermaNet marks the different part-of-speech (PoS) properties of the components being in the modifier position by using different cases: Upper case marks a noun (as this is the case for all the listed compounds), while lower case marks either a verb or an adjective.

We observe also that the modifier *rot* is often repeated (in fact much more often then in this slice taken from the list: there are also many compounds ending with the component *rot*).

In the following sections we present first the GermaNet formal representation of compounds in the full context of the lexical semantic net. Then we suggest our extensions to the GermaNet representation, utilizing modules of the *lemon*[2] approach to the encoding of lexical data.

2 Representation of Compounds in the GermaNet lexical semantic net

The structure of a GermaNet entry containing the compound word *Rotsperre* ('red card suspension') is shown in Example 1. The relevant information is to be found in the XML elements rendered in bold face.

```
<synset class="Geschehen"
    category="nomen" id="s21159">
  <lexUnit id="l29103"
      styleMarking="no"
      artificial="no"
      namedEntity="no" source="
      core" sense="1">
    <orthForm>Rotsperre</
      orthForm>
    <compound>
      <modifier category="
          Adjektiv">rot</
          modifier>
      <head>Sperre</head>
    </compound>
  </lexUnit>
  <paraphrase>beim Fussball</
      paraphrase>
</synset>
```

Example 1: A compound lexical unit in GermaNet: *Rotsperre* ('red card suspension')

In this formal representation, the PoS of the modifier element of the compound (*rot*, 'red') is explicitly given, while this is not the case for the head, as the PoS of the head element of a compound is identical to the PoS of the whole compound. However, we advocate that explicitly encoding the PoS information of the

---

[2]The *lexicon model for ontologies* (lemon) is resulting from the work of the W3C Ontology Lexicon Community Group; `https://www.w3.org/community/ontolex/wiki/Final_Model_Specification`.

head component can be necessary; for example if a tool would access only the repository of components. In this case, the tool would have to infer the PoS information of the head component from the compounds in which it occurs, adding thus an additional processing step, which can be avoided if the PoS of the head component is explicitly marked.

As already observed for the list of compounds in the tsv format, the GermaNet entry displays here the adjective modifier in lowercase. In this case we are loosing the information about the original use of the word form. We suggest to introduce an additional feature in which the original form of the component is preserved.

By observing the list of compounds provided by GermaNet, we noted that the modifier component of *Rotsperre* keep recurring in other compounds. This is for sure also the case for the head components. For example, the component *Sperre* ('suspension', 'block', ...) is repeated in the related word *Gelbsperre* ('yellow card suspension'). Such productively recurring components would be beneficial to have encoded in a repository so that they are included only once in a lexicon, possibly with links to the different components they can be combined with, depending on their related senses.

The use of a modifier in a compound can play a disambiguation role. While we can easily establish a relation between the reduced set of senses of the compound and the set of senses of the head of the compound, we have no immediate information on the synsets associated to the modifier of the compound. This is an information we would also like to explicitly encode.

Further, we consider the encoding of the *Fugenelement* ('connecting element') that is often used in the building of compounds; e.g. the *s* in *Führungstor* ('goal which gives the lead'). GermaNet does not include this information in its XML representation.

Finally, we notice that the ordering of components is not explicitly encoded.

In order to remedy the above issues, we suggest to adopt the recently published specifications of the *lemon* model. In the following section, we describe this model and our suggested representation of GermaNet compounds.

3 The *lemon* Model

The *lemon* model has been designed using the Semantic Web formal representation languages OWL, RDFS and RDF[3]. It also makes use of the SKOS vocabulary[4]. *lemon* is based on the ISO Lexical Markup Framework (LMF)[5] and the W3C Ontology Lexicon Community Group proposed an extension of the original *lemon* model[6], stressing its modular design.

The core module of *lemon*, called *ontolex*, is displayed in Figure 1. In *ontolex*, each element of a lexicon entry is described independently, while typed relation markers, in the form of OWL, RDF or *ontolex* properties, are interlinking these elements.

Additionally to the core module of *lemon*, we make use of its decomposition module, called *decomp*[7], designed for the representation of Multiword Expression lexical entries, and which we use for the representation of compound words.

---

[3]See respectively `http://www.w3.org/TR/owl-semantics/`, `https://www.w3.org/TR/rdf-schema/`, and `https://www.w3.org/RDF/`

[4]`https://www.w3.org/2004/02/skos/`

[5]See (Francopoulo et al., 2006) and `http://www.lexicalmarkupframework.org/`

[6]See (McCrae et al., 2012)

[7]`http://www.w3.org/community/ontolex/wiki/Final_Model_Specification`

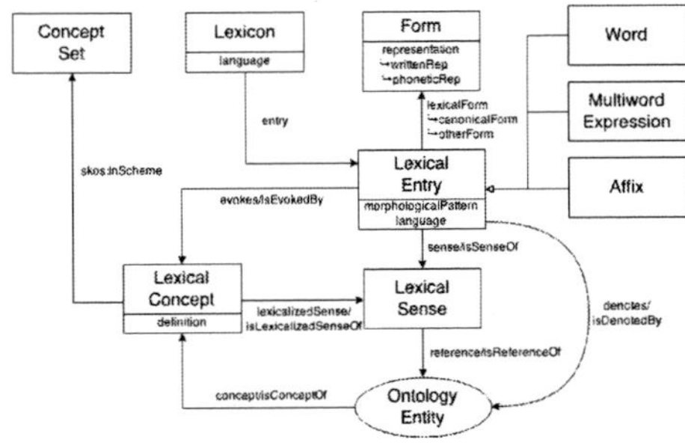

Figure 1: *ontolex*, the core module of *lemon*. Figure created by John P. McCrae for the W3C Ontolex Community Group.

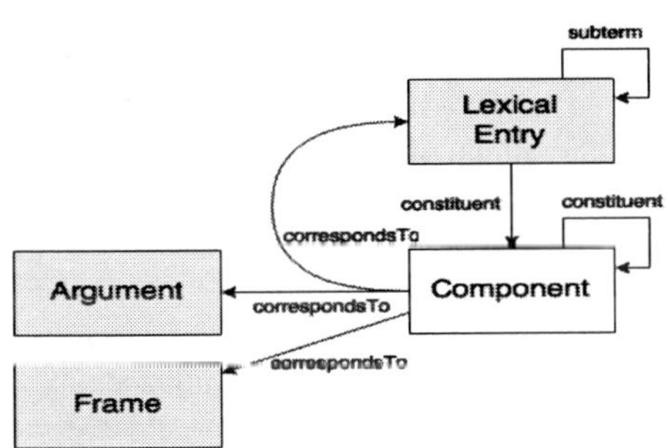

Figure 2: *decomp*, the decomposition module of *lemon*. Figure created by John P. McCrae for the W3C Ontolex Community Group.

The relation of *decomp* to the core module, and more particularly to the class ontolex:LexicalEntry, is displayed in Figure 2. Components of a compound (or a multiword) entry are pointed to by the property: decomp:constituent. The range of this property is an instance of the class decomp:Component.

Taking again *Rotsperre* ('red card suspension') as an example, and which is built of two components, we make use two times of the decomp:constituent property, the current values of it being :Rot_comp and :sperre_comp (see the corresponding RDF code given below in the entries (1-3), which are instances of the class ontolex:Component. This way we can encode the surface forms of the components, as they are used in compounds.

The relation between the ontolex:Component instances (the surface forms of the components occurring in the compounds) and the ontolex:Word instances (the full lexical entries corresponding the surface form of the components) follows the schema for the relation between the two classes ontolex:LexicalEntry and ontolex:Component, which is graphically shown in Figure 2. For our example *Rotsperre*, as shown in the entries (1-3) below, the elements *Rot* and *sperre* are instances of the class ontolex:Component, and as such *sperre* can be linked/related to other compounds like *Löschsperre* ('deletion block') or to the (semantically more closely related) *Gelbsperre* ('yellow card suspension'). The property decomp:correspondsTo links the components to the lexical entries that encode all the lexical properties of those surface forms used in the compound word.

A simplified representation of the compound entry *Rotsperre* and of its components is displayed below, in (1-3). In the entry (1) we use rdf_1 and rdf_2[8] for marking the order of the two components in the compound word. We assume that information on the position of the elements can be relevant for the interpretation of the compound.

```
(1)    :Rotsperre_lex
       rdf:type ontolex:LexicalEntry ;
       lexinfo:partOfSpeech lexinfo:noun ;
       rdf:_1 :Rot_comp ;
       rdf:_2 :sperre_comp ;
```

---

[8]As instances of the property rdfs:ContainerMembershipProperty, see http://www.w3.org/TR/rdf-schema/ for more details.

decomp:constituent :Rot_comp ;
decomp:constituent :sperre_comp ;
decomp:subterm :Sperre_lex ;
decomp:subterm :rot_lex ;
ontolex:denotes
<https://www.wikidata.org/wiki/
Q1827> .

Entries (2) and (3) below show the encoding of the instances of the class `decomp:Component`:

(2) :Rot_comp
     rdf:type decomp:Component ;
     decomp:correspondsTo :rot_lex .

(3) :sperre_comp
     rdf:type decomp:Component ;
     decomp:correspondsTo
     :Sperre_lex .

The proposed approach to the representation of elements of compounds seems intuitive and economical, since one component can be linked to a large number of other components, and, next to decomposition, can also be used for the generation of compound words, taking into account the typical position such components are taking in known compounds.

In the compound entry (1) we also make use of the property `decomp:subterm`. This property links the compound to the full lexical information associated to its components, including the senses of such components. The motivation of the *lemon* model is the determination of senses of lexical entries by reference to ontological entities outside of the lexicon proper. We can thus easily extend the representation of the compound word with sense information, by linking the components and the compound word to relevant resources in the Linked Open Data (LOD) cloud. The sense of `:Rot_comp` is given by a reference to `http://de.dbpedia.org/page/Rot`, where additional associations of *red* with political

parties or sports clubs, etc. can be found. The same holds for `:sperre_comp`, which can be linked to the LOD resource `http://de.dbpedia.org/page/Sperre`.

Additionally, for the sense of the complete compound word we link to the LOD resource: `https://www.wikidata.org/wiki/Q1827`, with the specific meaning of suspension from a sports game. The senses repository for *Sperre* can look as displayed in the lexicalSense entries (4) and (5).

(4) :sperre_sense1
     rdf:type ontolex:LexicalSense ;
     rdfs:label "A sense for the German word 'Sperre'" @en ;
     ontolex:isSenseOf :Sperre_lex ;
     ontolex:reference
     <http://de.dbpedia.org/resource/Lock>
     .

(5) :sperre_sense2
     rdf:type ontolex:LexicalSense ;
     rdfs:label "A sense for the German word 'Sperre'" @en ;
     ontolex:isSenseOf :Sperre_lex ;
     ontolex:reference
     <http://de.dbpedia.org/resource/
     Wettkampfsperre> .

Our current work includes associating GermaNet senses as values of the `ontolex:LexicalSense` property. We are also encoding connecting elements (*Fugenelemente* with the help of the `ontolex:Affix` class.

4 Conclusion

We presented an approach for the formal representation of elements that occur in compound words. Our motivation is to provide rules for computing compound words on the basis of their components.

Acknowledgments

Work presented in this paper has been supported by the PHEME FP7 project (grant No. 611233) and by the FREME H2020 project (grant No. 644771). The author would like to thank the anonymous reviewers for their very helpful comments.

References

Corina Dima and Erhard Hinrichs. 2015. Automatic noun compound interpretation using deep neural networks and word embeddings. In *Proceedings of the 11th International Conference on Computational Semantics*, pages 173–183, London, UK, April. Association for Computational Linguistics.

Corina Dima, Verena Henrich, Erhard Hinrichs, and Christina Hoppermann. 2014. How to tell a schneemann from a milchmann: An annotation scheme for compound-internal relations. In Nicoletta Calzolari (Conference Chair), Khalid Choukri, Thierry Declerck, Hrafn Loftsson, Bente Maegaard, Joseph Mariani, Asuncion Moreno, Jan Odijk, and Stelios Piperidis, editors, *Proceedings of the Ninth International Conference on Language Resources and Evaluation (LREC'14)*, Reykjavik, Iceland, may. European Language Resources Association (ELRA).

Christiane Fellbaum. 1998. *WordNet: An Electronic Lexical Database*. Bradford Books.

Gil Francopoulo, Monte George, Nicoletta Calzolari, Monica Monachini, Nuria Bel, Y Pet, and Claudia Soria. 2006. Lexical markup framework (lmf. In *In Proceedings of LREC2006*.

Birgit Hamp and Helmut Feldweg. 1997. Germanet - a lexical-semantic net for german. In *In Proceedings of ACL workshop Automatic Information Extraction and Building of Lexical Semantic Resources for NLP Applications*, pages 9–15.

Verena Henrich and Erhard W. Hinrichs. 2011. Determining immediate constituents of compounds in germanet. In Galia Angelova, Kalina Bontcheva, Ruslan Mitkov, and Nicolas Nicolov, editors, *RANLP*, pages 420–426. RANLP 2011 Organising Committee.

Erhard Hinrichs, Verena Henrich, and Reinhild Barkey. 2013. Using partwhole relations for automatic deduction of compound-internal relations in germanet. *Language Resources and Evaluation*, 47(3):839–858.

Claudia Kunze and Lothar Lemnitzer. 2002. Germanet - representation, visualization, application. In *Proceedings of the Third International Conference on Language Resources and Evaluation (LREC-2002)*, Las Palmas, Canary Islands - Spain, May. European Language Resources Association (ELRA). ACL Anthology Identifier: L02-1073.

John P. McCrae, Guadalupe Aguado de Cea, Paul Buitelaar, Philipp Cimiano, Thierry Declerck, Asunción Gómez-Pérez, Jorge Gracia, Laura Hollink, Elena Montiel-Ponsoda, Dennis Spohr, and Tobias Wunner. 2012. Interchanging lexical resources on the semantic web. *Language Resources and Evaluation*, 46(4):701–719.

Pedro Bispo Santos. 2014. Using compound lists for german decompounding in a back-off scenario. In *Workshop on Computational, Cognitive, and Linguistic Approaches to the Analysis of Complex Words and Collocations (CCLCC 2014)*, pages 51–55.

Towards robust cross-linguistic comparisons of phonological networks

Philippa Shoemark
School of Informatics
University of Edinburgh
`p.j.shoemark@sms.ed.ac.uk`

Sharon Goldwater
School of Informatics
University of Edinburgh
`sgwater@inf.ed.ac.uk`

James Kirby
Linguistics and English Language
University of Edinburgh
`j.kirby@ed.ac.uk`

Rik Sarkar
School of Informatics
University of Edinburgh
`rsarkar@inf.ed.ac.uk`

Abstract

Recent work has proposed using network science to analyse the structure of the mental lexicon by viewing words as nodes in a *phonological network*, with edges connecting words that differ by a single phoneme. Comparing the structure of phonological networks across different languages could provide insights into linguistic typology and the cognitive pressures that shape language acquisition, evolution, and processing. However, previous studies have not considered how statistics gathered from these networks are affected by factors such as lexicon size and the distribution of word lengths. We show that these factors can substantially affect the statistics of a phonological network and propose a new method for making more robust comparisons. We then analyse eight languages, finding many commonalities but also some qualitative differences in their lexicon structure.

1 Introduction

Studies suggest that the ease with which a word is recognised or produced is affected by the word's phonological similarity to other words in the mental lexicon (often operationalised as *neighbourhood density*, i.e., the number of words that differ from a target word by just a single phoneme) (Luce and Pisoni, 1998; Harley and Bown, 1998; Vitevitch, 2002; Ziegler et al., 2003). Yet the nature of these effects is not always consistent between languages. For example, in English, the neighbourhood density of a word was found to correlate positively with reaction times in a picture naming task (Vitevitch, 2002), and negatively with the speed and accuracy of participants' responses in a lexical decision task (Luce and Pisoni, 1998). However, in Spanish the opposite pattern was found: words with higher neighbourhood densities were produced less quickly in a picture naming task (Vitevitch and Stamer, 2006), and recognised more quickly and accurately in an auditory lexical decision task (Vitevitch and Rodríguez, 2005).

A possible explanation for such cross-linguistic variation is that the different effects of neighbourhood density (a *local* measure of lexicon structure) might result from differences in the *global* lexicon structure: for example, if one language exhibits much greater similarity between words overall, this could affect how language processing mechanisms develop, leading to qualitatively different behaviour.

One way to analyse the global phonological structure of the mental lexicon is by representing it as a *phonological network* (Vitevitch, 2008): a graph in which nodes correspond to the word-forms in a lexicon, and edges link nodes which are phonologically similar according to some metric (typically, words which differ by exactly one phoneme, i.e. they have a Levenshtein distance of one). The structure of the network can then be analysed quantitatively using measures from network science. While neighbourhood density (i.e., a node's degree) is one local measure of connectivity, other measures can better capture the global structure of the network. By comparing these measures across languages, we might find explanations for the behavioural differences mentioned above.

As well as providing insight into cross-linguistic variations in language processing, cross-linguistic comparisons of phonological network structure could also uncover universal properties of language

Proceedings of the 14th Annual SIGMORPHON Workshop on Computational Research in Phonetics, Phonology, and Morphology, pages 110–120,
Berlin, Germany, August 11, 2016. ©2016 Association for Computational Linguistics

or typological generalisations. Indeed, Arbesman et al. (2010) argued based on an analysis of phonological networks from five languages that these networks share several structural properties that distinguish them from other naturally occurring networks, suggesting some important underlying organisation. Though specific hypotheses were not presented in this work, one of the authors suggested in an earlier analysis of the English lexicon that such properties might arise due to particular learning processes (Vitevitch, 2008).

However, work by Gruenenfelder and Pisoni (2009) found that several of the structural properties discussed above were also found in a random pseudolexicon with the same word lengths as a real English lexicon, but with the phonemes in each word chosen at random. Thus, they argued that these structural properties are simply a by-product of the way phonological networks are defined (by connecting similar strings) and should not be taken as evidence of particular growth processes (or presumably, any other cognitive pressures Arbesman et al. might later have had in mind).

These studies highlight some important methodological issues that need to be resolved if we hope to use network analysis as a tool for cross-linguistic studies. In order to make meaningful comparisons between different languages' networks, we need to determine what constitutes a large or small difference in phonological network statistics by comparing *all* languages to appropriate random baselines. In addition, there are two other factors that have not been explicitly considered in previous studies of phonological networks. First, we don't know how the *size* of a phonological network (number of nodes) affects its statistics. The lexicons in Arbesman et al.'s study ranged from 2500 words (Hawaiian) to 122,000 words (Spanish), yet if the size of the Spanish lexicon had also been 2500 words, it might have yielded quite different statistics. Second, there is a lack of consensus about whether phonological networks should be constructed from *lemmas* or from *all wordforms* including morphological variants, and in some cases, datasets may only be available for one or the other option. Therefore, we need to understand how including or excluding inflectional variants affects the measured statistics of phonological networks.

In this paper, we investigate the questions above, synthesizing arguments from the literature with our own analyses to propose a new method for comparing phonological networks across languages. Using this method, we compare network statistics across eight different languages to appropriate baselines at a range of lexicon sizes. We show that Gruenenfelder and Pisoni's (2009) findings for English extend to the other seven languages we consider, supporting their argument that the small-world properties of phonological networks should not be used as evidence of particular cognitive/growth processes. We also find that network statistics vary with lexicon size within each language, but not always in the same way. These differences provide a first step in investigating the relationship between cross-linguistic variation in language processing and global lexicon structure.

2   Background

The use of network science to study the phonological structure of the lexicon was first proposed by Vitevitch (2008). He and later authors converged on using several standard measures from network science, which we will also employ. These are:

Degree assortativity coefficient   In some networks, nodes tend to connect to other nodes that have similar *degrees* (numbers of neighbours) to their own. The extent to which a network exhibits this property can be quantified using the *degree assortativity coefficient*, which is defined as the Pearson correlation coefficient r of the degrees of the nodes at either end of each edge. So, r lies between -1 (the higher a node's degree is, the lower the degrees of its neighbours) and 1 (nodes connect only to other nodes of the same degree), with $r = 0$ if there is no correlation between the degrees of neighbouring nodes.

Networks with positive degree assortativity are relatively robust. Empirical studies show that in such networks many nodes can be removed without substantially reducing their connectivity (Newman, 2003).

Fraction of nodes in the giant component   Complex networks often have many distinct connected components. Often, a single *giant component* contains a much larger fraction of the nodes than any other component, and this fraction helps characterise the global connectivity of the network.

Average shortest path length (ASPL)   The *shortest path length* between two nodes v and w, which we denote $d(v, w)$, is the minimum number of edges that must be traversed to get from node

v to node w. The ASPL is then the mean of the shortest path lengths between all pairs of nodes, and is given by the equation

$$\text{ASPL} = \sum_{v,w \in V} \frac{d(v, w)}{|V|(|V| - 1)},$$

where V denotes the set of all nodes in the network. Since paths do not exist between mutually disconnected components, there are different ways to compute ASPL for graphs with disconnected components; all values reported in this paper compute the average across all pairs of nodes in the giant component only.

Average clustering coefficient   A node's *clustering coefficient* measures the 'cliquishness' of its neighbourhood, and is defined as the number of edges that exist between its neighbours divided by the number of possible edges between them:

$$C(v) = \frac{2|\{ e_{u,w} \in E : e_{v,u} \in E, e_{v,w} \in E \}|}{k(v)(k(v) - 1)},$$

where E denotes the set of all edges in the network, $e_{x,y}$ denotes an edge between nodes x and y, and $k(x)$ denotes the degree of node x. The clustering coefficient is undefined for nodes with $k < 2$, since the denominator reduces to zero for such nodes. We report the mean clustering coefficient over all nodes in the giant component; nodes with fewer than two neighbours are assigned a coefficient of zero.[1]

A word's clustering coefficient has been found to predict behavioural measures in both lexical access (Chan and Vitevitch, 2009) and adult and child word learning (Goldstein and Vitevitch, 2014; Carlson et al., 2014).

Small-world property   Small world networks (Watts and Strogatz, 1998) are characterized by short ASPL relative to their size and high average clustering coefficients relative to what one would expect from an equivalent *Erdős-Rényi graph*—one with the same number of nodes and edges as the real graph, but where edges are placed randomly between pairs of nodes. A distinctive property of these networks is their easy searchability: it is usually possible to find short paths between nodes in a decentralized fashion using only small quantities of information per node when the network admits

embedding in a suitable space (Kleinberg, 2000; Sarkar et al., 2013). It has been suggested that easy searchability could be relevant for spreading-activation models of lexical processing (Chan and Vitevitch, 2009) and in lexical acquisition (Carlson et al., 2011).

Using the measures above, Vitevitch (2008) analysed a lexicon of English, and Arbesman et al. (2010) extended the analysis to five lexicons representing languages from different language families. They found several characteristics common to these networks. All five lexicons were found to exhibit the small-world property, having similar ASPLs to those expected in comparable Erdős-Rényi graphs, but average clustering coefficients that were several orders of magnitude larger. The phonological networks were also marked by high degree assortativity, with coefficients ranging from 0.56 to 0.76, in contrast to typical values of 0.1 to 0.3 for social networks, and -0.1 to -0.2 for biological and technical networks. The giant components in the phonological networks all contained less than 70% of nodes (in three cases, less than 40%), whereas the giant components of social, biological, and technical networks typically contain 80-90% of nodes. Arbesman et al. suggested that "together, these observed characteristics hint at some deeper organization within language" (2010: 683).

Nevertheless, Arbesman et al. also found some quantitative variation in the phonological network statistics across languages—for example, the Mandarin network had an ASPL almost twice that of the Hawaiian network, a clustering coefficient twice that of the Spanish network, and the fraction of nodes in its giant component was almost twice that of the English network. However, we don't know if these differences are meaningful, since the expected variability of these statistics in phonological networks has not been established. In addition, since the lexicon sizes varied widely across languages, the differences in network statistics may have been due to this variation rather than to more interesting differences between the languages.

Gruenenfelder and Pisoni (2009) started to address these issues by considering a random baseline network for English. They constructed a pseudolexicon by randomly generating phoneme sequences with the same lengths as the words in an English lexicon[2], and found that the phonological network

---

[1]Some researchers instead define the coefficient for such nodes to be one, whilst others exclude such nodes from the average (Schank and Wagner, 2004).

[2]Both the English lexicon and the pseudolexicon were limited to words of only 2 to 5 phonemes in length.

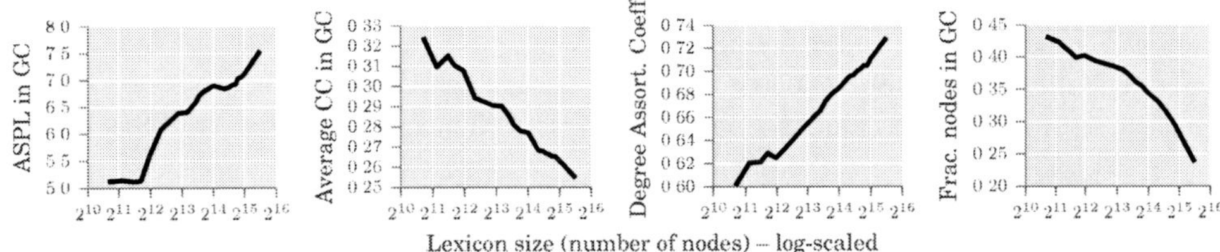

Figure 1: Phonological network statistics of English lemmas, as a function of lexicon size.

of this random pseudolexicon also exhibited the small-world property and a high degree assortativity coefficient. They concluded that these characteristics are likely to occur in any network whose nodes represent random sequences of parts (i.e., phonemes), and whose edges are determined by the overlap of these parts. Thus they argued that high assortative mixing by degree and small-world characteristics should not be taken to indicate a deeper organisational principle in the lexicon.

So, although Gruenenfelder and Pisoni (2009) have analysed some properties of a randomly generated lexicon with the same size, word-lengths, and phoneme inventory as a particular English lexicon, it remains to be seen whether these properties are characteristic of randomly generated lexicons in general, or to what extent they vary across different lexicon sizes, word-length distributions, and phoneme inventory sizes. In the following sections we show that all of these factors affect the statistics of both random and real lexicons; we then propose a more robust method for making cross-linguistic comparisons of phonological networks. While our method is still not enough to draw strong quantitative conclusions in all cases, we are able to shed further light on a number of the claims and questions raised above, and we also discover some cross-linguistic differences in lexicon structure that warrant further investigation.

3 Effect of lexicon size

We begin by asking whether the size of a phonological network may affect its statistics. For this analysis, we use only a single language (English).

3.1 Method

We start with the 44,841 English lemmas in the CELEX database (Baayen et al., 1995), which includes both word frequencies and phonemic transcriptions. We derive from this original lexicon a series of sublexicons of decreasing sizes, by progressively filtering out batches of words with the lowest frequencies. Thresholding a lexicon by frequency simulates drawing a lexicon from a smaller corpus or dictionary, since the more frequently a word is used, the more likely it is to appear in even a small corpus or dictionary. For each (sub)lexicon, we associate each distinct phonological form with a unique node and place edges between pairs of nodes that differ by one phoneme (insertion, deletion, or substitution). To construct the networks and compute their statistics we use the NetworkX Python package (Hagberg et al., 2008).

3.2 Results and discussion

Figure 1 shows the values of four network statistics as a function of lexicon size. All the values fall within the range found across languages by Arbesman et al. (2010). However, all four statistics do vary with lexicon size, suggesting that comparisons between networks should only be made between lexicons of similar size.

One way to attempt such quantitative comparisons across languages could be to subsample from each lexicon in order to obtain lexicons of the same size. However, we don't know if the slopes of these plots will be the same across languages. Consider the hypothetical plot in Figure 2:

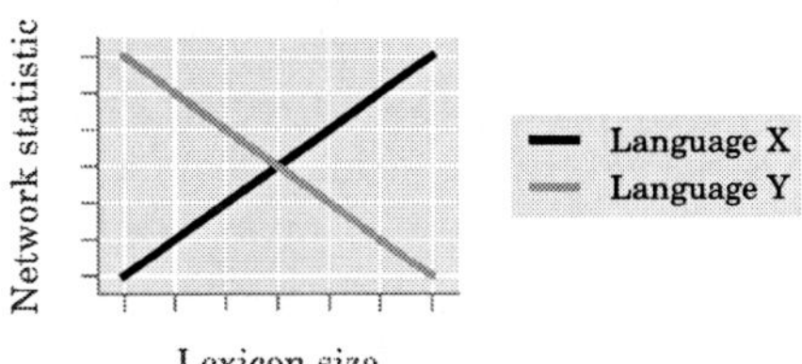

Figure 2: Hypothetical scenario where the value of a phonological network statistic is positively correlated with lexicon size in Language X, but negatively correlated in Language Y.

In this case, controlling for lexicon size is not enough, since if we choose a small lexicon size then Language X will have a smaller statistic than Language Y, whereas if we choose a large size then the opposite holds. This observation motivates us to compare statistics across a *range* of sizes rather than using point estimates as in previous work.

Indeed, an established technique for comparing the properties of real networks against random baselines is to plot the value of a network statistic as a function of network size, and compare the slope obtained for random networks against the trend observed in real networks (Albert and Barabási, 2002). However, care must be taken in choosing appropriate random baselines for phonological networks, due to the issues described next.

4 Effects of word-length distribution and phoneme inventory size

Recently, Stella and Brede (2015) pointed out that due to the way in which nodes and edges are typically defined in phonological networks, the statistics of such networks are highly sensitive to the distribution of word lengths in the lexicon, and to a lesser extent, the size of the phoneme inventory. Stella and Brede considered the set of all possible 'words' (i.e. possible sequences of phonemes) that could be formed using a given phoneme inventory, and noted that the number of possible n-phoneme words scales exponentially with n, while the number of possible neighbours of an n-phoneme word scales linearly with n. Hence, if we randomly sample a pair of words from the set of all possible words, then the shorter their lengths are, the more likely it is that the sampled words will be neighbours. Thus, lexicons with a higher proportion of short words will tend to be more densely connected, regardless of any other phonological properties. Also, since the number of possible n-phoneme words scales faster with the size of the phoneme inventory than does the number of possible neighbours of an n-phoneme word, we expect the size of the phoneme inventory to affect the connectivity of a phonological network, albeit by a smaller factor than the distribution of word lengths.

Unlike lexicon size, the word-length distribution and phoneme inventory size are inherent properties of a language, so these confounds make it difficult to directly compare network statistics across languages, even after controlling for lexicon size. In making cross-linguistic comparisions, we would like to be able to identify differences between languages beyond the fact that their lexicons have different word length distributions.

Therefore, rather than directly comparing the statistics of real lexicons across languages, we propose to generate separate pseudolexicons for each language that match the word-length distribution and phoneme inventory size of that language. We can then examine the differences between these pseudolexicons and the real lexicons over a range of lexicon sizes, and compare these differences across languages. Using this method we can better evaluate some of the claims made by previous authors and reveal some previously undetected variation in network structure across languages.

5 Cross-linguistic comparison

5.1 Data and method

We analyse phonological networks from eight different languages: English, Dutch, German, French, Spanish, Portuguese, Polish, and Basque. Where possible, we have obtained for each language a lexicon consisting only of lemmas, and another with separate entries for phonemically distinct inflectional variants.[3] Each lexical entry consists of a phonemically transcribed word and a corpus-derived estimate of its frequency. The sources and sizes of the lexicons are listed in Table 1. From each of these original lexicons, we derive a series of sublexicons of decreasing sizes, by progressively filtering out batches of low-frequency words.

For each real lexicon and derived sublexicon, we generate 20 random pseudolexicons with the same size, phoneme inventory size, and word-length distribution[4]. For each lexicon size in each language, we compute the mean and standard deviation of each statistic across the 20 pseudolexicons, as well as the statistics for the comparable real (sub)lexicon.

5.2 Results and discussion

We first consider how the average word length varies across our sample lexicons. Figure 3 shows that average word lengths vary with lexicon size (tending to increase as more infrequent words are included in the lexicon), as well as across languages (average word lengths in English and French are substantially shorter than in Spanish).

---

[3]We were unable to obtain phonemic transcriptions for Portuguese inflected wordforms, or reliable frequencies for Spanish lemmas.

[4]Specifically, we replicate Gruenenfelder and Pisoni's procedure for generating their 'Word Length Only' lexicon, except that we match the entire word-length distribution, not just the number of two-, three-, four-, and five-segment words.

Language	Lexicon Type	Size	Source of pronunciations	Source of frequencies
English	Lemmas	44,841	CELEX (Baayen et al., 1995)	CELEX
	All wordforms	87,263	CELEX	CELEX
Dutch	Lemmas	117,048	CELEX	CELEX
	All wordforms	300,090	CELEX	CELEX
German	Lemmas	50,481	CELEX	CELEX
	All wordforms	353,679	CELEX	CELEX
French	Lemmas	43,361	Lexique (New et al., 2001)	Lexique
	All wordforms	71,334	Lexique	Lexique
Portuguese	Lemmas	18,656	Porlex (Gomes and Castro, 2003)	CORLEX (Bacelar do Nascimento, 2003)
Spanish	All wordforms	42,461	CALLHOME (Garrett et al., 1996)	CALLHOME
Polish	Lemmas	6024	GlobalPhone (Schultz, 2002)	SUBTLEX-PL (Mandera et al., 2014)
	All wordforms	25,623	GlobalPhone	SUBTLEX-PL
Basque	Lemmas	9102	E-hitz (Perea et al., 2006)	E-hitz
	All wordforms	99,491	E-hitz	E-hitz

Table 1: Sources and sizes of lexicons. Sizes refer to the number of distinct *phonological* forms: sets of words which have distinct spellings and/or senses but the same phonemic transcription are conflated into a single phonological wordform.

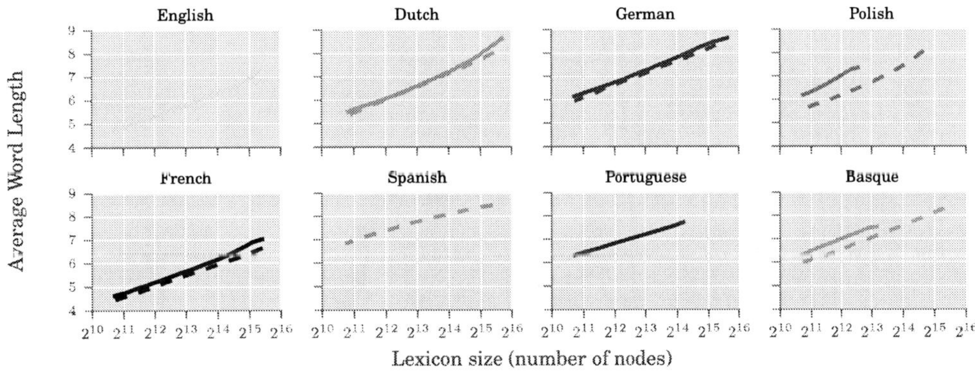

Figure 3: Average word length as a function of lexicon size. Solid lines are for lemmas; dashed lines are for all wordforms.

Results for the four measures of network structure and connectivity defined above are presented in Figure 4. We first discuss the similarities between different languages, focusing on the claims made by previous researchers; we then discuss some cross-linguistic differences.

5.2.1 Cross-linguistic similarities

As noted by Arbesman et al. (2010), there are some striking similarities across the languages, especially relative to other types of networks. To test for the small-word behaviour that Arbesman et al. found in their networks, we computed estimates of the ASPLs and clustering coefficients of Erdős-Rényi graphs matched to the giant components of each of our lexicons.[5] The ASPLs all ranged from 4 to 6,

which is somewhat smaller than in our real lexicons, but considered similar according to the conventions used to test for the small-world property (Watts and Strogatz, 1998). The clustering coefficients of the Erdős-Rényi graphs ranged between 0.0003 and 0.03, orders of magnitude smaller than the values of 0.17 to 0.37 for our real lexicons; again, according to the usual conventions (Watts and Strogatz, 1998), these results indicate that all of our real lexicons exhibit the small-world property.

However, all of our pseudolexicons are also small-world networks. This finding extends Gruenenfelder and Pisoni's result for English and sup-

---

[5]Following Gruenenfelder and Pisoni (2009), we estimate the ASPL of an Erdős-Rényi graph using the formula $ASPL_{ER} \approx \frac{ln(|V|)}{ln(\langle k \rangle)}$, where $\langle k \rangle = \frac{2|E|}{|V|}$ is the graph's average degree. The average clustering coefficient of an Erdős-Rényi graph is given by $C_{ER} = \frac{\langle k \rangle}{|V|}$ (Albert and Barabási, 2002).

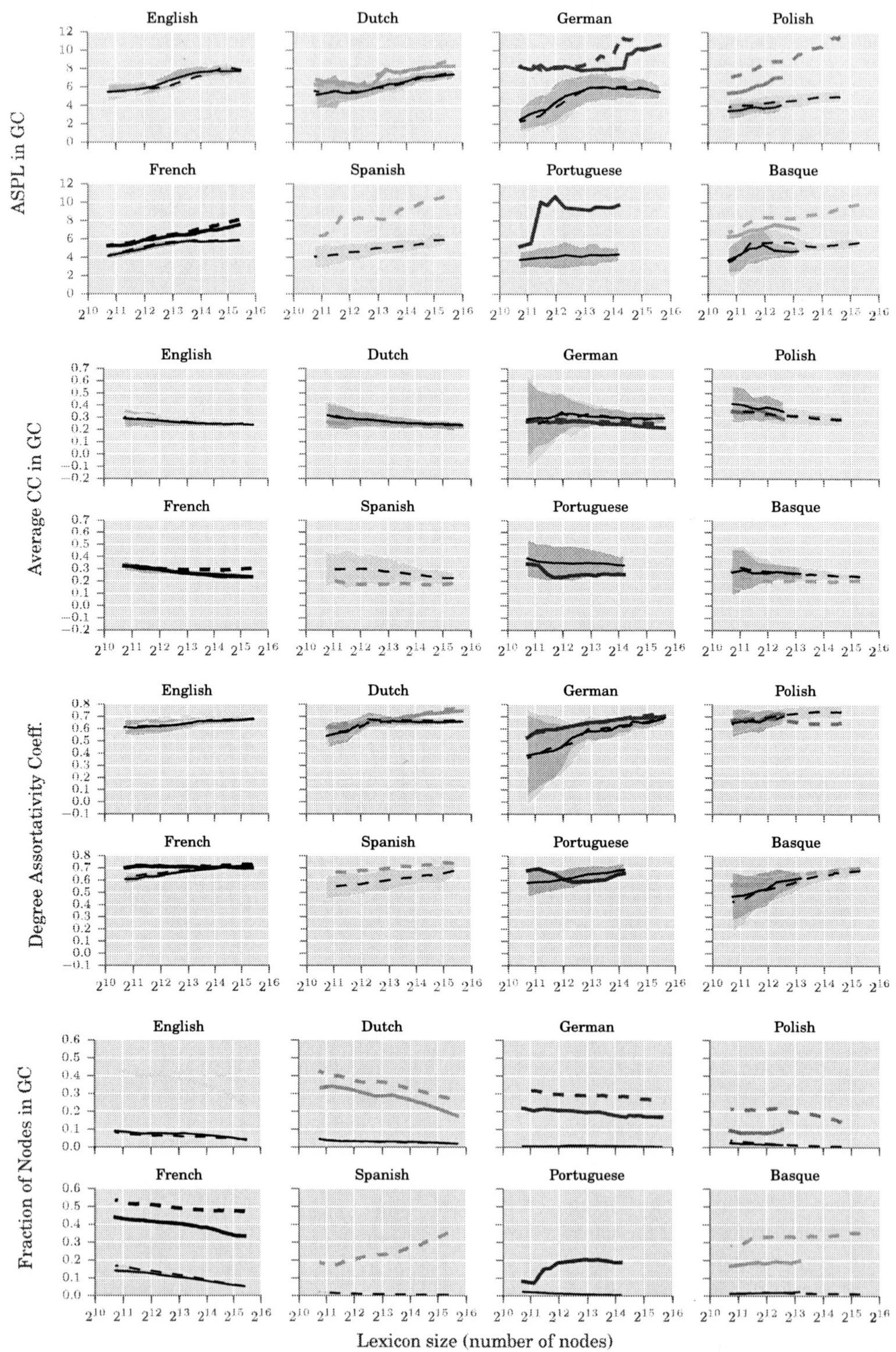

Figure 4: Thick, coloured lines show network statistics as a function of lexicon size in real lexicons. Thin, black lines show network statistics averaged across twenty random pseudolexicons, and the shaded regions indicate $\pm\,2$ standard deviations. Solid lines are for lemmas; dashed lines are for all wordforms.

ports their claim that the small-world properties arise naturally from the conventional definition of these networks, rather than suggesting a "deeper organization" as suggested by Arbesman et al.

Our results for degree assortativity also support Gruenenfelder and Pisoni's argument that substantial assortative mixing by degree can be expected in networks which are based on the overlap of parts randomly combined into wholes. The degree assortativity coefficients for all of the real lexicons lie between 0.5 and 0.8, which is higher than the values typically observed in social, biological, and technical networks. But again, the coefficients of the pseudolexicons are similar to those of the real lexicons, making these values less remarkable.

The final generalisation that Arbesman et al. made was that all the languages they examined had a smaller proportion of nodes in their giant components than the 80-90% that is typically observed in complex networks. We find the same, but as noted in Gruenenfelder and Pisoni's analysis of English, the fraction of nodes in the giant component of the real lexicons is actually much *greater* than in their matched pseudolexicons. This is not surprising, as the real lexicons have phonotactic constraints which would tend to make words more similar to one another than if phonemes were sampled at random. So again, the claim of a "deeper organisation" seems premature.

5.2.2 Cross-linguistic differences

The search for interesting universal properties is only half the motivation for making such cross-linguistic comparisons. Ideally, we also want to identify *differences* that might correlate with different behavioural patterns across languages. Two of our statistics don't reveal much on this point: average clustering coefficient (discussed above) and degree assortativity. There are some quantitative differences in degree assortativity between languages, but they seem mainly driven by differences in the word length distributions, since the differences across real lexicons pattern the same as the differences across pseudolexicons.

However, our results do reveal some more interesting cross-linguistic differences in the way the other two statistics vary across lexicon sizes and lexicon types (lemmas vs all wordforms).

Fraction of nodes in the giant component Some of the cross-linguistic differences in this statistic again seem driven by differences in word-

length distribution, since there are large cross-linguistic differences for this statistic even in the pseudolexicons. For example, pseudolexicons matched to French or English tend to contain around 10% of the nodes, whereas pseudolexicons matched to German or Spanish are an order of magnitude smaller. However, word lengths cannot account for all of the differences in giant component size across languages, because the magnitude of the difference in values between the real lexicons and their corresponding pseudolexicons also varies across languages. For example, the giant component sizes of the pseudolexicons matched to Basque and Polish lemmas are reasonably similar, but the giant component sizes of the real Basque lemma lexicons are twice as large as those of the real Polish lemma lexicons.

In most of the languages the fraction of nodes in the giant component tends to decrease with increasing lexicon size (i.e. as more infrequent words are included in the lexicon), which suggests that less frequent words are phonotactically unusual. In contrast, in Spanish, Portuguese, and to a lesser extent Basque, the less frequent words are more likely to be a part of the giant component, suggesting that they are more similar to other words in the language. These different trends do not appear to be solely a consequence of differences in word-length distributions, since in the pseudolexicons matched to Spanish, Portuguese, and Basque, the fraction of nodes in the giant component does tend to decrease slightly with increasing lexicon size. This finding could be important for understanding cross-linguistic differences in language processing, since both word frequency and phonotactic probability are thought to affect both recognition and production of words (Luce and Pisoni, 1998; Vitevitch and Sommers, 2003).

These results also provide a real example of the behaviour hypothesized in Figure 2, underscoring the danger of using a single lexicon size to compare phonological network statistics across languages: if we compared lexicons containing around 10,000 words, we might conclude that Dutch wordforms were more densely connected than Spanish wordforms; whereas if we compared lexicons containing 30,000 words, their giant component sizes would support the opposite conclusion.

Average shortest path length Arbesman et al. noted that the ASPL for Mandarin was double that of Hawaiian, and raised the question of whether this quantitative difference was significant. Our results suggest not: the sizes of the two lexicons they used (Hawaiian: 2578, Mandarin: 30,086) are similar to the smallest and largest sizes of the Polish and Spanish wordform lexicons used in our study (Polish: 1694 and 25,623, Spanish: 1694 and 42,461), and we see that for Polish and Spanish wordforms, as well as for Portuguese lemmas, the largest lexicon has almost twice the ASPL as the smallest one.

On the other hand, there do seem to be some meaningful differences in ASPL across languages. For the English lexicons, the ASPLs in the giant component are barely distinguishable from those of the corresponding random pseudolexicons. However, the values for Spanish and Polish lexicons are consistently higher than those of their respective pseudolexicons; while for German, Portuguese, and Basque, the differences between real and random lexicons are less stable across different lexicon sizes.

It should be noted that while the sizes of the pseudolexicons are matched to those of the real lexicons, the sizes of their giant components are not. Since the giant components of random pseudolexicons tend to be considerably smaller than those of real lexicons, it is unsurprising that their ASPLs tend also to be smaller. Nevertheless, our results show that the ASPL in the giant component of a phonological network is not a simple function of the giant component's size. Recall that the difference between the size of the giant component in the real lexicons and the size of the giant component in the corresponding random lexicons is smaller for Polish than for English or French. Hence, all else being equal, we would expect the difference in the ASPLs of real and random lexicons to be smaller for Polish too—but the ASPLs in the Polish giant components are actually larger, relative to the corresponding pseudolexicons, than those of English or French.

Polish also behaves differently from some of the other languages with respect to its morphology. In Polish, the magnitude of the difference in ASPL between real and random lexicons is greater when morphological variants are included than when the lexicons are restricted to lemmas, but this is not the case for English, Dutch, or French.

6 Conclusion

This paper has argued that, when making comparisons between phonological networks, researchers must consider that network statistics are affected by lexicon size, phoneme inventory size, the distribution of word lengths, and whether morphological variants are included or not. Since it is not possible to directly control for all of these in cross-linguistic comparisons, we have proposed that such comparisons need to be made indirectly, by looking at how each language's phonological network differs from a matched pseudolexicon across a range of lexicon sizes, and then comparing these differences across languages. While this approach doesn't permit simple comparisons of single numbers, nevertheless it can lead to insights regarding proposed universal properties as well as cross-linguistic differences.

In particular, our analysis of eight languages provides further support to Gruenenfelder and Pisoni's (2009) claim that the small-world and other properties discussed by Vitevitch (2008) and Arbesman et al. (2010) are a consequence of how phonological networks are defined, and do not necessarily reflect particular growth processes or cognitive pressures. At the same time, we did identify several differences in the behaviour of network statistics across different languages, which could provide an explanation for previously identified differences in language processing. We hope that our results will inspire further work to investigate these potential connections and to extend our analyses to additional languages.

7 Acknowledgements

This work was supported in part by a James S. McDonnell Foundation Scholar Award (#220020374) to Sharon Goldwater, and by the EPSRC Centre for Doctoral Training in Data Science, funded by the UK Engineering and Physical Sciences Research Council (grant EP/L016427/1) and the University of Edinburgh.

References

Réka Albert and Albert-László Barabási. 2002. Statistical mechanics of complex networks. *Reviews of Modern Physics*, 74(1):47.

Samuel Arbesman, Steven H. Strogatz, and Michael S. Vitevitch. 2010. The structure of phonological networks across multiple languages. *International Journal of Bifurcation and Chaos*, 20(03):679–685.

R Harald Baayen, Richard Piepenbrock, and Léon Gulikers. 1995. CELEX2, LDC96L14. *Web download, Linguistic Data Consortium, Philadelpha, PA*.

Maria Fernanda Bacelar do Nascimento. 2003. Um novo léxico de frequências do Português. *Revista Portuguesa de Filologia*, 25:341–358.

Matthew T Carlson, Max Bane, and Morgan Sonderegger. 2011. Global properties of the phonological networks in child and child-directed speech. In N Danis, K Mesh, and H Sung, editors, *Proceedings of the 35th Boston University Conference on Language Development*, volume 1, pages 97–109. Cascadilla Press Somerville, MA.

Matthew T Carlson, Morgan Sonderegger, and Max Bane. 2014. How children explore the phonological network in child-directed speech: A survival analysis of childrens first word productions. *Journal of Memory and Language*, 75:159–180.

Kit Ying Chan and Michael S Vitevitch. 2009. The influence of the phonological neighborhood clustering coefficient on spoken word recognition. *Journal of Experimental Psychology: Human Perception and Performance*, 35(6):1934.

Susan Garrett, Tom Morton, and Cynthia McLemore. 1996. CALLHOME Spanish lexicon, LDC96L16. *Web download, Linguistic Data Consortium, Philadelpha, PA*.

Rutherford Goldstein and Michael S Vitevitch. 2014. The influence of clustering coefficient on word-learning: how groups of similar sounding words facilitate acquisition. *Frontiers in Psychology*, 5.

Inês Gomes and São Luís Castro. 2003. Porlex, a lexical database in European Portuguese. *Psychologica*, 32:91–108.

Thomas M Gruenenfelder and David B Pisoni. 2009. The lexical restructuring hypothesis and graph theoretic analyses of networks based on random lexicons. *Journal of Speech, Language, and Hearing Research*, 52(3):596–609.

Aric A Hagberg, Daniel A Schult, and Pieter J Swart. 2008. Exploring network structure, dynamics, and function using NetworkX. In *Proceedings of the 7th Python in Science Conference (SciPy2008)*, pages 11–15, Pasadena, CA USA, August.

Trevor A Harley and Helen E Bown. 1998. What causes a tip-of-the-tongue state? evidence for lexical neighbourhood effects in speech production. *British Journal of Psychology*, 89(1):151–174.

Jon Kleinberg. 2000. The small-world phenomenon: An algorithmic perspective. In *Proceedings of the Thirty-Second Annual ACM Symposium on Theory of Computing*, pages 163–170. ACM.

Paul A Luce and David B Pisoni. 1998. Recognizing spoken words: The neighborhood activation model. *Ear and Hearing*, 19(1):1.

Paweł Mandera, Emmanuel Keuleers, Zofia Wodniecka, and Marc Brysbaert. 2014. Subtlex-pl: subtitle-based word frequency estimates for Polish. *Behavior Research Methods*, 47(2):471–483.

Boris New, Christophe Pallier, Ludovic Ferrand, and Rafael Matos. 2001. A lexical database for contemporary french on internet: Lexique. *Année Psychologique*, 101(3):447–462.

Mark EJ Newman. 2003. Mixing patterns in networks. *Physical Review E*, 67(2):026126.

Manuel Perea, Miriam Urkia, Colin J Davis, Ainhoa Agirre, Edurne Laseka, and Manuel Carreiras. 2006. E-hitz: A word frequency list and a program for deriving psycholinguistic statistics in an agglutinative language (Basque). *Behavior Research Methods*, 38(4):610–615.

Rik Sarkar, Xianjin Zhu, and Jie Gao. 2013. Distributed and compact routing using spatial distributions in wireless sensor networks. *ACM Transactions on Sensor Networks (TOSN)*, 9(3):32.

Thomas Schank and Dorothea Wagner. 2004. *Approximating clustering-coefficient and transitivity*. Universität Karlsruhe, Fakultät für Informatik.

Tanja Schultz. 2002. Globalphone: a multilingual speech and text database developed at karlsruhe university. In *INTERSPEECH*.

Massimo Stella and Markus Brede. 2015. Patterns in the English language: phonological networks, percolation and assembly models. *Journal of Statistical Mechanics: Theory and Experiment*, 2015(5):P05006.

Michael S Vitevitch and Eva Rodríguez. 2005. Neighborhood density effects in spoken word recognition in Spanish. *Journal of Multilingual Communication Disorders*, 3(1):64–73.

Michael S Vitevitch and Mitchell S Sommers. 2003. The facilitative influence of phonological similarity and neighborhood frequency in speech production in younger and older adults. *Memory & Cognition*, 31(4):491–504.

Michael S Vitevitch and Melissa K Stamer. 2006. The curious case of competition in Spanish speech production. *Language and Cognitive Processes*, 21(6):760–770.

Michael S Vitevitch. 2002. The influence of phonological similarity neighborhoods on speech production. *Journal of Experimental Psychology: Learning, Memory, and Cognition*, 28(4):735.

Michael S Vitevitch. 2008. What can graph theory tell us about word learning and lexical retrieval? *Journal of Speech, Language, and Hearing Research*, 51(2):408–422.

Duncan J Watts and Steven H Strogatz. 1998. Collective dynamics of 'small-world' networks. *Nature*, 393(6684):440–442.

Johannes C Ziegler, Mathilde Muneaux, and Jonathan Grainger. 2003. Neighborhood effects in auditory word recognition: Phonological competition and orthographic facilitation. *Journal of Memory and Language*, 48(4):779–793.

Morphotactics as Tier-Based Strictly Local Dependencies

Alëna Aksënova   Thomas Graf   Sedigheh Moradi

Department of Linguistics
Stony Brook University
Stony Brook, NY 11794, USA
`*mail@thomasgraf.net`
`alena.aksenova@stonybrook.edu,  sedigheh.moradi@stonybrook.edu`

Abstract

It is commonly accepted that morphological dependencies are finite-state in nature. We argue that the upper bound on morphological expressivity is much lower. Drawing on technical results from computational phonology, we show that a variety of morphotactic phenomena are tier-based strictly local and do not fall into weaker subclasses such as the strictly local or strictly piecewise languages. Since the tier-based strictly local languages are learnable in the limit from positive texts, this marks a first important step towards general machine learning algorithms for morphology. Furthermore, the limitation to tier-based strictly local languages explains typological gaps that are puzzling from a purely linguistic perspective.

1   Introduction

Different aspects of language have different levels of complexity. A lot of recent work in phonology (see Graf (2010), Heinz (2011a; 2011b; 2015), Chandlee (2014), Jardine (2015) and references therein) argues that phonological well-formedness conditions are subregular and hence do not require the full power of finite-state automata. This is particularly noteworthy because computational phonology still relies heavily on finite-state methods (Kaplan and Kay, 1994; Frank and Satta, 1998; Riggle, 2004). A similar trend can be observed in computational syntax, where the original characterization as mildly context-sensitive string languages (Huybregts, 1984; Shieber, 1985) is now being reinterpreted in terms of subregular tree languages (Graf, 2012; Graf and Heinz, 2015). Curiously missing from these investigations is morphology.

While linguistic theories sometimes consider morphology a part of syntax, computational morphology recognizes that the weak generative capacity of morphology is much closer to phonology than syntax. Consequently, computational morphology involves largely the same finite-state methods as computational phonology (Koskenniemi, 1983; Karttunen et al., 1992). This raises the question whether morphology, just like phonology, uses only a fraction of the power furnished by these tools. A positive answer would have important repercussions for linguistics as well as natural language processing. The subregular classes identified in computational phonology are learnable in the limit from positive text (Heinz et al., 2012), so a subregular theory of morphology would greatly simplify machine learning while also explaining how morphological dependencies can be acquired by the child from very little input. A subregular model of morphology would also be much more restricted with respect to what processes are predicted to arise in natural languages. It thus provides a much tighter typological fit than the regular languages. In this paper, we argue that the subregular view of morphology is indeed correct, at least for morphotactics.

Morphotactics describes the syntax of morphemes, that is to say, their linear order in the word and the conditions that license their presence or enforce their absence. One can distinguish *surface morphotactics* from *underlying morphotactics*. The former regulates the shape of the pronounced surface strings, whereas the latter is only concerned with the arrangements of the morphemes in the initial representation rather than how said morphemes are realized in specific environments. We only consider underlying morphotactics in this paper.

The following example may clarify the distinction. In German, the past participle of a verb is

Proceedings of the 14th Annual SIGMORPHON Workshop on Computational Research in Phonetics, Phonology, and Morphology, pages 121–130,
Berlin, Germany, August 11, 2016. ©2016 Association for Computational Linguistics

formed via a circumfix. The first part of the circumfix is always the prefix *ge-*, whereas the second part may be the suffix *-en* or *-t* depending on the verb stem. In addition, the suffixes can also occur on their own, e.g. on infinitives or the third person singular form of the verb. Surface morphotactics thus has to ensure that *ge-* always appears with one of these two suffixes, and that the form of the suffix matches the stem. At the same time, it does not need to worry about matching *-en* or *-t* with *ge-* since these forms can occur independently as realizations of different morphemes. Underlying morphotactics, on the other hand, is unaware of the surface realizations and only knows that some abstract prefix *GE-* must always occur with the abstract suffix *-EN*, and the other way round. The fact that *-EN* has a surface realization that is indistinguishable from the infinitival marker, which does not require the prefix *GE-*, is irrelevant for underlying morphotactics. More succinctly: underlying morphotactics regulates the distribution of morphemes, surface morphotactics the distribution of allomorphs.

This paper considers a variety of phenomena — circumfixation, variable affix ordering, unbounded prefixation — and concludes that they all belong to the class of tier-based strictly local languages. We first show that even though many morphotactic dependencies are strictly local, that is not the case for all of them (Sec. 2.1). While some of these outliers are strictly piecewise (Sec. 2.2), tier-based strictly local grammars are needed to handle the full range of data points (Sec. 2.3). This prompts our conjecture that all dependencies that are part of underlying morphotactics stay within the class of tier-based strictly local languages. We then use this hypothesis in Sec. 3 to explain two typological gaps with respect to compounding markers and circumfixation.

2 Subregular Patterns in Morphology

The regular languages are one of the best understood language classes, with many attractive properties. Yet it is often forgotten that this class properly includes many weaker ones (McNaughton and Pappert, 1971), some of which have recently attracted much interest in computational phonology. At the very bottom of the hierarchy one finds strictly local and strictly piecewise languages (Rogers et al., 2010), and a little bit higher up the tier-based strictly local languages (Heinz et al.,

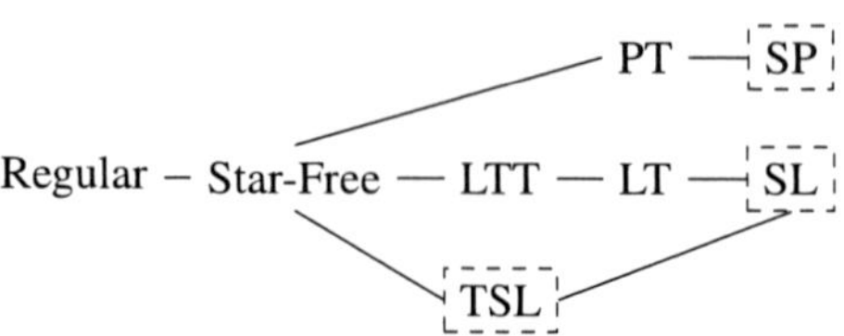

Figure 1: The subregular hierarchy as given in Heinz et al. (2011); language classes in dashed boxes are studied in this paper

2011). The subregular hierarchy includes many other classes (see Fig. 1), but the previous three are noteworthy because they are conceptually simple and efficiently learnable in the limit from positive data (Heinz et al., 2012; Jardine and Heinz, 2016) while also furnishing sufficient power for a wide range of phonological phenomena (Heinz, 2015; Jardine, 2015).

In this section, we investigate the role of strictly local, strictly piecewise and tier-based strictly local patterns in morphotactics. We show that some but not all patterns are strictly local or strictly piecewise, whereas all typologically instantiated patterns seem to fit in the class of tier-based strictly local languages.

2.1 Strictly Local

A string language L over alphabet Σ is *strictly local* (SL) iff there is some $k \in \mathbb{N}$ such that L is generated by a strictly k-local grammar G. Such a grammar consists of a finite set of k-grams, each one of which describes an illicit substring. More precisely, given a string $w \in \Sigma^*$, let $\hat{w}^k :=$ $\rtimes^k w \ltimes^k$ (where $\rtimes, \ltimes \notin \Sigma$) and k-grams$(w) :=$ $\{s \mid s$ is a substring of $\hat{w}^{k-1}$ of length $k\}$. Then G generates string w iff k-grams$(w) \cap G = \emptyset$. That is to say, G generates every string over Σ that does not contain an illicit substring.

Most phonological dependencies can be described in strictly local terms — see Heinz (2015) for numerous examples. Consider for instance the well-known process of *word-final obstruent devoicing* that forces voiced obstruents at the end of the word to be realized as voiceless: moroz [maros] 'frost' in Russian, Ba**d** [bat] 'bath' in German). If one considers phonotactics rather than mappings from underlying representations to surface forms, this is tantamount to a ban against word-final voiced obstruents. Said ban, in turn, is captured by a strictly 2-local grammar G that contains all bigrams of the form $v\ltimes$, with v a voiced obstruent.

The specification of SL grammars can be simplified by applying mappings. In the case at hand, one could define a function f that replaces every voiced obstruent by the designated symbol $\Diamond$ so that the grammar G can be reduced to the single bigram $\Diamond \ltimes$. One has to be careful, though. The SL languages are not closed under relabelings, in fact, every regular language is the image of a strictly 2-local language under some relabeling. However, the directionality of the $\Diamond$-relabeling above is the opposite: first the relabeling is applied, and then the grammar filters out strings in the image of that relabeling. As long as the relabeling is a many-to-one map between alphabets (and thus does not introduce distinctions that weren't already part of the original alphabet), this provably does not increase weak generative capacity for any of the formalisms discussed in this paper.

We make use of such relabelings in the following sections in order to convert natural language patterns into more easily described formal languages. For morphotactics, though, this raises the issue how the size of the atomic units should be chosen. One could posit that morphology, just like phonology, treats every phonological segment as a symbol. In that case, stems and morphemes are strings of symbols. Alternatively, one may treat each morpheme, including stems, as an atomic symbol. This is an important decision when it comes to modeling the interactions of morphology and phonology such as phonologically conditioned allomorphy. Fortunately our results are independent of this choice, due to the productive nature of compounding.

To better understand why different representations could in principle affect subregular complexity, note first that whether a stem is represented as a single, atomic symbol or as a sequence of phonological segments seems to determine if prefixes and suffixes might be separated by an unbounded amount of symbols. Consider a circumfix u- -v, where neither part of the affix may occur without the other. A concrete example is the nominalization circumfix ke- -an in Indonesian (Mahdi, 2012; Sneddon, 1996):

(1)   a.   tingii
         high

      b.   ke-   tinggi -an
         NMN- high   -NMN
         'altitude'

If a stem is a single symbol x, then x and uxv are well-formed whereas ux and xv are not due to u- -v being a circumfix whose subparts cannot occur in isolation. This generalization is easily captured by the strictly 3-local grammar $\{\rtimes xv, ux \ltimes\}$. However, if stems are sequences of symbols, then the well-formed patterns are of the form x^+ or ux^+v (since the length of stems is in principle unbounded). The illict strings, on the other hand, are of the form $\rtimes x^+ v$ and $ux^+ \ltimes$. But no strictly local grammar can generate the former patterns without also generating the latter. That is due to the strictly local languages being closed under suffix substitution closure.

Suffix Substitution Closure Language L is SL iff there exists a $k \in \mathbb{N}$ such that for all strings u_1, v_1, u_2, v_2 and any string x of length $k - 1$, if $u_1 x v_1$, $u_2 x v_2 \in L$, then $u_1 x v_2 \in L$.

If there is no upper bound on the length of stems, then we can infer from $x^k \in L$ and $ux^k v \in L$ that both $x^k v \in L$ and $ux^k \in L$. It seems, then, that circumfixes are strictly local only if each stem is an atomic symbol.

But this line of reasoning erroneously assumes that the circumfix can only apply to individual stems, which ignores the availability of compounding. Returning to Indonesian, we see that its nominalization marker is not restricted to single stems and can also apply to compounds.

(2)   a.   maha siswa
         big   pupil
         'student'

      b.   ke-   maha siswa -an
         NMN- big   pupil -NMN
         'student affairs'

Compounding is an unbounded process, so even if each stem is mapped to a single symbol x, one ends up with the same patterns as with the segmental mapping approach: x^+ and ux^+v are well-formed, while ux^+ and x^+v are ill-formed. Since the choice of representation does not affect the subregular complexity results, we opt for the segmental mapping, which does not require us to use compounding in all our natural language data points.

The details of the segmental mapping are as follows: within a stem, all segments are replaced by some distinguished symbol. We choose x for this purpose. All morphemes, on the other hand, are replaced by single symbols. Symbols are chosen to maximize clarity of exposition, so that we sometimes assign each morpheme a unique symbol and sometimes map irrelevant morphemes to a randomly chosen filler symbol. For some linguistic phenomena we follow linguistic convention in assuming that the underlying representations contain additional distinguished symbols to mark the edges of the stem — this will be mentioned explicitly for all relevant cases.

The preceding discussion yielded as a nice side-result that circumfixation is not SL unless each part of the circumfix can also occur on its own. Few circumfixes display that kind of freedom, wherefore not all aspects of morphotactics are SL. However, large swaths of morphology still are, with a couple of examples from English given below:

(3) a. un- do
         a- xx

     b. break -able
         xxxxx -b

(4) a. punch -ed
         xxxxx -c

     b. put -ε
         xxx -c

Any kind of affix that only consists of one part and whose distribution is determined within a locally bounded domain is part of strictly local morphotactics. Although we did not carry out any rigorous quantitative comparisons, we believe the majority of morphological dependencies to belong to this class.

2.2 Strictly Piecewise

While SL covers a wide range of phenomena, it isn't just circumfixes that require more power. Problems arise whenever a dependency involves both the domain of prefixes and the domain of suffixes — because they can be separated by arbitrarily many symbols — and such configurations are not limited to circumfixes. In most languages the ordering of affixes tends to be fixed, but there are languages in which affixes are ordered relatively freely and do not follow a strict template, thereby creating non-local dependencies.

Let us consider the following data from Swahili:

(5) a. a-   vi-   soma
         SBJ:CL.1- OBJ:CL.8- read
         -vyo
         -REL:CL.8
         u-v-xxxx-c
         'reads'

     b. a-   si-   vyo-   vi-
         SBJ:CL.1- NEG- REL:CL.8- read
         soma
         -OBJ:CL.8
         u-w-c-v-xxxx
         'doesn't read'

This data is taken from Stump (2016). Based on his discussion of *vyo*, the following forms are ungrammatical.

(6) a. * a-   vyo-   vi-
           SBJ:CL.1- REL:CL.8- OBJ:CL.8-
           soma
           read
           u-c-v-xxxx

     b. * a-   vyo-   vi-
           SBJ:CL.1- REL:CL.8- OBJ:CL.8-
           soma -vyo
           read -REL:CL.8
           u-c-v-xxxx-c

     c. * a-   si-   vyo-
           SBJ:CL.1- NEG- REL:CL.8-
           vi-   soma -vyo
           OBJ:CL.8- read REL:CL.8-
           u-w-c-v-xxxx-c

     d. * a-   si-   vi-   soma
           SBJ:CL.1- NEG- OBJ:CL.8- read
           -vyo
           REL:CL.8-
           u-w-v-xxxx-c

Different generalizations can be drawn from these data sets, some of which are more complex than others.

The first generalization states that *vyo* is only licensed if it follows either a segment that is part of a stem or the prefix *si*. This is a strictly 2-local pattern, and it explains both (6a) and (6b). Alternatively, one may conclude that (6b) is ill-formed because there is more than one occurrence of *vyo*. Such a ban against two instances of *vyo* is also supported by the ill-formedness of (6c), which is unexpected under the first generalization. Preventing the presence of two instances of *vyo* is beyond the power of any SL grammar G: if $uvx^{+}c \subset L(G)$

and $uwcvx^+ \subset L(G)$, then $L(G)$ must also contain strings of the form $uwcvx^+c$ (due to suffix substitution closure).

The second generalization is similar to the phonological requirement that no word may contain more than one primary stress, which is *strictly piecewise* (SP; Heinz (2010), Rogers et al. (2010)). SP grammars work exactly the same as SL grammar except that instead of illicit substrings they list illicit subsequences. Given a string w, its set of k-sequences is $k\text{-seqs}(w) := \{s \mid s \text{ is a subsequence of } \hat{w}^{k-1} \text{ of length } k\}$. A strictly k-piecewise grammar G is a finite set of k-grams over $\Sigma \cup \{\rtimes, \ltimes\}$, and the language generated by G is $L := \{w \mid k\text{-seqs}(w) \cap G = \emptyset\}$.

The ban against two occurrences of *vyo* is strictly 2-piecewise — the grammar only need to contain the bigram *vyo vyo*. The intersection of the strictly 2-local and strictly 2-piecewise languages does not contain (6a)–(6c), as desired. But it does contain (6d). Both generalizations miss that even though *vyo* can occur as a prefix and as a suffix, it is a prefix if and only if *si* is present. This kind of conditional positioning cannot be captured by SL grammars, and the culprit is once again suffix substitution closure. But SP grammars by themselves are not sufficient, either.

Suppose we increase the locality rank from 2 to 3 and include *si x vyo* as an illicit subsequence in our SP grammar. This forces *vyo* to be a prefix in the presence of *si*. However, it still incorrectly allows for *vyo* to be a prefix in the absence of *si*. No SP grammar can prevent this outcome. The problem is that any word of the form u *vyo* v x contains only subsequences that also occur in the well-formed u *si vyo* v x. Consequently, any SP grammar that generates the latter also generates the former. It is only in combination with the SL grammar that we can correctly rule out prefix *vyo* without a preceding *si*. Swahili's inflectional morphology thus provides evidence that SL is not enough to handle all aspects of morphotactics and must be supplemented by some mechanism to handle long-distance dependencies, with SP being one option.

But even the combination of SL and SP cannot capture all non-local dependencies. In Swahili, the inability of SP mechanisms to enforce the presence of *si* with prefix *vyo* could be remedied by the strictly local requirement that *vyo* may only occur after *si* or a stem. This elegant interaction of SL and SP is not always possible, however. The most noteworthy case are circumfixes. Consider some arbitrary circumfix *u- -v*. Clearly all subsequences of ux^+ are subsequences of ux^+v, so if the latter is generated by some SP grammar then by definition the former must be, too. The underlying problem is that SP grammars can only enforce the absence of an affix, not its presence. Circumfixes where the presence of one affix entails the presence of the other affix thus are not SP. It seems that we must move higher up the subregular hierarchy in order to accommodate circumfixes, which will also have the welcome side-effect of providing a simpler account for the distribution of Swahili *vyo*.

2.3 Tier-Based Strictly Local

As pointed out in the previous section, the Swahili pattern isn't too dissimilar from the phonological requirement that no word has more than one primary stress. However, the distribution of primary stress is more specific than that: every phonological word has exactly one primary stress. Ensuring the presence of at least one primary stress is beyond the capabilities of SP grammars — once again this holds because every subsequence of an ill-formed word without primary stress is also a subsequence of the well-formed counterpart with exactly one primary stress. A better model for primary stress assignment is furnished by *tier-based strictly local* (TSL; Heinz et al. (2011)) grammars, which also happen to be powerful enough for circumfixation.

A TSL grammar is an SL grammar that operates over a *tier*, a specific substructure of the string. Given a tier-alphabet $T \subseteq \Sigma$, let E_T be a mapping that erases all symbols in a string that do not belong to T. First, $E_T(\varepsilon) = \varepsilon$. Then for $a \in \Sigma$ and $w \in \Sigma^*$,

$$E_T(aw) := \begin{cases} a \cdot E_T(w) & \text{if } a \in T \\ E_T(w) & \text{otherwise} \end{cases}$$

The T-tier of a string w is its image under E_T. A tier-based strictly k-local grammar G is a pair $\langle K, T \rangle$ where K is a strictly k-local grammar over tier-alphabet T. The grammar generates the language $L(G) := \{w \mid E_T(w) \in L(K)\}$. Note that every SL language is a TSL language with $T = \Sigma$.

The distribution of primary stress is tier-based strictly 2-local. Assuming that primary stress is indicated as some diacritic on symbols, the tier-alphabet T contains all symbols with this diacritic.

This is tantamount to projecting a tier that only contains segments with primary stress. The grammar then contains the bigram ⋊⋉ to block words with an empty primary stress tier, i.e. words that contain no primary stress. In addition, every bigram uv for $u, v \in T$ is added to rule out words with more than one primary stress. The requirement of exactly one primary stress per word thus boils down to having exactly one segment on the primary stress tier, which is a strictly local dependency over that tier.

The Swahili pattern from the previous section can also be analyzed as tier-based strictly local, and the same is true for circumfixation. For Swahili we project a tier that contains only the affix *vyo*, and we do not allow more than one segment on this tier. As a result, *vyo* occurs at most once per word. To ensure that *vyo* is a prefix whenever *si* is present, we furthermore postulate a marker # that indicates the edges of the stem. The projected tier then includes all instances of *vyo*, *si* and the marker # (of which there are exactly two). On this tier, the 4-gram *si##vyo* correctly excludes all ill-formed cases of *vyo* as a suffix, whereas ⋊*vyo*## prevents *vyo* from occurring as a prefix in the absence of *si*. Adapting the ban against two instances of *vyo* to this slightly expanded tier is left as an exercise to the reader.

In order to regulate the distribution of circumfixes such as *u- -v*, we have to project a tier that contains only those subparts *u* and *v*. If the affixes can never occur by themselves, then we block ⋊v and u⋉. Removing one of those two bigrams creates asymmetric cases where one of the affixes — but not the other — is sometimes allowed to be present by itself. We also add uu and vv to block strings where the prefix parts outnumber or are outnumbered by the suffix parts of the circumfix. Note that this has the side effect of also prohibiting unbounded circumfixation, a point we return to in Sec. 3.2.

At this point, we can safely say that natural language morphotactics is at least TSL (barring the discovery of any intermediate classes between SL and TSL, or SP and TSL). SL is sufficiently powerful for large parts of morphology, but any kind of dependency that involves both prefixes and suffixes is likely not SL. Some patterns that are not SL are SP, but these also turn out to be TSL. To the best of our knowledge, there are no morphological dependencies that are SP but not TSL (even

though the two language classes are incomparable). We thus put forward the following conjecture:

Subregular Morphotactics All morphotactic dependencies are tier-based strictly local.

As any universal claim about the real world, our conjecture cannot be proved conclusively — the fact that no counterexamples have been encountered does not guarantee that counterexamples will never be encountered. But there are additional reasons to consider TSL a better fit for morphotactics than one of the more powerful classes.

Moving beyond TSL in the subregular hierarchy would take us into the class of star-free languages, which are equivalent to the string sets definable in first-order logic with the transitive closure of the successor relation. As mentioned before, every language that is generated by a tier-based strictly k-local grammar can be identified in the limit from positive text, provided the learner knows the value of k. The class of star-free languages, on the other hand, is not learnable in the limit from positive text. It also makes largely incorrect typological predictions: Unlike TSL, the class of star-free languages is closed under union and relative complement. But the union or relative complement of two morphotactic systems attested in natural languages rarely yields linguistically plausible morphotactics. Similarly, it is trivial to write first-order formulas for highly unnatural patterns, e.g. that every word containing two instances of a but less than three bs must contain no substring of the form cd^+c. These points show that moving from TSL to star-free means losing essential properties of natural language morphotactics.

Future work may of course identify more adequate classes in the vicinity of TSL. Given our current, more limited knowledge of the subregular hierarchy, however, the strongest empirically defensible stance is that tier-based strict locality is both sufficient and necessary for natural language morphotactics.

3   Beyond Tier-Based Strictly Local?

If the subregular hypothesis is correct, then no morphological pattern may exceed the computational power furnished by tier-based strictly local grammars. In particular, whenever the combination of two attested TSL patterns is not TSL, that combination should not be attested. The subregular hypothesis thus provides a principled explanation for typological gaps. In this section we consider two such cases related to compounding markers and the limits of circumfixation.

3.1 Case Study 1: Compounding Markers

Compounding describes the combination of two or more stems to form a compound lexeme, where the stems may belong to different categories. Languages differ with respect to whether compounding is (at least sometimes) explicitly marked. In the following we exhibit two TSL compounding patterns from Turkish and Russian whose combination is not typologically attested. We then explain why this combined pattern is not TSL, deriving the otherwise puzzling typological gap.

Turkish possessive compounds (see Aslan and Altan (1998) for a detailed description) obey the general pattern *stem-stem$^+$-o*, where *o* stands for the compounding marker *-sı*.

(7)   a. bahçe kapı -sı
           garden gate -COMP
           xxxxx-xxxx-o

           'garden gate'

    b. türk   kahve -sı
          turkish coffee -COMP
          xxxx-xxxxx-o

          'Turkish coffee'

    c. türk   bahçe kapı -sı   (*-sı)
          turkish garden gate -COMP (*-COMP)
          xxxx-xxxxx-xxxx-o(-*o)

          'Turkish garden gate'

The compounding marker is added when two stems are combined. Addition of further stems does not increase the number of compounding markers, it is always a single marker for the whole word. The resulting pattern *stem-(stem$^+$-o)* is tier-based strictly 2-local under the assumption that a designated symbol occurs between stems, say □. For then we can project a tier that contains only □ and *o*, with the only illicit bigrams on this tier being ⋊*o*, *o*□, and □⋉.

Russian compounding, on the other hand, follows the pattern *(stem-o)*-stem*, which means that the addition of a new stem to the compound requires the appearance of the compounding marker *-o-* between the stems:

(8)   a. vod -o-   voz
          water -COMP- carry
          xxx-o-xxx

          'water-carrier'

    b. vod -o- voz -o- voz
          water -COMP- carry -COMP- carry
          xxx-o-xxx-o-xxx

          'carrier of water-carriers'

Assuming once again the presence of the special symbol # — which marked the edges of stems in the previous section — we can show this pattern to also be tier-based strictly 2-local. In this case, the illicit bigrams are ##, *oo*, ⋊*o*, and *o*⋉. Observe that we can remove the first one of these bigrams to allow for cases where the compounding marker is optional.

One may wonder now whether it is possible for natural languages to display a combination of the compounding patterns seen with Russian and Turkish. From a linguistic perspective, the expected answer is yes. If compounding can be marked by a suffix as in Turkish, and compounding can introduce a marker with each step as in Russian, then it should be possible to introduce a suffix with each compounding step. But to the best of our knowledge, no language instantiates this system. From a computational perspective, on the other hand, this typological gap is expected because the described system is not TSL — as a matter of fact, it isn't even regular.

A language L that suffixes a marker to a compound with each compounding step would produce compounds where the number of compound markers is proportional to the number of stems. Let h be a map that replaces all stems by s, all compound markers by o, and all other material by some other symbol. Intersecting $h(L)$ with the regular language s^+o^+ yields the language $s^m o^n$, $m > n$. This string set is easily shown to be context-free (e.g. via the Myhill-Nerode theorem), and since regular languages are closed under homomorphisms and intersection, it follows that L cannot be regular. But every TSL language is regular, so the combination of Russian and Turkish outlined above is not TSL. The absence of this compounding pattern in the typology of natural languages thus lends further support to our conjecture that natural language morphotactics is limited to TSL dependencies.

3.2 Case Study 2: Unbounded Affixation

Circumfixation already played an important role in motivating TSL as a reasonable lower bound on how much power is required for natural language morphotactics. We now show that just like compounding markers, circumfixation also suggests that TSL marks the upper bound on required expressivity. In particular, unbounded affixation is widely attested across languages, whereas unbounded circumfixation is not.

A number of languages allow some of their affixes to occur multiple times. For instance, the Russian temporal prefix *posle-* can appear iteratively in the beginning of a word like *zavtra* 'tomorrow'.

(9)   a. posle- zavtra
         AFTER- tomorrow
         a-xxxxxx

         'the day after tomorrow'

      b. posle- posle- zavtra
         AFTER- AFTER- tomorrow
         a-a-xxxxx

         'the day after the day after tomorrow'

The very same pattern is also found in German, with *morgen* 'tomorrow', *über-morgen* 'the day after tomorrow', *über-über-morgen* 'the day after the day after tomorrow', and so on. German also has the pattern *ur-groß-vater*, *ur-ur-groß-vater*, which is the analog of English *great grandfather*, *great great grandfather* and its iterations (various linguistic diagnostics show that these are morphological words rather than phrases). Note that in all those cases it is impossible to insert other prefixes between the iterated prefix: **ur-groß-ur-ur-groß-vater*. In sum, some affixes can be freely iterated as long as no other affixes intervene.

These patterns are all TSL by virtue of being strictly 2-local. We illustrate this claim with German. We ignore the problem of how *groß* can be restricted to occur only with specific stems (if stems are atomic symbols, this is trivial, otherwise it requires a strictly k-local grammar over the string of phonological segments where k is large enough to contain both *groß* and the relevant stems). We also assume, as before, that there is some marker $\#$ that marks the edges of stems. Then to ensure that the relevant strings of prefixes follow the pattern *ur*groß\#*, the sequences *großur*, *großgroß*, and *ur\#* are marked as illicit. Unbounded prefixation thus stays within the class of TSL dependencies.

An interesting counterpart to Russian and German is Ilocano (Galvez Rubino, 1998), which uses the circumfix *ka- -an* with a function similar to *posle* and *über*.

(10) a. bigat
         morning
         xxxxx

         'morning'

      b. ka-   bigat   -an
         NEXT- morning -NEXT
         a-xxxxx-a$'$

         'the next morning'

Crucially, Ilocano differs from Russian and German in that the circumfix cannot be iterated.

(11) * ka-   ka-   bigat   -an   -an
       NEXT- NEXT- morning -NEXT -NEXT
       a-a-xxxxx-a$'$-a$'$

       'the next morning after the next one'

Given our previous discussion of circumfixation in Sec. 2.3, Ilocano clearly instantiates a tier-based strictly 2-local pattern, too.

As before, there is little linguistic reason why unbounded circumfixation should be blocked. If affixation can be unbounded to construct more and more complex versions of *day after tomorrow*, and *day after tomorrow* can be derived via circumfixation, then one would expect unbounded circumfixation to be a viable option. But once again there is a clear computational reason as to why this does not happen: the corresponding morphotactic system would no longer be TSL.

Let L be some minor variant of Russian where *posle-* is instead a circumfix *pos- -le*. As before we let h be a homomorphism that replaces all stems by s, the two parts of the circumfix by o, and all other material by some distinct symbol. The intersection of $h(L)$ with the regular language o^+so^+ is the context-free string set $o^n so^n$. Therefore L is supra-regular and cannot be tier-based strictly local. Unbounded circumfixation simply cannot be reconciled with the subregular hypothesis.

4   Conclusion

The received view is that all of morphology is easily modeled with finite-state machines (Koskenniemi, 1983; Karttunen et al., 1992). We contend that this view is overly generous and that tighter bounds can be established, at least for specific subparts of morphology. Morphotactics defines the restrictions on the possible orderings of morphological units, and we argued based on data from typologically diverse languages that the power of natural language morphotactics is severely restricted:

Subregular Morphotactics All morphotactic dependencies are tier-based strictly local.

In contrast to regular languages, tier-based strictly local languages are efficiently learnable in the limit from positive text (Heinz et al., 2012; Jardine and Heinz, 2016). Our result thus marks a first step towards provably correct machine learning algorithms for natural language morphology.

Admittedly, morphotactics is just one of several parts of morphology. We put aside allomorphy and only considered the distribution of morphemes in the underlying forms. Even within that narrow area we did not thoroughly explore all facets, for instance infixation and incorporation. Nonetheless our results show that the success of the subregular perspective need not be limited to phonology. At least morphotactics can be insightfully studied through this lens, too. In addition, there has been a lot of progress in extending the subregular hierarchy from languages to transductions (see Chandlee (2014) and references therein), and we are confident that these results will allow us to expand the focus of investigation from morphotactics to morphology at large.

It will also be interesting to see how uniform the complexity bounds are across different modules of morphology. In phonology, suprasegmental dependencies tend to be more complex than segmental ones (Jardine, 2015). Most constructions in this paper involve derivational morphology, but the affix *vyo* in Swahili is related to inflectional morphology and turned out to have a distribution that is neither SL nor SP (although it can be captured with a combination of the two). So both derivational and inflectional morphotactics occupy points in TSL \ (SL ∪ SP). In this regard it is also worth noting that some phonological processes such as tone plateauing belong to SP \ TSL, whereas no morphological dependencies seem to be part of this subclass. We hope to address these and related issues in future work.

References

Erhan Aslan and Asli Altan. 1998. The role of *-(s)ı* in turkish indefinite nominal compounds. *Dil*, 131:57–75.

Jane Chandlee. 2014. *Strictly Local Phonological Processes*. Ph.D. thesis, University of Delaware.

Robert Frank and Giorgio Satta. 1998. Optimality theory and the generative complexity of constraint violability. *Computational Linguistics*, 24:307–315.

Carl R. Galvez Rubino. 1998. *Ilocano: Ilocano-English, English-Ilocano: Dictionary and Phrasebook*. Hippocrene Books Inc., U.S.

Thomas Graf and Jeffrey Heinz. 2015. Commonality in disparity: The computational view of syntax and phonology. Slides of a talk given at GLOW 2015, April 18, Paris, France.

Thomas Graf. 2010. Logics of phonological reasoning. Master's thesis, University of California, Los Angeles.

Thomas Graf. 2012. Locality and the complexity of minimalist derivation tree languages. In Philippe de Groot and Mark-Jan Nederhof, editors, *Formal Grammar 2010/2011*, volume 7395 of *Lecture Notes in Computer Science*, pages 208–227, Heidelberg. Springer.

Jeffrey Heinz, Chetan Rawal, and Herbert G. Tanner. 2011. Tier-based strictly local constraints in phonology. In *Proceedings of the 49th Annual Meeting of the Association for Computational Linguistics*, pages 58–64.

Jeffrey Heinz, Anna Kasprzik, and Timo Kötzing. 2012. Learning with lattice-structure hypothesis spaces. *Theoretical Computer Science*, 457:111–127.

Jeffrey Heinz. 2010. Learning long-distance phonotactics. *Linguistic Inquiry*, 41:623–661.

Jeffrey Heinz. 2011a. Computational phonology — part I: Foundations. *Language and Linguistics Compass*, 5:140–152.

Jeffrey Heinz. 2011b. Computational phonology — part II: Grammars, learning, and the future. *Language and Linguistics Compass*, 5:153–168.

Jeffrey Heinz. 2015. The computational nature of phonological generalizations. Ms., University of Delaware.

M. A. C. Huybregts. 1984. The weak adequacy of context-free phrase structure grammar. In Ger J. de Haan, Mieke Trommelen, and Wim Zonneveld, editors, *Van Periferie naar Kern*, pages 81–99. Foris, Dordrecht.

Adam Jardine and Jeffrey Heinz. 2016. Learning tier-based strictly 2-local languages. *Transactions of the ACL*, 4:87–98.

Adam Jardine. 2015. Computationally, tone is different. *Phonology*. to appear.

Ronald M. Kaplan and Martin Kay. 1994. Regular models of phonological rule systems. *Computational Linguistics*, 20(3):331–378.

Lauri Karttunen, Ronald M. Kaplan, and Annie Zaenen. 1992. Two-level morphology with composition. In *COLING'92*, pages 141–148.

Kimmo Koskenniemi. 1983. Two-level morphology: A general computational model for word-form recognition and production. Publication 11, University of Helsinki, Department of General Linguistics, Helsinki.

Waruno Mahdi. 2012. Distinguishing cognate homonyms in Indonesian. *Oceanic Linguistics*, 51(2):402–449.

Robert McNaughton and Seymour Pappert. 1971. *Counter-Free Automata*. MIT Press, Cambridge, MA.

Jason Riggle. 2004. *Generation, Recognition, and Learning in Finite-State Optimality Theory*. Ph.D. thesis, University of California, Los Angeles.

James Rogers, Jeffrey Heinz, Gil Bailey, Matt Edlefsen, Molly Vischer, David Wellcome, and Sean Wibel. 2010. On languages piecewise testable in the strict sense. In Christan Ebert, Gerhard Jäger, and Jens Michaelis, editors, *The Mathematics of Language*, volume 6149 of *Lecture Notes in Artificial Intelligence*, pages 255–265. Springer, Heidelberg.

Stuart M. Shieber. 1985. Evidence against the context-freeness of natural language. *Linguistics and Philosophy*, 8(3):333–345.

James Neil Sneddon. 1996. *Indonesian Comprehensive Grammar*. Routledge, London and New York.

Greg Stump. 2016. Rule composition in an adequate theory of morphotactics. Manuscript, University of Kentucky.

A Multilinear Approach to the Unsupervised Learning of Morphology

Anthony Meyer
Indiana University
antmeyer@indiana.edu

Markus Dickinson
Indiana University
md7@indiana.edu

Abstract

We present a novel approach to the unsupervised learning of morphology. In particular, we use a Multiple Cause Mixture Model (MCMM), a type of autoencoder network consisting of two node layers—hidden and surface—and a matrix of weights connecting hidden nodes to surface nodes. We show that an MCMM shares crucial graphical properties with autosegmental morphology. We argue on the basis of this graphical similarity that our approach is theoretically sound. Experiment results on Hebrew data show that this theoretical soundness bears out in practice.

1 Introduction

It is well-known that Semitic languages pose problems for the unsupervised learning of morphology (ULM). For example, Hebrew morphology exhibits both agglutinative and fusional processes, in addition to non-concatenative root-and-pattern morphology. This diversity in types of morphological processes presents unique challenges not only for unsupervised morphological learning, but for morphological theory in general. Many previous ULM approaches either handle the concatenative parts of the morpholgy (e.g., Goldsmith, 2001; Creutz and Lagus, 2007; Moon et al., 2009; Poon et al., 2009) or, less often, the non-concatenative parts (e.g., Botha and Blunsom, 2013; Elghamry, 2005). We present an approach to clustering morphologically related words that addresses both concatenative and non-concatenative morphology via the same learning mechanism, namely the Multiple Cause Mixture Model (MCMM) (Saund, 1993, 1994). This type of learning has direct connections to autosegmental theories of morphology

(McCarthy, 1981), and at the same time raises questions about the meaning of morphological units (cf. Aronoff, 1994).

Consider the Hebrew verbs $zwkr$[1] ('he remembers') and $mzkir$ ('he reminds'), which share the root $z.k.r$. In neither form does this root appear as a continuous string. Moreover, each form interrupts the root in a different way. Many ULM algorithms ignore non-concatenative processes, assuming word formation to be a linear process, or handle the non-concatenative processes separately from the concatenative ones (see survey in Hammarstrom and Borin, 2011). By separating the units of morphological structure from the surface string of phonemes (or characters), however, the distinction between non-concatenative and concatenative morphological processes vanishes.

We apply the Multiple Cause Mixture Model (MCMM) (Saund, 1993, 1994), a type of autoencoder that serves as a disjunctive clustering algorithm, to the problem of morphological learning. An MCMM is composed of a layer of hidden nodes and a layer of surface nodes. Like other generative models, it assumes that some subset of hidden nodes is responsible for generating each instance of observed data. Here, the surface nodes are features that represent the "surface" properties of words, and the hidden nodes represent units of morphological structure.

An MCMM is well-suited to learn non-concatenative morphology for the same reason that the autosegmental formalism is well-suited to representing it on paper (section 2): the layer of morphological structure is separate from the surface layer of features, and there are no dependencies between nodes within the same layer. This intra-layer independence allows each hidden node to associate with any subset of features, con-

---

[1] We follow the transliteration scheme of the Hebrew Treebank (Sima'an et al., 2001).

131

Proceedings of the 14th Annual SIGMORPHON Workshop on Computational Research in Phonetics, Phonology, and Morphology, pages 131–140,
Berlin, Germany, August 11, 2016. ©2016 Association for Computational Linguistics

tiguous or discontiguous. We present details of the MCMM and its application to morphology in section 3. Our ultimate goal is to find a ULM framework that is theoretically plausible, with the present work being somewhat exploratory.

1.1 Targets of learning

Driven by an MCMM (section 3), our system clusters words according to similarities in form, thereby finding form-based atomic building blocks; these building blocks, however, are not necessarily morphemes in the conventional sense. A morpheme is traditionally defined as the coupling of a form and a meaning, with the meaning often being a set of one or more morphosyntactic features. Our system, by contrast, discovers building blocks that reside on a level between phonological form and morphosyntactic meaning, i.e., on the *morphomic* level (Aronoff, 1994).

Stump (2001) captures this distinction in his classification of morphological theories, distinguishing *incremental* and *realizational* theories. Incremental theories view morphosyntactic properties as intrinsic to morphological markers. Accordingly, a word's morphosyntactic content grows monotonically with the number of markers it acquires. By contrast, in realizational theories, certain sets of morphosyntactic properties *license* certain morphological markers; thus, the morphosyntactic properties cannot be inherently present in the markers. Stump (2001) presents considerable evidence for realizational morphology, e.g., the fact that "a given property may be expressed by more than one morphological marking in the same word" (p. 4).

Similarly, Aronoff (1994) observes that the mapping between phonological and morphosyntactic units is not always one-to-one. Often, one morphosyntactic unit maps to more than one phonological form, or vice versa. There are even many-to-many mappings. Aronoff cites the English past participle: depending on the verb, the past participle can by realized by the suffixes *-ed* or *-en*, by ablaut, and so on. And yet for any given verb lexeme, the *same* marker is used for the both the perfect tense and the passive voice, despite the lack of a relationship between these disparate syntactic categories. Aronoff argues that the complexity of these mappings between (morpho-)syntax and phonology necessitates an intermediate level, namely the morphomic level.

	MASC	FEM
SG	mqwmi	mqwmi-**t**
PL	mqwmi-im	mqwmi-w**t**

(a) *mqwmi* 'local'

	MASC	FEM
SG	gdwl	gdwl-h
PL	gdwl-im	gdwl-w**t**

(b) *gdwl* 'big'

Figure 1: The *t* quasi-morpheme

Our system's clusters correspond roughly to Aronoff's morphomes. Hence, the system does not require building blocks to have particular meanings. Instead, it looks for *pre-morphosyntactic* units, i.e., ones assembled from phonemes, but not yet assigned a syntactic or semantic meaning. In a larger pipeline, such building blocks could serve as an interface between morphosyntax and phonology. For instance, while our system can find Hebrew's default masculine suffix *-im*, it does not specify whether it is in fact masculine in a given word or whether it is feminine, as this suffix also occurs in idiosyncratic feminine plurals.

Our system also encounters building blocks like the *t* in fig. 1, which might be called "quasi-morphemes" since they recur in a wide range of related forms, but fall just short of being entirely systematic.[2] The *t* in fig. 1 seems to be frequently associated with the feminine morphosyntactic category, as in the feminine nationality suffix *-it* (*sinit* 'Chinese (F)'), the suffix *-wt* for deriving abstract mass nouns (*bhirwt* 'clarity (F)'), as well as in feminine singular and plural present-tense verb endings (e.g., *kwtb-t* 'she writes' and *kwtb-wt* 'they (F.PL) write', respectively).

In fig. 1(a), note that this *t* is present in both the F.SG and F.PL forms. However, it cannot be assigned a distinct meaning such as "feminine," since it cannot be separated from the *w* in the F.PL suffix *-wt*.[3] Moreover, this *t* is not always the F.SG marker; the ending *-h* in fig. 1(b) is also common. Nevertheless, the frequency with which *t* occurs in feminine words does not seem to be accidental. It seems instead to be some kind of building block, and our system treats it as such.

---

[2] Though, see Faust (2013) for an analysis positing /-t/ as Hebrew's one (underlying) feminine-gender marker.

[3] If the *w* in *-wt* meant "plural," we would expect the default M.PL suffix to be *-wm* instead of *-im*.

Because our system is not intended to identify morphosyntactic categories, its evaluation poses a challenge, as morphological analyzers tend to pair form with meaning. Nevertheless, we tentatively evaluate our system's clusters against the *modified* output of a finite-state morphological analyzer. That is, we map this analyzer's abstract morphosyntactic categories onto categories that, while still essentially morphosyntactic, correspond more closely to distinctions in form (see section 4).

2 Morphology and MCMMs

In this section, we will examine autosegmental (or *multi-linear*) morphology (McCarthy, 1981), to isolate the property that allows it to handle non-concatenative morphology. We will then show that because an MCMM has this same property, it is an appropriate computational model for learning non-concatenative morphology.

First, we note some previous work connecting autosegmental morphology to computation. For example, Kiraz (1996) provides a framework for autosegmental morphology within two-level morphology, using hand-written grammars. By contrast, Fullwood and O'Donnell (2013) provide a learning algorithm in the spirit of autosegmental morphology. They sample templates, roots, and residues from Pitmor-Yor processes, where a *residue* consists of a word's non-root phonemes, and a *template* specifies word length and the word-internal positions of root phonemes. Botha and Blunsom (2013) use mildly context-free grammars with crossing branches to generate words with discontiguous morphemes. The present work, in contrast, assumes nothing about structure beforehand.

Other works implement certain components of autosegmental theory (e.g., Goldsmith and Xanthos, 2009) or relegate it to a certain phase in their overall system (e.g., Rodrigues and Ćavar, 2005). The present work seeks to simulate autosegmental morphology in a more general and holistic way.

2.1 Multilinear morphology

The central aspect of autosegmental theory (McCarthy, 1981) is its multi-linear architecture, i.e., its use of a *segmental tier* along with many *autosegmental tiers* to account for morphological structure. The segmental tier is a series of placeholders for consonants and vowels, often called the *CV skeleton*. The other tiers each represent a particular morpheme. Fig. 2(a) shows four tiers.

One is the CV skeleton. The other three, labeled μ_1, μ_2, and μ_3, are morphemes.[4]

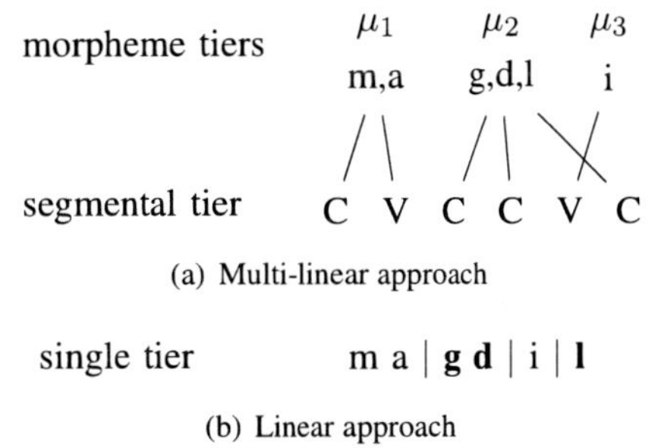

(a) Multi-linear approach

single tier   m a | **g d** | i | **l**

(b) Linear approach

Figure 2: Multiple tiers vs. a single tier

Notice that μ_2, the consonantal root, is discontinuous; it is interrupted by μ_3. If a model has only one tier, as in fig. 2(b), there would be no way of representing the unity of μ_2, i.e., that *g*, *d*, and *l* all belong to the same morpheme. With this multi-tier aspect of autosegmental morphology in mind, we can now state two criteria for a model of non-concatenative morphology:

(1)   a. Morphemes are represented as being separate from the segmental tier.

       b. Each morpheme tier (or node) is orthogonal to all other morpheme tiers.

Criterion (1b) implies that the morpheme tiers are unordered. Without sequential dependencies between morpheme tiers, crossing edges such as those in fig. 2(a) are made possible. We should note that autosegmental morphology has other properties to constrain morphological structure, e.g., the well-formedness principle; at present, we are not concerned with capturing all aspects of autosegmental morphology, but instead in building a generic system to which one can later add linguistically motivated constraints.

2.2 A graph-theoretic interpretation

In graph-theoretic terms, the multi-linear formalism of McCarthy (1981) is a type of *multipartite* graph. This is a graph whose nodes can be partitioned into N sets of *mutually nonadjacent* nodes, i.e., N sets such that no two nodes within the *same* set are connected by an edge. Fig. 3, for example, shows a *bipartite* graph, i.e., a graph with two partitions, in this case the sets M and R. Within each

---

[4]Although McCarthy uses the term *morpheme* rather than *morphome*, the same principles apply.

set, all nodes are independent; the only connections are between nodes of different sets.

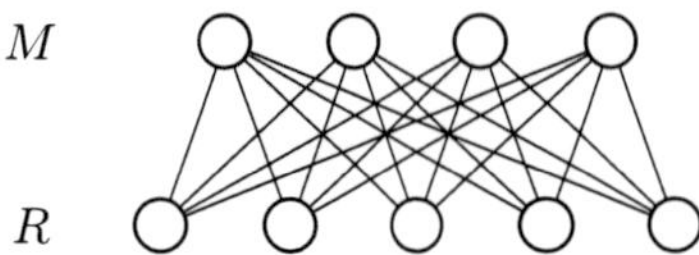

Figure 3: Bipartite graph

As it turns out, a bipartite graph suffices to capture the essential properties of McCarthy's autosegmental framework, for a bipartite graph meets the two criteria stated in (1). We can reformulate the morpheme tiers and the segmental tier in fig. 2(a) as the sets M and R, respectively, in fig. 3—disjoint by the definition of *bipartite*. This satisfies the first criterion. For the second, each node in M represents a morpheme (or morpheme tier), and, by the definition of *bipartite*, the nodes within M are independent and thus orthogonal.

An MCMM (section 3) is well-suited for the learning of non-concatenative morphology because it is bipartite graph. It has two *layers* (equivalently, sets) of nodes, a hidden layer and a surface layer—corresponding, respectively, to M and R in fig. 3. There are no intra-layer connections in an MCMM, only connections between layers.

We will henceforth refer to an MCMM's two partitions of nodes as *vectors* of nodes and will use matrix and vector notation to describe the components of an MCMM: uppercase boldface letters refer to matrices, lowercase boldface letters refer to vectors, and italicized lowercase letters refer to the individual elements of vectors/matrices. For example, $m_{i,k}$ is the kth element in the vector $\mathbf{m}_i$, which is the ith row in the $I \times K$ matrix $\mathbf{M}$. Thus, we will henceforth write the M and R in fig. 3 as $\mathbf{m}$ and $\mathbf{r}$, respectively (or $\mathbf{m}_i$ and $\mathbf{r}_i$, where i is the index of the ith word).

3 The Multiple Cause Mixture Model

A Multiple Cause Mixture Model (MCMM) (Saund, 1993, 1994) is a graphical model consisting of a layer of surface nodes and a hidden layer of causal nodes. The hidden nodes (or units) are connected to surface nodes by weights. Each surface node is either ON (active) or OFF (inactive) depending on the hidden-node activities and the weights connecting hidden nodes to surface nodes.

3.1 Architecture

An MCMM can be viewed as a variation of the classical autoencoder network (Dayan and Zemel, 1995), a type of neural network used for unsupervised learning. In autoencoders, a hidden layer is forced to learn a compression scheme, i.e., a lower-dimensional encoding, for a dataset.

MCMMs are called *Multiple Cause* Mixture Models because more than one hidden unit can take part in the activation of a surface unit. This is illustrated in figure 4, where the nodes $\mathbf{m}$ are the hidden units, and $\mathbf{r}$ is the (reconstructed) surface vector. Each arc $c_{j,k}$ represents the weight on the connection between m_k and r_j. The activity of r_j is determined by a mixing function (section 3.2).

The MCMM learns by comparing the reconstructed vector $\mathbf{r}_i$ to its corresponding original datapoint $\mathbf{d}_i$. The discrepancy between the two is quantified by an *objective function*. If there is a discrepancy, the values of the nodes in $\mathbf{m}_i$ as well as the weights $\mathbf{C}$ are adjusted in order to reduce the discrepancy as much as possible. See section 3.3 for more on the learning process.

Suppose data points $\mathbf{d}_u$ and $\mathbf{d}_v$ have some features in common. Then, as the MCMM tries to reconstruct them in $\mathbf{r}_u$ and $\mathbf{r}_v$, respectively, similarities will emerge between their respective hidden-layer vectors $\mathbf{m}_u$ and $\mathbf{m}_v$. In particular, the vectors $\mathbf{m}_u$ and $\mathbf{m}_v$ should come to share at least one active node, i.e., at least one $k \in K$ such that $m_{u,k} = 1$ and $m_{v,k} = 1$. This can serve as a basis for clustering; i.e., $m_{i,k}$ indicates whether $\mathbf{d}_i$ is a member of cluster k.

3.2 Mixing Function

The mapping between the layer of hidden nodes $\mathbf{m}$ and the layer of surface nodes $\mathbf{r}$ is governed by a *mixing function*, which is essentially a voting rule (Saund, 1994); it maps from a set of input "votes" to a single output decision. The output decision is the activity (or inactivity) of a node r_{ij} in the surface layer. Following Saund (1994), we use the Noisy-Or function:

$$r_{i,j} = 1 - \prod_k (1 - m_{i,k}c_{j,k}) \qquad (1)$$

Note that the input to this function includes not only the hidden nodes $\mathbf{m}$, but also the *weights* $\mathbf{c}_j$ on the hidden nodes. That is, the activity of the hidden node m_k is weighted by the value c_{jk}. A classical autoencoder also has a mixing function,

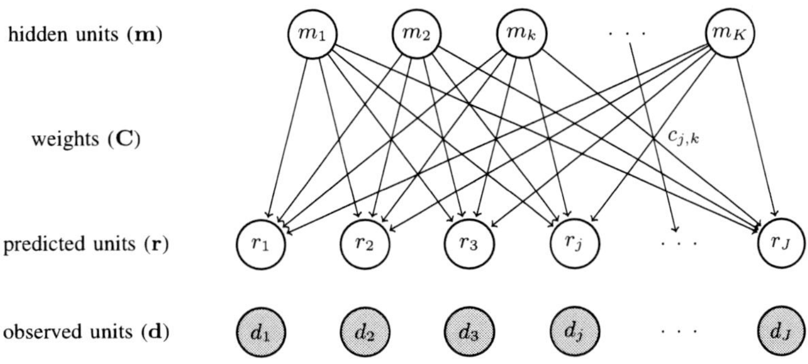

Figure 4: Architecture of a Multiple Cause Mixture Model (MCMM).

though it is more commonly called an *activation function* in autoencoders. The most common activation function involves a simple weighted sum of the hidden layer **m**'s activations. The entirely linear weighted sum is then passed to the logistic sigmoid function σ, which squashes the sum to a number between 0 and 1:

$$r_{i,j} = \sigma\left(\sum_k m_{i,k} c_{j,k}\right) \qquad (2)$$

Notice that both (1) and (2), have the same three primary components: the output (or surface node) $r_{i,j}$, the hidden layer of nodes **m**, and a matrix of weights **C**. Both are possible mixing functions.

3.3 Learning

In both the classical autoencoder and the MCMM, learning occurs as a result of the algorithm's search for an optimal valuation of key variables (e.g., weights), i.e., a valuation that minimizes the discrepancy between reconstructed and original data points. The search is conducted via numerical optimization; we use the nonlinear conjugate gradient method. Our objective function is a simple error function, namely the normalized sum of squares error:

$$E = \frac{1}{I \times J} \sum_i \sum_j \left(r_{i,j} - d_{i,j}\right)^2 \qquad (3)$$

where $I \times J$ is the total number of features in the dataset. The MCMM's task is to minimize this function by adjusting the values in **M** and **C**, where **M** is the $I \times K$ matrix that encodes each data point's cluster-activity vector, and **C** is the $J \times K$ matrix that encodes the weights between $\mathbf{m}_i$ and $\mathbf{r}_i$ for every $i \in I$ (see fig. 5).

The MCMM's learning process is similar to Expectation Maximization (EM) in that at any given time it is holding one set of variables fixed while optimizing the other set. We thus have two functions, OPTIMIZE-M and OPTIMIZE-C, which take turns optimizing their respective matrices.

The function OPTIMIZE-M visits each of the I cluster-activity vectors $\mathbf{m}_i$ in **M**, optimizing each one separately. For each $\mathbf{m}_i$, OPTIMIZE-M enters an optimization loop over its K components, adjusting each $m_{i,k}$ by a quantity proportional to the negative gradient of E at $m_{i,k}$. This loop repeats until E ceases to decrease significantly, whereupon OPTIMIZE-M proceeds to the next $\mathbf{m}_i$.

The function OPTIMIZE-C consists of a single optimization loop over the entire matrix **C**. Each $c_{j,k}$ is adjusted by a quantity proportional to the negative gradient of E at $c_{j,k}$. Unlike OPTIMIZE-M, which comprises I separate optimization loops, OPTIMIZE-C consists of just one, When each of its $J \times K$ components has been adjusted, one round of updates to **C** is complete. E is reassessed only between completed rounds of updates. If the change in E remains significant, another round begins.

Both OPTIMIZE-M and OPTIMIZE-C are enclosed within an "alternation loop" that alternates between the two functions, holding **C** fixed during OPTIMIZE-M, and vice versa. This alternation continues until E cannot be decreased further. At this point, an "outer loop" splits the cluster which contributes the most to the error, adds one to the cluster count K, and restarts the alternation loop. The outer loop repeats until it reaches an overall stopping criterion, e.g., $E = 0$.

The optimization task is subject to the constraint that no value in **M** or **C** may exceed 1 or fall below 0. In other words, it is a task of bound constrained optimization. Thus, whenever a value in either **M** or **C** is about to fall below 0, it is set to 0. Likewise, whenever a value is about to exceed 1, it is set to 1 (Ni and Yuan, 1997).

3.4 A Simple MCMM Example

Fig. 5 shows an example of an MCMM for two data points (i.e., $I = 2$). The hidden cluster activities **M**, the weights **C**, and the mixing function r constitute a model that reproduces the observed data points **D**. The nodes $m_{i,k}$ represent cluster activities; if $m_{1,2} = 1$, for instance, the second cluster is active for $\mathbf{d}_1$ (i.e., $\mathbf{d}_1$ is a member of cluster 2). Note that the $J \times K$ weight matrix **C** is the same for all data points, and the kth row in **C** can be seen as the kth cluster's "average" vector: the jth component in $\mathbf{c}_k$ is 1 only if all data points in cluster k have 1 at feature j.

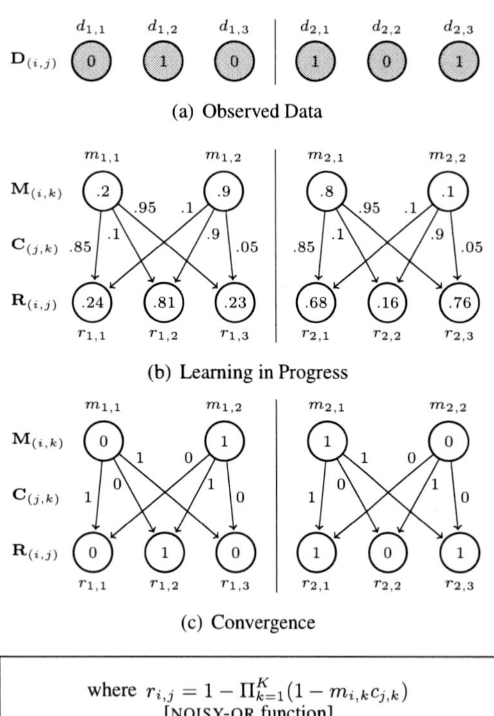

(a) Observed Data

(b) Learning in Progress

(c) Convergence

$$r_{i,j} = 1 - \Pi_{k=1}^{K}(1 - m_{i,k}c_{j,k})$$
[NOISY-OR function]

Figure 5: A simple MCMM example

We can see that while learning is in progress, the cluster activities $(m_{i,k})$ and the cluster centers $(c_{j,k})$ are in flux, as the error rate is being reduced, but that they converge to values of 0 and 1. At convergence, a reconstruction node $(r_{i,j})$ is 1 if at least one $m_{i,k}c_{j,k} = 1$ (and 0 otherwise).

3.5 MCMMs for Morphology

To apply MCMMs to morphological learning, we view the components as follows. For each word i, the observed (d_j) and reconstructed (r_j) units refer to binary surface features extracted from the word (e.g., "the third character is s"). The hidden units (m_k) correspond to clusters of words which, in the ideal case, contain the same morpheme (or morphome). The weights $(c_{j,k})$ then link specific morphemes to specific features.

For an example, consider the English word *ads*. Ideally, there would be two clusters derived from the MCMM algorithm, one for the stem *ad* and one clustering words with the plural ending *-s*. Fig. 6 shows a properly learned MCMM, based upon *positional* features: one feature for each letter in each position. Note that *ads* does not have partial membership of the *ad* and *-s* hidden units, but is a full member of both.

4 Experiments

4.1 Gold Standard

Our dataset is the Hebrew word list (6888 unique words) used by Daya et al. (2008) in their study of automatic root identification. This list specifies the root for the two-thirds of the words that have roots. Only the roots are specified, however, and not other (non-root) properties. To obtain other morphological properties, we use the MILA Morphological Analysis tool (MILA-MA) (Itai and Wintner, 2008). Because its morphological knowledge is manually coded and its output deterministic, MILA-MA provides a good approximation to human annotation. The system is designed to analyze morphemes, not morphomes, an issue we partially account for in our category mappings and take up further in section 4.4.

As an example of the way we use MILA-MA's output, consider the word *bycim* ('in trees'), which MILA-MA analyzes as a M%P1 noun bearing the prefixal preposition *b-* ('in'). Given this analysis, we examine each MCMM-generated cluster that contains *bycim*. In particular, we want to see if *bycim* has been grouped with other words that MILA-MA has labeled as M%P1 or as having *b-*.

Category mappings MILA-MA outputs 22 possible feature labels. Four of these (`id`, `undotted`, `transliterated`, `register`)

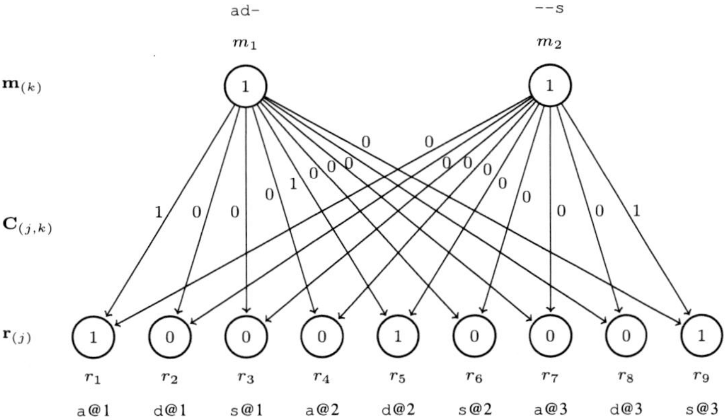

Figure 6: An MCMM example for the word *ads*, with nine features (three letters, each at three positions), and two clusters "causing" the word

are irrelevant and are discarded. Each of the 18 remaining features has at least two values, and some have many more, resulting in a great many feature-value pairs, i.e., categories.

Most part-of-speech (POS) categories are rather abstract; they often cannot be linked to particular elements of form. For example, a noun can be masculine or feminine, can be singular or plural, and can bear one of a variety of derivational affixes. But there is no *single* marker that unifies *all* nouns. The situation with verbs is similar: every Hebrew verb belongs to one of seven classes (*binyanim*), each of which is characterized by a distinctive vowel pattern.

We thus replace "super-categories" like NOUN and VERB with finer-grained categories that point to actual distinctions in form. In fact, the only POS categories we keep are those for adverbs, adjectives, and numerals (ordinal and cardinal). The rest are replaced by composite (sub-)categories (see below) or discarded entirely, as are negative categories (e.g., `construct:false`) and unmarked forms (e.g., M%Sg in nominals).

Sometimes two or more morphosyntactic categories share an element of form; e.g., the future-tense prefix *t-* can indicate the 2nd person in the MASC gender or, in the FEM gender, either the 2nd or 3rd person:

temwr	'you (M.SG) will keep'
temwr	'she will keep'
temwrw	'you (F.PL) will keep'

Verb inflections are thus mapped to composite categories, e.g., `future%(2%M)|(2|3%F)`, where the symbol | means 'or'. We also map MILA-MA's `binyan` and `tense` feature-value pairs to `stem_type`, since the shape of a verb's stem follows from its binyan, and, in some binyanim, past and future tenses have different stems. Both the composite-inflectional and `stem_type` categories represent complex mappings between morphosyntax and phonology.

However, since it is not yet entirely clear what would constitute a fair evaluation of the MCMM's clusters (see section 5), we generally try to retain the traditional morphosyntatctic labels in some form, even if these traditional labels exist only in combination with other labels. Most of our mappings involve fusing "atomic" morphosyntactic categories. For example, to capture Hebrew's fusional plural suffixes for nominals, we combine the atomic categories FEM or MASC with PL; i.e., MASC + PL $\mapsto$ M%Pl and FEM + PL $\mapsto$ F%Pl.

Whenever ambiguity is systematic and thus predictable, we choose the most general analysis. For instance, participle analyses are always accompanied by adjective and noun analyses (cf. English *-ing* forms). Since a participle is always both a noun and an adjective, we keep the participle analysis and discard the other two. Finally, we use `rootless:Nominal` to capture orthographic regularities in loan words. In sum, we employ reasonably motivated and informative categories, but the choice of mappings is nontrivial and worthy of investigation in its own right.

4.2 Thresholds and Features

The MCMM begins the learning process with a single cluster, and whenever its error stops decreasing significantly, it adds a cluster. It is supposed to continue to add clusters until it converges, i.e., until the error is (close to) 0, but so far our MCMM has never converged. As the number of clusters increases, the MCMM becomes increasingly encumbered by the sheer number of computations it must perform. We thus stop it when the number of clusters K reaches a pre-set limit: for this paper, the limit was $K = 100$. Such a cut-off leaves most of the cluster activities in $\mathbf{M}$ between 0 and 1. We set a threshold for cluster membership at 0.5: if $m_{i,k}c_{j,k} \geq 0.5$ for at least one index j in J, then $\mathbf{d}_i$ is a member of the kth cluster.

If $m_{i,k}c_{j,k} \leq 0.5$ for all j in J, we say that the kth cluster is *inactive* in the ith word. If a cluster is inactive for *every* word, we say that it is currently only a *potential* cluster rather than an *actual* one.

Each word is encoded as a vector of features. This vector is the same length for all words. For any given word, certain features will be ON (with values $= 1$), and the rest—a much greater portion—will be OFF (with values $= 0$). Each feature is a statement about a word's form, e.g., "the first letter is b" or "i occurs before t". In our features, we attempt to capture some of the information implicit in a word's visual representation.

A **positional feature** indicates the presence of a particular character at a certain position, e.g., `m@[0]`, for 'm at the first position' or `l@[-2]` for 'l at the second-to-last position'. Each data point $\mathbf{d}_i$ contains positional features corresponding to the first s and the final s positions in word i, where s is a system parameter (section 4.4). With 22 letters in the Hebrew alphabet, this amounts to $22 \times s \times 2$ positional features.

A **precedence feature** indicates, for two characters a and b, whether a precedes b within a certain distance (or number of characters). This distance is the system parameter δ. We define δ as the difference between the indices of the characters a and b. For example, if $\delta = 1$, then characters a and b are adjacent. The number of precedence features is the length of the alphabet squared ($22^2 = 484$).

4.3 Evaluation Metrics

We evaluate our clustering results according to three metrics. Let U denote the set of M returned clusters and V the set of N gold-standard categories. The idea behind *purity* is to compute the proportion of examples assigned to the correct cluster, using the most frequent category within

a given cluster as gold. Standard purity assumes each example belongs to only one gold category. For a dataset like ours consisting of multi-category examples, this can yield purities greater than 1. We thus modify the calculations slightly to compute **average cluster-wise purity**, as in (4), where we divide by M. While this equation yields purities within $[0, 1]$, even when clusters overlap, it retains the metric's bias toward small clusters.

$$\text{pur}_{\text{avg}}(U, V) = \frac{1}{M} \sum_{m \in M} \frac{\max_n |u_m \cap v_n|}{M} \quad (4)$$

Given this bias, we incorporate other metrics: **BCubed precision** and **BCubed recall** (Bagga and Baldwin, 1998) compare the cluster mappings of x with those of y, for every pair of data points x and y. These metrics are well-suited to cases of overlapping clusters (Artiles and Verdejo, 2009). Suppose x and y share m clusters and n categories. BCubed precision measures the extent to which $m \leq n$. It is 1 as long there are not more clusters than gold-standard categories. BCubed Recall measures the extent to which $m \geq n$. See Artiles and Verdejo (2009) for calculation details.

4.4 Results

With a cut-off point at $K = 100$ clusters, we ran the MCMM at different valuations of s and δ. The results are given in table 1, where "$\delta = *$" means that δ is the entire length of the word in question, and "n/a" means that the feature type in question was left out; e.g., in the s column, "n/a" means that no positional features were used. Depending upon the threshold (section 4.2), a cluster may be empty: K' is the number of *actual* clusters (see section 4.2). *Cov(erage)*, on the other hand, is the number of words that belong to least one cluster. The valuations $s = 1$ and $\delta = 1$ or 2 seem to produce the best overall results.[5]

Some of the clusters appear to be capturing key properties of Hebrew morphology, as evidenced by the MILA-MA categories. For example, in one cluster, 677 out of 942 words turn to be of the composite MILA-MA category M%P1, a purity of 0.72.[6] In another cluster, this one containing 584 words, 483 are of the MILA-MA category

---

[5]While $s = 1$ indicates an preference for learning short prefixes and suffixes, it is important to note that more than one-letter affixes may be learned through the use of the precedence features, which can occur anywhere in a word.

[6]Recall that M%P1 is merger of the originally separate MILA-MA categories M and P1 .

`preposition:l` (the prefixal preposition *l*-), a purity of 0.83.

Thus, in many cases, the evaluation recognizes the efficacy of the method and helps sort the different parameters. However, it has distinct limitations. Our gold standard categories are modified categories from MILA-MA, which are not entirely form-based. For example, in one 1016-word cluster, the three most common gold-standard categories are `F%Pl` (441 words), `F%Sg` (333 words), and `pos:adjective` (282 words). Taking the most frequent category as the correct label, the purity of this cluster is $\frac{441}{1016} = 0.434$. However, a simple examination of this cluster's words reveals it to be more coherent than this suggests. Of the 1016 words, 92% end in *t*; in 96%, *t* is one of the final two characters; and in 98%, one of the final three. When *t* is not word-final, it is generally followed by a morpheme and thus is stem-final. Indeed, this cluster seems to have captured almost exactly the "quasi-morpheme" *t* discussed in section 1. Thus, an evaluation with more form-based categories might measure this cluster's purity to be around 98%—a point for future work.

None of the experiments reported here produced *actual* (section 4.2) clusters representing consonantal roots. However, past experiments did produce some consonantal-root clusters. In these clusters, the roots were often discontinuous, e.g., *z.k.r* in the words *lizkwr*, *lhzkir*, and *zikrwn*. It is not yet clear to us why these past experiments produced actual root clusters and the present ones did not, but, in any case, we expect to see more root clusters as K (and especially K') increases.

s	δ	Purity	BP	BR	Cov.	K'
n/a	1	0.394	0.456	0.223	3279	12
n/a	2	0.330	0.385	0.218	4002	14
n/a	3	0.396	0.423	0.261	4214	19
n/a	*	0.379	0.422	0.319	4495	20
1	n/a	0.576	0.599	0.458	3577	4
2	n/a	0.428	0.488	0.396	5942	12
3	n/a	0.429	0.508	0.370	6384	18
1	1	0.463	0.580	0.325	5760	16
1	2	0.443	0.540	0.358	5401	14
1	3	0.458	0.500	0.369	5144	12
1	*	0.456	0.518	0.383	5096	14
2	1	0.371	0.460	0.298	6316	26
2	2	0.401	0.481	0.291	5728	20
2	3	0.392	0.465	0.366	5509	17
2	*	0.412	0.474	0.347	5366	18
3	1	0.399	0.461	0.334	6102	19
3	2	0.403	0.474	0.326	5756	19
3	3	0.364	0.438	0.345	5164	17
3	*	0.391	0.463	0.390	5496	17

Table 1: Results at $K = 100$

5 Summary and Outlook

We have presented a model for the unsupervised learning of morphology, the Multiple Cause Mixture Model, which relies on hidden units to generate surface forms and maps to autosegmental models of morphology. Our experiments on Hebrew, using different types of features, have demonstrated the potential utility of this method for discovering morphological patterns.

So far, we have been stopping the MCMM at a set number (K) of clusters because computational complexity increases with K: the complexity is proportional to $I \times J \times K$, with $I \times J$ already large. But if the model is to find consonantal roots along with affixes, K is going to have to be much larger. We can attack this problem by taking advantage of the nature of bipartite graphs (section 2): with intra-layer independence, every $r_{i,j}$ in the vector $\mathbf{r}_i$—and thus each element in the entire matrix $\mathbf{R}$—can be computed *in parallel*. We are currently parallelizing key portions of our code, rewriting costly loops as kernels to be processed on the GPU.

In a different vein, we intend to adopt a better method of evaluating the MCMM's clusters, one more appropriate for the *morphome*-like nature of the clusters. Such a method will require gold-standard categories that are morphomic rather than morphosyntactic, and we anticipate this to be a nontrivial undertaking. From the theoretical side, an exact inventory of (Hebrew) morphomes has not been specified in any work we know of, and annotation criteria thus need to be established. From the practical side, MILA-MA provides neither segmentation nor derivational morphology for anything other than verbs, and so much of the annotation will have to built from scratch.

Finally, our data for this work consisted of Modern Hebrew words that originally appeared in print. They are spelled according to the orthographic conventions of Modern Hebrew, i.e., without representing many vowels. As vowel absences may obscure patterns, we intend to try out the MCMM on phonetically transcribed Hebrew.

References

Mark Aronoff. 1994. *Morphology by Itself: Stems and Inflectional Classes*, volume 22 of *Linguistic Inquiry Monograph*. MIT Press, Cambridge, MA.

Enrique Amigó Julio Gonzalo Javier Artiles and Felisa Verdejo. 2009. A comparison of extrinsic clustering evaluation metrics based on formal constraints. *Information Retrieval* 12(4):353–371.

Amit Bagga and Breck Baldwin. 1998. Entity-based cross-document coreferencing using the vector space model. In *Proceedings of the 17th international conference on Computational linguistics: Volume 1*. Association for Computational Linguistics, pages 79–85.

Jan A. Botha and Phil Blunsom. 2013. Adaptor grammars for learning non-concatenative morphology. In *Proceedings of the 2013 Conference on Empirical Methods in Natural Language Processing (EMNLP-13)*. Seattle, pages 345–356.

Mathias Creutz and Krista Lagus. 2007. Unsupervised models for morpheme segmentation and morphology learning. *ACM Transactions on Speech and Language Processing* 4(1):3.

Ezra Daya, Dan Roth, and Shuly Wintner. 2008. Identifying semitic roots: Machine learning with linguistic constraints. *Computational Linguistics* 34(3):429–448.

Peter Dayan and Richard S Zemel. 1995. Competition and multiple cause models. *Neural Computation* 7:565–579.

Khaled Elghamry. 2005. A constraint-based algorithm for the identification of arabic roots. In *Proceedings of the Midwest Computational Linguistics Colloquium*. Indiana University.

Noam Faust. 2013. Decomposing the feminine suffixes of modern hebrew: a morpho-syntactic analysis. *Morphology* 23(4):409–440.

Michelle Fullwood and Tim O'Donnell. 2013. Learning non-concatenative morphology. In *Proceedings of the Fourth Annual Workshop on Cognitive Modeling and Computational Linguistics (CMCL)*. Sofia, Bulgaria, pages 21–27.

John Goldsmith. 2001. Unsupervised learning of the morphology of a natural language. *Computational Linguistics* 27:153–198.

John Goldsmith and Aris Xanthos. 2009. Learning phonological categories. *Language* 85(1):4–38.

Harald Hammarstrom and Lars Borin. 2011. Unsupervised learning of morphology. *Computational Linguistics* 37(2):309 – 350.

Alon Itai and Shuly Wintner. 2008. Language resources for Hebrew. *Language Resources and Evaluation* 42(1):75–98.

George Anton Kiraz. 1996. Computing prosodic morphology. In *Proceedings of the 16th International Conference on Computational Linguistics (COLING 1996)*. Copenhagen, pages 664–669.

Andreas Klöckner, Nicolas Pinto, Yunsup Lee, B. Catanzaro, Paul Ivanov, and Ahmed Fasih. 2012. PyCUDA and PyOpenCL: A Scripting-Based Approach to GPU Run-Time Code Generation. *Parallel Computing* 38(3):157–174.

John J McCarthy. 1981. A prosodic theory of nonconcatenative morphology. *Linguistic inquiry* 12:373–418.

Taesun Moon, Katrin Erk, and Jason Baldridge. 2009. Unsupervised morphological segmentation and clustering with document boundaries. In *Proceedings of the 2009 Conference on Empirical Methods in Natural Language Processing: Volume 2*. Association for Computational Linguistics, pages 668–677.

Q Ni and Y Yuan. 1997. A subspace limited memory quasi-newton algorithm for large-scale nonlinear bound constrained optimization. *Mathematics of Computation of the American Mathematical Society* 66(220):1509–1520.

Hoifung Poon, Colin Cherry, and Kristina Toutanova. 2009. Unsupervised morphological segmentation with log-linear models. In *In ACL. Ariya Rastrow, Abhinav Sethy, and Bhuvana Ramabhadran*.

Paul Rodrigues and Damir Ćavar. 2005. Learning arabic morphology using information theory. In *Proceedings from the Annual Meeting of the Chicago Linguistic Society*. Chicago Linguistic Society, pages 49–58.

Eric Saund. 1993. Unsupervised learning of mixtures of multiple causes in binary data. In *NIPS*. pages 27–34.

Eric Saund. 1994. A multiple cause mixture model for unsupervised learning. *Neural Computation* 7(1):51–71.

Khalil Sima'an, Alon Itai, Yoad Winter, Alon Altman, and N. Nativ. 2001. Building a tree-bank of Modern Hebrew text. *Traitement Automatique des Langues* 42(2).

Gregory T Stump. 2001. *Inflectional morphology: A theory of paradigm structure*, volume 93. Cambridge University Press.

Inferring Morphotactics from Interlinear Glossed Text: Combining Clustering and Precision Grammars

Olga Zamaraeva
University of Washington
Seattle, WA, USA
`olzama@uw.edu`

Abstract

In this paper I present a k-means clustering approach to inferring morphological position classes (morphotactics) from Interlinear Glossed Text (IGT), data collections available for some endangered and low-resource languages. While the experiment is not restricted to low-resource languages, they are meant to be the targeted domain. Specifically my approach is meant to be for field linguists who do not necessarily know how many position classes there are in the language they work with and what the position classes are, but have the expertise to evaluate different hypotheses. It builds on an existing approach (Wax, 2014), but replaces the core heuristic with a clustering algorithm. The results mainly illustrate two points. First, they are largely negative, which shows that the baseline algorithm (summarized in the paper) uses a very predictive feature to determine whether affixes belong to the same position class, namely edge overlap in the affix graph. At the same time, unlike the baseline method that relies entirely on a single feature, k-means clustering can account for different features and helps discover more morphological phenomena, e.g. circumfixation. I conclude that unsupervised learning algorithms such as k-means clustering can in principle be used for morphotactics inference, though the algorithm should probably weigh certain features more than others. Most importantly, I conclude that clustering is a promising approach for diverse morphotactics and as such it can facilitate linguistic analysis of field languages.

1 Introduction

Morphological analysis is a critical component in NLP systems for morphologically rich languages (Daille et al., 2002). Yet, while automatic morphological analysis may be well-developed for languages like English and Spanish, the list of these languages is rather short. There are at least two reasons for that. One is that high-resource languages offer big training corpora. This makes the use of various machine learning algorithms easier. Another reason is that many high-resource languages, most notably English, happen to feature fairly simple morphology. A morphological analyzer for a language like English does not need

to model complex *morphotactics*, the constraints on the ordering of the morphemes types.

While there are many systems which are capable of segmenting words into morphemes (Creutz and Lagus, 2006; Johnson, 2008) and some systems which include more sophisticated morphological analyzers and use supervised machine learning for some tasks (Pasha et al., 2014), there do not seem to be many systems out there which can actually infer morphotactics in an unsupervised fashion. Yet many languages exhibit complex morphotactics. Furthermore, most of the world's languages are low-resource, meaning that there are few digitized resources that can be used in computational projects. Many are also understudied, meaning that the properties of the language including its morphotactics are not well-documented or well-understood.

Documenting morphological rules of understudied languages which often also have endangered status is of critical importance for the purposes of both linguistic research and cultural diversity conservation efforts (Krauss, 1992). At the same time, the scarcity of data makes many modern learning approaches that rely on big data inapplicable in this domain. However, field linguists who work on these languages have small sized but richly annotated data, Interlinear Glossed Text (IGT), and so the richness can be leveraged to compensate for the modest size of the corpora. An example of IGT from Chintang [ctn][1] is given below as (1):

(1) unisaŋa   khatte
      u-nisa-ŋa   khatt-e
      3sPOSS-younger.brother-ERG.A take-IND.PST
      mo   kosi?   moba
      mo   kosi-i   mo-pe
      DEM.DOWN river-LOC DEM.DOWN-LOC

      'The younger brother took it to the river.' [ctn]
      (Bickel et al., 2013)

---

[1] Spoken in Nepal.

Proceedings of the 14th Annual SIGMORPHON Workshop on Computational Research in Phonetics, Phonology, and Morphology, pages 141–150,
Berlin, Germany, August 11, 2016. ©2016 Association for Computational Linguistics

I take an existing approach to automatically extracting morphological rules from IGT as the baseline (Wax, 2014) and present a k-means clustering approach to the same problem. I evaluate the results by morphological parsing (analyzing a list of verbs by finding for each verb a sequence of morphological rule applications that would produce this form) on several languages from different language families, including some low-resource languages. I show that grammars obtained using k-means are generally worse than the baseline though they can be on par with it in a particularly noisy setting. K-means still strongly outperforms a grammar hand-built by language experts because automated processing ensures better recall. I notice that, unlike the baseline approach, k-means is capable of picking up non-canonical phenomena like circumfixation. I conclude that unsupervised classification methods like k-means clustering can help the field linguists come up with more complete hypotheses about morphotactics (accounting for more affixes and more relationships between them) and also discover non-canonical morphological phenomena in their data.

2 Background

This section briefly explains the theoretical assumptions about morphology that are used in this paper, looks at related work, presents the evaluation framework, and finally goes over the baseline system.

2.1 Canonical and Non-Canonical Morphotactics

Position classes, or *morphotactics*, are slots for groups of morphemes (affixes) that are in complementary distribution. The slots can have strict or variable ordering, and an affix that attaches to another affix is said to take the second affix as *input*. For example, Finnish [fin] is known to have the following order of position classes for finite verbs (Karlsson, 2008):

(2) *root + passive + tense/mood + person + particle*

Here, the root serves as input to the passive marker, the passive marker is input to the tense/mood marker, etc.

Canonical morphotactics, in Stump's (1993) terminology used also in works like Crysmann and

Bonami (2015),[2] assume a strict ordering of position classes (for example, if the affix that means tense always follows the one that means aspect, as in Finnish above). Deviations from that which involve variable morpheme ordering can be called *non-canonical* morphotactics (Stump, 1993). Another type of non-canonical phenomena is circumfixation, when a prefix always comes together with a certain suffix, or in other words an affix can be said to split into two parts. For a more complete review of non-canonical phenomena, see Crysmann and Bonami (2015). Non-canonical morphotactics are found very often in the world's languages yet they are often overlooked in implemented systems which tend to be biased towards Indo-European and even just English characteristics (Bender, 2011).

2.2 Morphological Analysis in NLP

The big body of research about automatic morphological analysis that exists today is mostly not concerned with morphotactics. Automatic segmentation, which admittedly is a necessary step in any morphological analysis system, is probably the most developed area. In my study, I assume that the segmentation has already been done, and the goal is to capture relationships between groups of morphemes. There are approaches which advertise themselves as deep morphological analysis (Yarowsky and Wicentowski, 2000; Schone and Jurafsky, 2001), but they focus on well-studied and high-resource Indo-European languages, and mostly aim to learn a maximally broad-coverage table of mappings from stems and affix combinations to some linguistic tag (e.g. a Penn TreeBank POS tag). What they don't yield is a generative model of the language's morphology which would contain information about the position or inflectional classes.

Work that is most similar to mine in what it aims for is Oflazer and Gokhan (1996) and Oflazer, Nirenburg and McShane (2001). Oflazer and Gokhan (1996) use constraints to model morphotactics, but the constraints are hand-built and unsupervised learning is used only for segmentation. Oflazer, Nirenburg and McShane (2001) combine rule-based and machine learning techniques and include elicitation in the loop in order to build finite state automata for low-density languages.

---

[2]Cf. a broader term for canonical morphology as in Corbett (2009).

Their FSAs encode non-canonical morphotactic phenomena such as conditioning, and they induce morphological rules using transformation-based learning (Brill, 1995). Still, their approach focuses more on identifying affixes and roots than on paradigms and position classes, while the latter is necessary for the rules to become part of a morphological grammar.

2.3 Precision Grammars and Evaluation by Parsing

For evaluation, I use automatically generated precision grammars (Bender et al., 2008), a type of digitized language resource. A precision grammar consists of a lexicon and a hierarchy of lexical and phrasal rules written according to the HPSG theory of syntax (Pollard and Sag, 1994). The term 'precision' is meant to emphasize that any parse or generation by the grammar will comply with the rules and will in that sense be linguistically sound, or precise. The grammar is machine-readable. In combination with software such as the LKB system (Copestake, 2002), precision grammars can generate syntactic trees of complete feature structures[3] along with semantic representations. Lexical morphological rules apply first to construct words, and then phrasal rules apply to construct sentences. Such grammars are useful to evaluate the quality of linguistic analyses (Bender et al., 2008). In particular, I used precision grammars to evaluate my results by parsing.

I used the Grammar Matrix customization system (Bender et al., 2002; Bender et al., 2010) to compile precision grammars from the specifications which were output by either the baseline (Wax, 2014) or by my k-means system. In both cases, the morphotactics is represented internally as a directed acyclic graph (DAG) where nodes are affix types (position classes) and edges mean that one class serves as input to another. Cycles are not allowed mainly because of the internal Grammar Matrix restrictions, though iterating position classes are indeed rare.[4] The DAG implementation is provided entirely by the customization system, as are all the other functional parts of the grammar. The baseline and the k-means system

supply only the specification for the DAG in form of nodes and edges. Below are a sample entry for a verb position class from a specification file (Figure 1) and the relevant snippet from the grammar itself, in HPSG-style (Pollard and Sag, 1994) type description language (Figure 2) (Copestake, 2000). The customization system reads in the specification file and, in this case, it would create a node in the DAG that corresponds to verb-slot1 (verb position class 1) and an edge to it from the stems node (called simply 'verb' in the figure).

```
verb-slot1_name=non-fin
verb-slot1_order=after
  verb-slot1_input1_type=verb
  verb-slot1_morph1_name=prp
  verb-slot1_morph1_orth=ing
    verb-slot1_morph1_feat1_name=aspect
    verb-slot1_morph1_feat1_value=prog
    verb-slot1_morph1_feat1_head=verb
    verb-slot1_morph1_feat2_name=form
    verb-slot1_morph1_feat2_value=prp
    verb-slot1_morph1_feat2_head=verb
```

Figure 1: Sample precision grammar specification for a file verb position class entry

```
prp-lex-rule := infl-lex-rule & non-fin-lex-rule-super &
[ SYNSEM.LOCAL [ CONT.HOOK.INDEX.E.ASPECT prog,
                 CAT.HEAD.FORM prp ] ].
```

Figure 2: HPSG grammar snippet in type description language (Copestake, 2000)

For clarity, the examples are from a toy English grammar. The lexical rule which is illustrated will add a suffix *ing* to verbs to produce the participial form. This way a string like *walking* will be parsed and a feature structure will be produced which will capture the fact that this is a non-finite verb form, for example.[5]

2.4 Baseline: Inferring Position Classes DAG by Input Overlap

One approach to inferring the morphotactic DAG from IGT that has been tried is Wax (2014), and I use it as the baseline. The code for the baseline system was shared by its author. It was also used by Bender et al. (2014) in their set of experiments with automatically generated grammars of Chintang. Wax (2014) processes the input IGT (which already have segmentation and alignment between the language line and the gloss line) to identify the

---

[3] A feature structure is the form of linguistic unit description in HPSG. Feature structures can combine with each other by constraint unification to form phrase structures.

[4] Chintang [ctn] has them (Schikowski (2012) as cited in Bender et al. (2012)), but it may be one of very few languages with this feature.

[5] There would have to be a separate lexical rule for gerund, because the morphosyntactic constraints are distinct.

original affix types: affix instances which share the same orthography, gloss, and input relations. The original DAG is a function of these affix types, with affixes being nodes and input relations between them being directed edges. The system then takes a minimum input (edge) overlap value from the user (e.g. 80%, 50%, 20%) and compresses the graph according to this value, i.e. two nodes which share more than a certain percentage of edges will be considered the same position class. The principle is illustrated in the figures below on a toy Russian morphology graph which assumes an input of two verbs: *vy-kup-i-l* and *po-kup-a-et*.

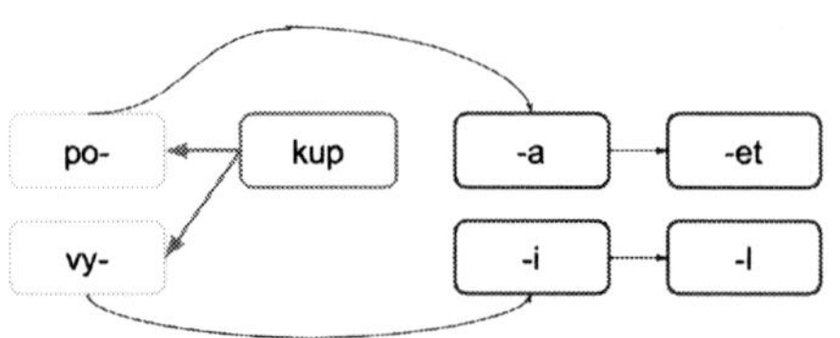

Figure 3: Two affix nodes (*po-* and *vy-*) are detected to have a 100% overlap (*kup*).

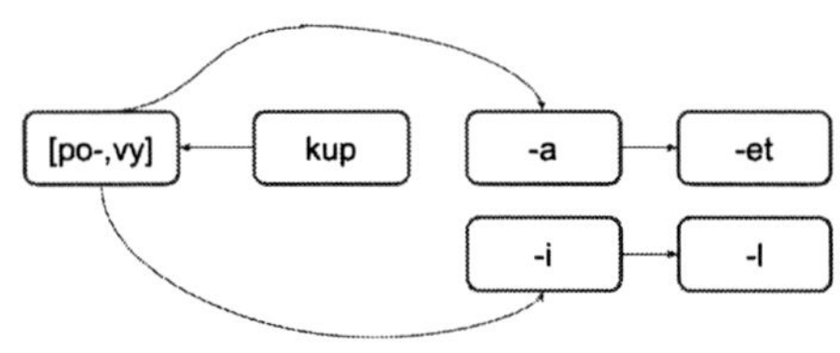

Figure 4: Two affix nodes are collapsed into one. Then the previous step is repeated with the next pair of affixes which share the minimum edge overlap.

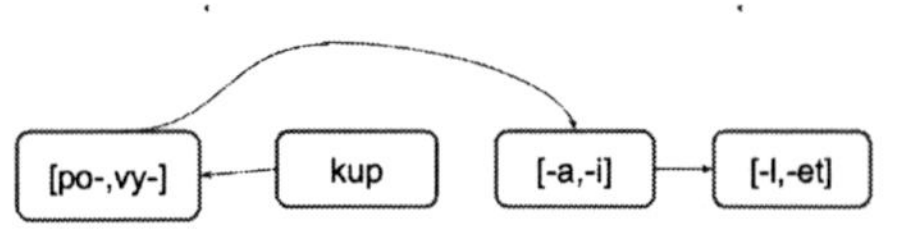

Figure 5: Eventually, the entire graph consists of classes of affixes, which can also be mapped from orthography to linguistic features through the IGT glossing.

Since the system will not allow a cycle in the graph, the compression is limited. If the system is trying to merge nodes A and B and one of B's edges would create a cycle if added to A's edges, such edge will not be added to A (it will there be lost). For example, the minimum number of nodes

in the compressed graph of Chintang is 48 while the literature reports 13 position classes (Bickel et al., 2007). One advantage of the k-means approach is that it allows the user to pick any number of position classes directly, though a smaller number means more edges may be sacrificed.

Wax's (2014) system outputs a grammar specification where the lexicon and the morphology sections are filled out, and the rest of the settings are set to default. In particular, subject and object drop are allowed in all cases, and this makes it possible to parse stand-alone verbs. Then the specification is compiled into grammar rules by the Grammar Matrix (Bender et al., 2002; Bender et al., 2010) and this grammar can be used for parsing with software such as the LKB (Copestake, 2002) or ACE (Crysmann and Packard, 2012).

3 Data

Chintang

The most interesting results were obtained on the Chintang [ctn] data, possibly because it is the biggest and the highest quality IGT collection that I had. I used 8667 sentences for "training" (in this case to learn the morphological rules) and 708 verbs for testing by morphological parsing. The collection was used with permission from the field linguists who created it (Bickel et al., 2013). Chintang was shown to have free prefix ordering (Bickel et al., 2007) and is a morphologically rich agglutinative language. The position classes for Chintang are described in Bickel et al. (2007). Furthermore, Bender et al. (2012) hand-built an Oracle morphological precision grammar based on this description, accounting for certain phenomena such as position classes iteration. I used this grammar in evaluation.

Matsigenka

Another low-resource language that I used for this study was Matsigenka [mcb]. The IGT collection was again obtained from the field linguists who created it (Michael et al., 2013). I used a part of the collection which had English translations (376 sentences for training and 47 for testing, which results in 118 verbs for testing). Matsigenka is also an agglutinative, morphologically rich language with possibly variable morpheme ordering (Michael, p.c.).

ODIN: Turkish, Tagalog, and Russian

ODIN (Lewis and Xia, 2010) is a database of
IGT obtained from crawling linguistic papers online. Though the particular languages which I used
from ODIN are not low-resource, the datasets still
represent noisy and scarce data. Because it comes
from examples in linguistic papers, ODIN data is
fairly homogeneous and not necessarily representative of natural language use, but it does provide a
big selection of different languages IGT (currently
1497 datasets). For this experiment, I used three
ODIN datasets: Turkish [tur], Tagalog [tgl], and
Russian [rus]. Turkish and Tagalog can be seen
as being on the opposite sides of the morphotactic spectrum: Turkish has many position classes
but the morphotactics is mostly canonical, while
Tagalog only basically has one prefix and one suffix position class but features infixes and redupli-
cation.[6] In addition to Turkish and Tagalog, I used
the Russian dataset from ODIN. Russian is a morphologically rich language with a few prefixal and
a few suffixal position classes and a native speaker
was available to perform qualitative error analysis,[7] so it was included for the diversity of the test
set.

4 Method

The method and the evaluation process are illustrated in Figure 6 and described in the subsections
below.

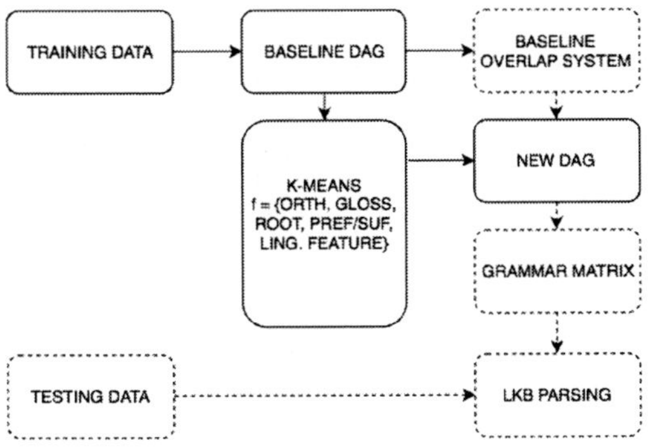

Figure 6: General method. The steps relevant only to evaluation are indicated by dotted lines.

---

[6]There is also a historical reason for using Turkish and
Tagalog: Wax originally tested his system on them. However,
he used the data in a different form and his original results are
not directly comparable to mine.

[7]Results for Russian turned out to be uninteresting.

4.1 Training/Testing Split and the Effect of the Random Split on the Results

The Chintang and Matsigenka datasets were split
randomly into training and testing for the purposes
of other projects, and these were the splits that I
used. The ODIN data I split myself. The split
has a noticeable effect on the results. Namely,
different splits result in a different number of position classes with the same minimum overlap
value. Poor alignment between the language and
the gloss line in the ODIN data leads to different items being discarded as the affix objects are
added to the system, depending on which IGTs are
originally in the training set.

There does not seem to be a strong correlation
between the number of position classes that the
baseline system comes up with and with either the
number of IGT in the training set or the number
of nodes in the original graph (Pearson coefficient
between -0.08 and +0.13). The effect is probably
just due to the randomness of the split. For all the
three ODIN datasets, I report the numbers and analyze the results for the training-testing split which
corresponds to a representative run. The representative run is one that resulted in the average value
for the final number of position classes over 100
runs.

4.2 Affix Objects

The k-means system takes as input the original affix DAG created by Wax's (2014) system as described in section 2.4. The baseline system reads
in the IGT and identifies affixes using the segmentation that is already in the IGT, the alignment with
the gloss line, and a list of known glosses. The
affixes then are stored in a DAG as nodes, and a
directed edge between two nodes means that one
affix can serve as input to the other. Stems are also
part of the DAG, though they only have outgoing
edges and no incoming edges. An affix instance is
mapped to an existing node if it is associated with
the same gloss, orthography, and inputs. Otherwise a new affix node is created. After the original
DAG is built, instead of compressing the graph by
using edge (input) overlap, I apply k-means clustering to merge the nodes based on a number of
features described below.

145

4.3 Clustering

4.3.1 k-means

I used classical k-means clustering in form of a package for the Python programming language (Pedregosa et al., 2011)[8] with the following feature set where each feature is binary: affix's orthography, affix's gloss, linguistic feature type (e.g. tense, number), immediate context (previous morpheme, or the input, the only feature that the baseline also uses), the root of the word the affix occurred in, and whether the affix is a prefix (occurs to the left of the root). I run k-means on affix instances rather than on the DAG nodes, but each affix instance had been associated with a particular node in the DAG as described in the previous section. The nodes are then merged as described below.

4.3.2 Applying Clustering Labels to the Affix DAG

After a label is obtained for each affix instance, a new DAG is constructed as follows: I take a collection of new nodes, based on the clustering labels. Nodes from the old DAG for which the clustering label is the same are merged, with all inputs and outputs kept, regardless of cycles. If a certain node from the old DAG is associated with two different clusters, the node is split into two copy-nodes. Then a spanning tree is constructed by breadth-first search using the 'heaviest' outgoing edge for each node, where the weight is the outdegree of the node to which the edge is pointing. Then all other possible outgoing edges, sorted by weight and starting from the heaviest, are added for all nodes so long as they don't create a cycle in the graph. Some have to be sacrificed.

4.3.3 Choosing k

One goal was to evaluate the system using k equal to the number of position classes that the baseline system produces, so that they can be compared. Since the baseline system's result depends on the minimum overlap choice, that had to be fixed at a particular value. At the same time, for Chintang, there exists an Oracle precision grammar built by language experts (Bender et al., 2012). The baseline system is limited in how small of a graph it can produce. In particular, when run on the Chintang data, it produced a minimum of 48 position

classes when input overlap is less or equal to 0.1, and 55 position classes with overlap = 0.2. Fifty-five is close to 54, the number of position classes in the Oracle grammar. Therefore I decided to use this 0.2 value for all languages to be able to compare the Oracle grammar to both the baseline system and the k-means system as well as to be consistent with respect to all other parts of the experiment. In addition, for Chintang I used k=13, the number which does not account for iterating affixes but is nonetheless the number that is hypothesized in the literature (Bickel et al., 2007).

5 Results and Discussion

5.1 Evaluation Method

It should be stated upfront that the results of this study seem most interesting if analyzed qualitatively, in terms of what kind of affixes get clustered together and whether this can be helpful to a filed linguist in any way. At the same time, it is appropriate to include quantitative results. For this, I use morphological parsing.

Morphological parsing is analyzing isolated words (e.g. extracted from a held-out test set) lexically, defaulting the phrase structure rules, in that each word (such as a verb) can be analyzed as a full sentence, provided there is a path in the morphotactic DAG that generates this word. This is an appropriate evaluation method given that labeled data for morphotactic inference virtually does not exist for most languages, be it high-resource or not. I am assuming that a grammar which achieves better coverage on a held out dataset may better represent the real grammar of the language, especially if k is kept modest.[9] The Chintang Oracle grammar I also use indirectly, looking at its performance in terms of morphological parsing and comparing to both the baseline and the k-means systems.

All grammars, including the Oracle, were normalized with respect to the lexicon and only differ in morphological rules. The test sets were filtered to just contain one instance of each verb. As such, the evaluation does not take into account how frequent the verbs are. The test sets for most languages are rather small (Chintang is the biggest with 708 unique verbs in the set). This is a realistic setting for low-resource language research.

---

[8] http://scikit-learn.org/stable/
modules/clustering.html

[9] If k is very big, the grammar is likely to parse more but it cannot be easily mapped to the language's actual morphology.

Language	System	k/PC	% parsed
ctn	Oracle	54	75.5
	Wax (2014)	55	**90.8**
	k-means	55	86.1
	k-means	13	83.3
mcb	Wax (2014)	23	**78.4**
	k-means	23	56.8
tgl	Wax (2014)	6	**67.9**
	k-means	6	50.9
tur	Wax (2014)	21	53.4
	k-means	21	53.4
rus	Wax (2014)	5	**47.9**
	k-means	5	47.1

Table 1: Morphological parsing results.

5.2 Results

The results are summarized in Table 1. The results show that, in terms of morphological parsing, a k-means grammar is generally worse than the baseline system, though it can sometimes achieve similar coverage (in the noisy ODIN setting). However both the baseline and the k-means systems strongly outperform the hand-built Oracle grammar of Chintang. Furthermore, the resulting grammars can be examined by hand, not in terms of parsing but in terms of what they look like and how they compare to the languages' actual morphological rules. In case of Chintang at least, k-means clusters together affixes which constitute circumfixes, while the baseline grammar cannot possibly do that because it will never cluster together a prefix and a suffix.

5.3 Analysis and Discussion

Given largely negative results, the main points of this paper are given in qualitative linguistic analysis of concrete examples, mainly from the Chintang experiments. In most cases, the k-means algorithm and the baseline come up with different sets of morphological rules. While the baseline system clearly is better at parsing, Chintang and Matsigenka have examples which the k-means can parse and the baseline system cannot. That the baseline is usually better at parsing suggests that input overlap is an important feature and possibly the strongest predictor of whether two affixes belong to the same position graph. However, the k-means system is capable of picking up phenomena which the input overlap will never detect, because they are related to variable order and gener-

ally non-canonical phenomena. For such phenomena to be detected, the algorithm should consider features beyond the affix's immediate context. The clearest example of this is the Chintang circumfix *mai-/-yokt* which is consistently put in the same cluster by the k-means. Below I mostly talk about the Chintang results, as they provide the most insight into the difference between the baseline and the k-means.[10]

5.3.1 Chintang

Oracle Grammar versus Automatically Induced Grammars

In terms of morphological parsing, both the k-means morphological grammar and the baseline grammar clearly outperform the Oracle grammar. The main reason for this is that an automatic procedure which goes through the entire dataset in a consistent fashion picks up a lot more affixes than is described in the sources used by Bender et al. (2014). In part, that is because Chintang employs nominalization, compounding, and also features many phonological variations, but there are also indications that there are true verbal inflections that are missing in the Oracle. While the Oracle grammar cannot parse 158 items out of 708, the baseline only misses 65, and the k-means system misses 92. Examples of affixes which both automatic grammars pick up which the Oracle grammar misses include -*ʔ* (glossed EMPH), -*ko* (nominalizer), and, most interestingly, -*en*, which is glossed PST.NEG, so it is clearly an affix that has something to do with verb inflection and as such should probably have been included in the Oracle grammar but was missed for some reason. This suggests that either the description of the grammar in the literature is incomplete, or there are errors in the corpus which should be corrected. In either case, identifying verb inflections candidates automatically would be helpful for the field linguist who is working with the data.

Baseline Overlap=0.2 vs. k=55

The baseline system ended up compressing the original graph to a number of nodes similar to the Oracle number (55 instead of 54) when input overlap was set to 0.2. There are 7 items which the k-means system parses and the baseline grammar does not in this setting. A few of them, like *a-lis-a-hat-a-ce-e*, require that there be two nodes for

---

[10] Admittedly, more analysis could be done on Matsigenka. This remains part of future work.

the *-a* orthography, such that one takes the root (in this case *lis*) as input and the other takes the complementizer *hat*. The baseline grammar does not have an edge from the complementizer slot to the tense slot. There are 34 items which the baseline grammar parses and the k-means grammar does not. This is because the k-means ends up sacrificing more of the useful edges to avoid cycles in the graph. Neither grammar parses 58 items. Of these, some are due to unseen lexemes but most are due to discarded edges (since the baseline also discards edges when merging nodes).

The True Number of Position Classes: k=13

The most interesting (from the linguistic perspective) k-means result is the one with k=13. First of all, it is not possible to obtain this number using the baseline grammar, since the smallest number it produces is 48. Secondly, the resulting graph has some resemblance to Chintang morphotactics as described in the literature, and that can be seen more easily in a smaller graph. This means that the k-means system can be useful to a researcher who is trying to come up with hypotheses about the language's morphotactics and may have an idea about roughly how many position classes there are but not necessarily which affixes belong together and what the input relationships are. I evaluate this scenario with k=13, the number of position classes in Chintang suggested by Bickel et al. (2007).

There is some resemblance between the system's output and Chintang morphotactics as described by Bickel et al. (2007). An abridged version of the results is presented in Figure 7. Three of the clusters (not shown) are very heterogeneous and contain stems as well as different kinds of morphemes. These cannot be directly mapped to actual Chintang morphotactics, though they are useful in parsing compound verbs. There are a few clusters that k-means seems to get roughly right (all of them are in the figure), and some of the input edges (also in the figure) reflect actual Chintang morphotactics as well. One cluster, namely 9, has affixes that are clearly glossed as a verb inflection in the data (*3, 3s, 3p*) but are not accounted for in Bickel et al. (2007). One especially interesting cluster is the one presented in Figure 8. It captures the fact that *-yokt* and *mai-* behave as a circumfix, i.e. they tend to occur only together, one to the right and one to the left of the root. Clustering in this case is not necessarily helpful for parsing, but it is helpful for identifying morphotactic con-

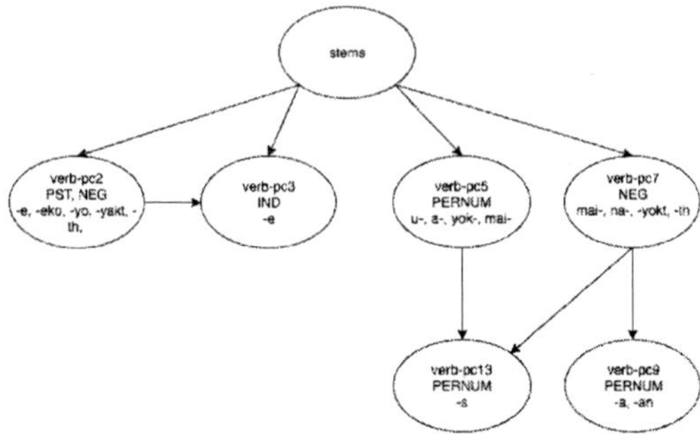

Figure 7: A part of the morphotactic graph output by k-means with k=13. Dotted ellipse (verb-pc9) shows a cluster which is not accounted for in the Chintang literature but seems plausible as a position class. All the rest included clusters at least roughly correspond to the position classes in the literature. Some clusters and edges are not shown.

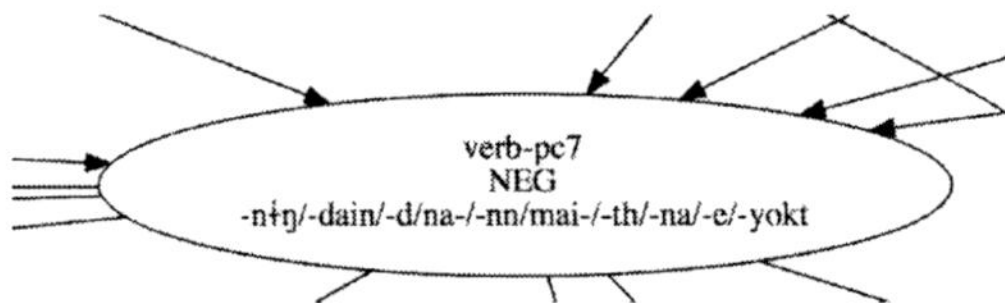

Figure 8: Chintang cluster containing circumfix *mai- -yokt.*

straints generally.

5.4 Matsigenka

While the k-means grammar lacks some productive edges that the overlap grammar has, it gains at least some others, which makes it possible for the k-means to parse *i-tsarog-a-i-t-an-ak-e*, since the k-means grammar does not lose the edge from *-i* class to *-t* class. With only one such example, it is difficult to conclude anything. No qualitative analysis of smaller Matsigenka graphs was done at this point. In future work, it will be possible to use a larger Matsigenka dataset, and hopefully the results will be more interesting.

5.5 ODIN Data

The ODIN datasets do not contain much variety, since the IGT come from linguistic papers' examples, and those tend to not be very diverse. At the same time, the ODIN data is rather noisy and often times it is not easy to align the gloss line to the language line. This way, many affixes never make it into the grammars and many items are not parsed. Interestingly, k-means comes closest to the baseline in this setting. The items that are parsed by both grammars are the ones that are seen in the data a lot and are therefore fairly simple for both systems to get. It seems that k-means could be used on small and noisy field datasets, often as successfully as the baseline system, and the hope of discovering non-canonical phenomena will be higher.

6 Conclusion

The experiments described in this paper show that unsupervised methods such as clustering can be used somewhat successfully on smaller scale data such as field languages IGT collections. In case with Chintang at least, the clusters of affixes yielded by k-means sometimes roughly correspond to the position classes described in the literature. Both the baseline and the k-means systems are able to morphologically analyze (parse) more verbs than a hand-built grammar, which confirms that automatic processing is useful for field research.

Strict ordering of affixes that is easily accounted for by heuristic methods such as Wax (2014) is generally a very strong predictor for whether two affixes belong to the same position class or not. Systems that rely solely on inferring such ordering perform better than k-means in all the cases presented in this paper, but k-means achieves comparable results in noisy settings. Furthermore, approaches such as input overlap are by definition hopeless for discovering non-canonical morphotactics, while k-means seems to discover some correlations between positions that are conditioned on each other (e.g. Chintang *-yokt* and the negative prefixes). An improvement to the current approach would be weighted k-means, where immediate context (input) can be given more weight.

A system like the one described in this paper can be a useful component of an interactive linguistic analysis tool for field linguists. Kim (2015) showed that clustering results can be made more interpretable for humans in the education domain with the aid of Bayesian Case Modeling. It is possible that the same is applicable to the domain of field linguistics and morphological analysis. I showed that clusters suggest correlations between morphological features; designing a BCM-based interactive system where the linguist could guide the algorithm and look at automatically generated hypotheses in the process is a tempting direction for future work. As it is at present, k-means is a simple and extensible alternative to heuristic algorithms of inferring position classes from IGT and can serve as a stepping stone for developing expert linguistic analyses, as it can form preliminary buckets of affixes that can be considered candidates for either true position classes or for positions that are related to each other in some non-obvious way.

References

Emily M. Bender, Dan Flickinger, and Stephan Oepen. 2002. The Grammar Matrix: An open-source starter-kit for the rapid development of cross-linguistically consistent broad-coverage precision grammars. In John Carroll, Nelleke Oostdijk, and Richard Sutcliffe, editors, *Proceedings of the Workshop on Grammar Engineering and Evaluation at the 19th International Conference on Computational Linguistics*, pages 8–14, Taipei, Taiwan.

Emily M Bender, Dan Flickinger, and Stephan Oepen. 2008. Grammar engineering for linguistic hypothesis testing. In *Proceedings of the Texas Linguistics Society X conference: Computational linguistics for less-studied languages*, pages 16–36. Citeseer.

Emily M Bender, Scott Drellishak, Antske Fokkens, Laurie Poulson, and Safiyyah Saleem. 2010. Grammar customization. *Research on Language & Computation*, 8(1):23–72. 10.1007/s11168-010-9070-1.

Emily M. Bender, Robert Schikowski, and Balthasar Bickel. 2012. Deriving a lexicon for a precision grammar from language documentation resources: A case study of Chintang. In *COLING*, pages 247–262.

Emily M. Bender, Joshua Crowgey, Michael Wayne Goodman, and Fei Xia. 2014. Learning grammar specifications from igt: A case study of chintang. In *Proceedings of the 2014 Workshop on the Use of Computational Methods in the Study of Endangered Languages*, pages 43–53, Baltimore, Maryland, USA, June. Association for Computational Linguistics.

Emily M. Bender. 2011. On achieving and evaluating language-independence in NLP. *Linguistic Issues in Language Technology*, 6(3):1–26.

Balthasar Bickel, Goma Banjade, Martin Gaenszle, Elena Lieven, Netra Prasad Paudyal, Ichchha Purna Rai, Manoj Rai, Novel Kishore Rai, and Sabine Stoll. 2007. Free prefix ordering in Chintang. *Language*, pages 43–73.

Balthasar Bickel, Martin Gaenszle, Novel Kishore Rai, Vishnu Singh Rai, Elena Lieven, Sabine Stoll, G. Banjade, T. N. Bhatta, N. Paudyal, J. Pettigrew, M. Rai, and I. P. Rai. 2013. Tale of a poor guy. Accessed online on 15-January-2013.

Eric Brill. 1995. Transformation-based error-driven learning and natural language processing: A case study in part-of-speech tagging. *Computational linguistics*, 21(4):543–565.

Ann Copestake. 2000. Appendix: Definitions of typed feature structures. *Natural Language Engineering*, 6(01):109–112.

Ann Copestake. 2002. The LKB system.

Greville G Corbett. 2009. Canonical inflectional classes. *Selected proceedings of the 6th Décembrettes: Morphology in Bordeaux*, pages 1–11.

Mathias Creutz and Krista Lagus. 2006. Morfessor in the morpho challenge. In *Proceedings of the PASCAL Challenge Workshop on Unsupervised Segmentation of Words into Morphemes*. Citeseer.

Berthold Crysmann and Olivier Bonami. 2015. Variable morphotactics in information-based morphology. *Journal of Linguistics*, pages 1–64.

Berthold Crysmann and Woodley Packard. 2012. Towards efficient hpsg generation for german, a non-configurational language. In *COLING*, pages 695–710.

Béatrice Daille, Cécile Fabre, and Pascale Sébillot. 2002. Applications of computational morphology. *Many morphologies*, pages 210–234.

Mark Johnson. 2008. Unsupervised word segmentation for sesotho using adaptor grammars. In *Proceedings of the Tenth Meeting of ACL Special Interest Group on Computational Morphology and Phonology*, pages 20–27. Association for Computational Linguistics.

Fred Karlsson. 2008. *Finnish: An essential grammar*. Routledge.

Been Kim. 2015. *Interactive and interpretable machine learning models for human machine collaboration*. Ph.D. thesis, Massachusetts Institute of Technology.

Michael Krauss. 1992. The world's languages in crisis. *Language*, 68(1):4–10.

William D. Lewis and Fei Xia. 2010. Developing ODIN: A multilingual repository of annotated language data for hundreds of the world's languages. *Literary and Linguistic Computing*, 25(3):303–319.

Lev Michael, Christine Beier, Zachary O'Hagan, Harold Vargas Pereira, and Jose Vargas Pereira. 2013. Matsigenka text written by Matsigenka authors. Accessed online on 15-September-2015: http://www.cabeceras.org/ldm_publications/mcb_text_collection_30jun2013_v1.pdf.

Kemal Oflazer and Gokhan Tur. 1996. Combining hand-crafted rules and unsupervised learning in constraint-based morphological disambiguation. *arXiv preprint cmp-lg/9604001*.

Kemal Oflazer, Sergei Nirenburg, and Marjorie McShane. 2001. Bootstrapping morphological analyzers by combining human elicitation and machine learning. *Computational linguistics*, 27(1):59–85.

Arfath Pasha, Mohamed Al-Badrashiny, Mona T Diab, Ahmed El Kholy, Ramy Eskander, Nizar Habash, Manoj Pooleery, Owen Rambow, and Ryan Roth. 2014. Madamira: A fast, comprehensive tool for morphological analysis and disambiguation of arabic. In *LREC*, pages 1094–1101.

F. Pedregosa, G. Varoquaux, A. Gramfort, V. Michel, B. Thirion, O. Grisel, M. Blondel, P. Prettenhofer, R. Weiss, V. Dubourg, J. Vanderplas, A. Passos, D. Cournapeau, M. Brucher, M. Perrot, and E. Duchesnay. 2011. Scikit-learn: Machine learning in Python. *Journal of Machine Learning Research*, 12:2825–2830.

Carl Pollard and Ivan A. Sag. 1994. *Head-Driven Phrase Structure Grammar*. Studies in Contemporary Linguistics. The University of Chicago Press and CSLI Publications, Chicago, IL and Stanford, CA.

Robert Schikowski. 2012. Chintang morphology. *Unpublished ms, University of Zürich*.

Patrick Schone and Daniel Jurafsky. 2001. Knowledge-free induction of inflectional morphologies. In *Proceedings of the second meeting of the North American Chapter of the Association for Computational Linguistics on Language technologies*, pages 1–9. Association for Computational Linguistics.

Gregory T Stump. 1993. Position classes and morphological theory. In *Yearbook of Morphology 1992*, pages 129–180. Springer.

David Wax. 2014. Automated grammar engineering for verbal morphology. Master's thesis, University of Washington.

David Yarowsky and Richard Wicentowski. 2000. Minimally supervised morphological analysis by multimodal alignment. In *Proceedings of the 38th Annual Meeting on Association for Computational Linguistics*, pages 207–216. Association for Computational Linguistics.

Author Index